T0320134

Pragmatism and Political Crisis Management

SUCCESSFUL PUBLIC GOVERNANCE

Series Editors: Paul 't Hart, *Professor, Utrecht School of Governance, Utrecht University, the Netherlands* and Tina Nabatchi, *Maxwell School of Citizenship and Public Affairs, Syracuse University, USA*

Societies have the best shot at thriving when they are governed through public institutions that are trustworthy, reliable, impartial, and competent. Yet in the first decades of the 21st century, governments and public institutions worldwide have been challenged by deep and fast changes in their operating environments. Thus, there is an urgent need for concepts, designs, and practices for successful public governance, which this groundbreaking new book series will seek to present.

Under the direction of the Series Editors, the series will present a number of approaches to the topic of successful public governance, including:

- *Conceptualizations* and critiques of the notion and ideal of 'success' in public sector and political settings;
- *Methodological strategies* for designing and conducting 'positive' evaluations of public policies, organisations, networks, initiatives, and other forms of public governance;
- *Empirical studies* that provide close-up, comparative, experimental, and large-n/big data research identifying, describing, explaining, and/or interpreting highly effective, highly adaptive, highly democratic, highly reputed, highly resilient public governance institutions and practices;
- *Pleas, proposals, designs* giving ideational accounts of 'what should and might be' when it comes to successful public governance.

Pragmatism and Political Crisis Management

Principle and Practical Rationality During the Financial Crisis

Christopher Ansell

University of California, Berkeley, USA

Martin Bartenberger

RATIS, Germany

SUCCESSFUL PUBLIC GOVERNANCE

Cheltenham, UK • Northampton, MA, USA

Published by
Edward Elgar Publishing Limited
The Lypiatts
15 Lansdown Road
Cheltenham
Glos GL50 2JA
UK

Edward Elgar Publishing, Inc.
William Pratt House
9 Dewey Court
Northampton
Massachusetts 01060
USA

A catalogue record for this book
is available from the British Library

Library of Congress Control Number: 2019948960

This book is available electronically in the **Elgar**online
Social and Political Science subject collection
DOI 10.4337/9781788978569

ISBN 978 1 78897 855 2 (cased)
ISBN 978 1 78897 856 9 (eBook)

Printed and bound by CPI Group (UK) Ltd, Croydon, CR0 4YY

Contents

Figures

Tables

Acknowledgments

We were first brought together by our shared interest in the philosophy of Pragmatism. Coincidentally, we both discovered that interest at the University of Chicago, though in different generations. Chris was at the University of Chicago in the late 1980s and early 1990s, a time he remembers for its deep exploration of the rationality of human action. The Political Science Department and the University were renowned at the time for their investigations into the power, but also the limits, of rational choice theory. At the same time, scholars like David Greenstone, David Laitin, John Padgett, Susanne and Lloyd Rudolph and William Sewell were exploring the linguistic, cultural and relational bases of human action. Chris's interest in Pragmatism eventually grew out of his attempt to bring these ideas together.

As an exchange student at Chicago in 2012, Martin engaged with a new generation of scholars. Benjamin McKean, Eric Oliver and Betsy Sinclair got him started thinking about the relationship between Pragmatism, politics and crisis management and, in the best Pragmatist spirit, Will Howell encouraged him to develop his idea that Pragmatism might play a role in crisis management, saying "I like it. I don't think it's true but I like it." Interestingly, there was one Chicago scholar who spanned across these two intellectual generations: Gary Herrigel was a new Assistant Professor at the end of Chris's time at Chicago and a Full Professor when Martin was in residence. Gary's interest in Pragmatism inspired both of us.

We were also brought together by our interest in crisis management. Chris's interest in crisis management grew out of a joint project with David Vogel on the political fallout of Europe's "mad cow" crisis, which eventually led to a small project with Jane Gingrich on how British government ministries made sense of the crisis as it unfolded. This work eventually led to a much larger project with Ann Keller and others about how governments respond to novel infectious disease outbreaks, which in turn led to a project with Arjen Boin on transboundary crises. In the meantime, Martin came to Berkeley in 2013 as a visiting scholar and Chris and Martin began a series of small joint projects on policy experimentation and political problem-solving. After stints as a researcher and lecturer at the University of Vienna and the Vienna University of Business and Economics, Martin decided to pursue his goal of developing a PhD dissertation on the relationship between Pragmatism and crisis management. Fortuitously, he chose to work on this project with Arjen Boin, Paul 't Hart and Paul Nieuwenburg at Utrecht and Leiden Universities in the Netherlands. All three proved to be great mentors.

This book took its initial form as Martin's dissertation at Leiden University, completed in 2017. Independently, Chris had been working with Arjen Boin and Moshe Farjoun on developing a Pragmatist approach to organization theory, work that eventually led Arjen and Chris to envision applying those ideas to crisis management (Chris fondly recalls a back-of-the-napkin outline being worked out at a coffee shop in a cold and blustery Leiden). It was Arjen who suggested that Chris and Martin team up, making Arjen the proverbial "silent partner" in this project—though no one would characterize our engaging mentor and friend as "silent"! At around the same time, Paul 't Hart was also developing his agenda for a "positive" approach to public policy and public administration and he noted that our Pragmatist approach represents a positive and constructive engagement with uncertainty. He suggested that this book project would make a nice contribution to his *Successful Public Governance* series. We thank Paul, Rachel Downie of Edward Elgar Publishing and reviewers for their good offices in realizing this book project.

In less direct ways, others have also made important contributions to this project. Chris feels fortunate to have the camaraderie of a small group of scholars at Berkeley—Ann Keller, Todd LaPorte, Paul Schulman and Louise Comfort—who have themselves made important contributions to our understanding of crisis management. A more extended network of scholars working on related topics have also enriched this work, including Mathilde Bourrier, Tom Christensen, Moshe Farjoun, Per Lægreid, Charles Parker, Eva Sørensen, Jacob Torfing and Jarle Trondal.

Martin is greatly indebted to many friends and former colleagues who have supported and inspired his research. Among his earliest supporters, he would specifically like to name the "Vienna Circle" of Georg Gangl, Christoph Wendler and Elmar Flatschart. In Chicago, Zeeshan Aleem, Roscoe Nicholson and Olivia Woolam nurtured his interest in Pragmatism and American politics.

Finally, we would both like to thank our families. Chris thanks his wife Suzanne and his daughters Ella and Lillian for keeping him smiling and not letting him take himself too seriously, and his dog Duke for occasionally taking him on (slow) walks. He dedicates this work to the memory of Bernie Silberman and Gene Rochlin, who both taught him a thing or two about organizational rationality.

Martin feels lucky to have the everlasting support of the love of his life and now wife Isabel. He also is deeply thankful to his parents who—despite the fact that they never went to university—have supported his academic musings in the most generous and caring way. Finally, he dedicates his work on Pragmatism and crisis management to his daughter Laila. Maybe philosophical

Pragmatism can help her generation steer mankind through these turbulent times.

1. Strategic crisis management in the public domain

For the first three quarters of 2007, the American economy was humming along. Unemployment was an enviable 4.5 percent in the summer of 2007 and the economy was steadily growing. But an overheated US homebuilding market then faltered, sending shock waves through the economy (Stock and Watson 2012). Although a few iconoclasts had seen the proverbial "writing on the wall," most political and economic elites were deeply surprised by the magnitude of the crisis (Lewis 2011). The *Great Recession*, as it is now known, produced deep pain for American workers and businesses and had terrifying spillover effects that cascaded through the entire global economy.

Government crisis managers quickly stepped into the breach. By early 2008, the US Federal Reserve Bank, led by the economist Ben Bernanke, a scholar of the Great Depression, had entered crisis management mode. The challenges were formidable. In March 2008, Bear Stearns, the smallest of the Big Five investment banks and heavily invested in the housing market, suffered a classic run on its holdings. The government intervened to prop it up. Then in September 2008, an even larger investment bank, Lehman Brothers, faced insolvency. Chastened by criticism of the Bear Stearns' "bailout," the government decided to let it fail. "Immediately thereafter," writes economist Alan Blinder, "the whole U.S. economy fell off the table" (2013, 19).

Clearly, much is at stake in crisis management. Although the Great Recession was unusual in both its scale and magnitude, it is hardly unique. Indeed, crises of all types have become one of the core challenges facing government. Recent examples are manifold. Terrorist attacks have hit many countries, including the US, France, Belgium, Germany, Turkey, Iraq and Pakistan. The European "refugee crisis" has given rise to right-wing movements that challenge elected governments, established political norms and values, and even the coherence of the European Union. Natural disasters like Hurricane Matthew in Haiti or the earthquakes in Nepal and Italy remind us that modern civilization remains vulnerable to the follies of nature. Today's "risk society" (Beck 1992) harbors a whole range of novel threats, from state-sponsored hacking and cyberwarfare to data breaches and information leaks (Schulman and Roe 2007; Perrow 2008; Van Eeten and Bauer 2009; Boin et al. 2014; Harknett and Stever 2011; Robinson et al. 2015).

It is a truism to say that crisis management is challenging. But why is it challenging? One reason is that crises demand that highly consequential decisions and authoritative public communications be made under urgent, uncertain and turbulent circumstances. In his memoir about the financial crisis, New York Federal Reserve President and later Secretary of Treasury Timothy Geithner captures the challenge well: "I had lived through enough crises to know that they're always unpredictable and blanketed with fog. Americans desperately wanted assurances that things would get better soon, and I wasn't sure how to project an air of confidence I didn't feel" (2014, 11). Crises make decision making and public communications much more difficult, while also magnifying the consequences of getting those decisions or communications wrong.

Successful public governance during a crisis requires that leaders find an effective path through the fog of uncertainty. When pushed to their limits and facing unenviable choices, what resources can crisis leaders call upon to meet these challenges? There are many possible answers to this question, but we focus on how leaders like Geithner *think* and *act*. While there are no magic bullets here, we argue that cultivating a deeper understanding of everyday problem-solving skills can help leaders to successfully navigate crises. The trick is to recognize the *hidden resources* of practical problem-solving.

THE MEANING OF CRISIS

Crises are not a recent phenomenon. The term "crisis" dates back to Ancient Greece where it "meant not only 'divorce' and 'quarrel', but also 'decision' in the sense of reaching a crucial point that would tip the scales" (Koselleck 2006, 358). The term crisis has since become part of the different national languages in Europe, expanding during the social revolutions and economic depressions of the 18th and 19th century to become a key term in modern political-economic thought (Masur 1968). As a result, the term has increasingly been taken up by the social sciences (Robinson 1968). By the 1960s "crisis had become a broad and expanding catchword ... for practically any challenge-and-response situation or scenario" (Starn 2005, 501).

As the term evolved over time, it has absorbed several layers of meaning. First, crises were understood as conflicts that could be a threat or an opportunity to an established order (Robinson 1968; Lalonde 2004). Second, the concept of crisis included the idea of judgment as a decision point both in the judicial and theological sense. Finally, crises were always seen as situations of high uncertainty (Koselleck 2006). These meanings clearly resonate with one of the dominant definitions of crisis in the academic literature on crisis management, as offered by Boin and 't Hart (2007, 42): "We speak of crisis when a community of people—an organization, a town, or a nation—perceives an urgent threat to core values or life-sustaining functions, which must be dealt with under conditions of uncertainty."

Three elements are crucial in this definition of crisis: urgency/time pressure, threat and uncertainty. *Urgency* refers to the idea that crises are situations where decisions have to be made under high time pressure. *Threat* highlights that crises challenge a society's core values, norms and beliefs or—in the case of terrorist attacks and natural disasters—the conditions of its survival.

Uncertainty plays a key role in all phases of a crisis. We understand uncertainty as the general unpredictability and uncontrollability of our environment which varies in degree and perception over time. In the words of former Defense Secretary Donald Rumsfeld, this understanding of deep uncertainty mainly points to the "unknown unknowns," the things "we don't know we don't know" (Rumsfeld 2002; also see Žižek 2004). Before a crisis even happens, uncertainty is present in the impossibility of predicting the next crisis while knowing that it will eventually come. During crises, uncertainty arises in the form of a broad set of questions: "[W]hat is happening and how did it happen? What's next? How bad will it be? More importantly, uncertainty clouds the search for solutions: what can we do? What happens if we select this option?" (Boin et al. 2005, 3–4).

This definition of crisis differs from two related concepts—*disaster* and *catastrophe*. A *disaster*, in the understanding of this study, is regarded "as a crisis with a devastating ending" (Boin and 't Hart 2007, 42). A *catastrophe* is qualitatively different from a disaster because of its scope and intensity. A catastrophe such as Hurricane Katrina is different from a disaster because of its massive physical impact, the insufficiency of local organizations in coping with it and the fact that most everyday community functions are interrupted (Quarantelli 1998, 2000; Rodríguez et al. 2006, 87).

This indicates that every disaster or catastrophe is a crisis, or more precisely, began as a crisis—but not every crisis necessarily turns out to become a disaster or catastrophe. As crisis researchers have argued, by concentrating on the broader concept of crisis we can learn more "about the origins and development of disaster" (Boin and 't Hart 2007, 42). We can also begin to investigate the factors that prevent a crisis from becoming a disaster or catastrophe. One key success factor, we believe, is effective crisis leadership.

THE IMPORTANCE OF CRISIS LEADERSHIP

Public leadership is often thought to be crucial in handling crises (Janis 1989; Rosenthal et al. 1989, 2001; Rosenthal and Kouzmin 1997; Boin and 't Hart 2003). In times of crisis, citizens expect their political leaders to mitigate the threats and dangers of a crisis, to explain why it happened in the first place. We also expect them to take action to prevent similar crises from occurring again in the future. We understand public leadership as "a number of distinctive functions that need to be performed in order for a polity to govern itself effectively and democratically" ('t Hart and Uhr 2008, 3).

It is useful for analytical purposes to distinguish two different levels of crisis management—strategic and operational. *Strategic crisis management* is concerned with setting the general parameters of a crisis response, but also with making the critical decisions that shape that society's future commitments. *Operational crisis management* focuses on the response's implementation by crisis responders "on the ground" ('t Hart et al. 2008, 230; Boin and Renaud 2013).

Our focus in this book is on strategic crisis management, which we understand to require the preparation, organization and execution of a set of critical tasks that, together, will likely lead to a "better" response (in terms of effectiveness and legitimacy). While public leaders do not themselves need to execute all of these tasks, they have the formal responsibility as elected or appointed officials to ensure that these tasks are addressed (Boin et al. 2005). Strategic crisis management is typically closely associated with managing "issues of authority, legitimacy and power that are inextricably connected to the way in which crises are defined and handled" ('t Hart 2008, 100). At its heart then, strategic crisis management can be understood to be *political crisis management*.

Since we are primarily concerned with strategic and political dimensions of crisis management in this study, our focus is on a particular subset of public leaders in crisis—political crisis managers who are typically top-level elected or appointed officials. For this subset of public leaders, managing a crisis is a credibility and legitimacy challenge. Public leaders and the institutions they command are measured by how they perform during crises. Under the scrutiny of the general public and the media, effective crisis management is critical for fostering public trust in democratic leadership and institutions (Boin et al. 2005, 8; OECD 2015). Effective crisis management may also have significant implications for public leaders' chances for reelection or continued public service (Chanley 2002; Bytzek 2008; Olmeda 2008). Crises can thus be regarded as stress tests for modern democracies and their leaders.

We focus on two particular executive tasks that political crisis managers must discharge during a crisis—decision making and meaning making.

Decision making is probably the most salient and most thoroughly explored aspect of public leadership during crises and regarded as one of the main tasks of public leaders (see Allison 1971 for one of the most prominent examples). Crisis scholars often describe a tendency towards political centralization during crises ('t Hart et al. 2008). Carl Schmitt has developed this argument most systematically in his theory of the "state of exception" (Schmitt 1985). For Schmitt, crises are states of exception that require temporary dictatorship in order to lead a democracy out of a crisis. Such a temporary dictatorship has to (partially) suspend the existing constitution of a polity in order to defend it (Schmitt 1988). Other scholars, while rejecting Schmitt's authoritarianism, have agreed that crises require an increased level of political centralization (Corwin 1947; Rossiter 1948). Studies on the American presidency have added empirical substance to this argument by showing an increased level of presidential power during wartime (Schlesinger 1973, 2004; Howell et al. 2013).

While most democratic systems have mechanisms in place to concentrate decision-making power in the hands of leaders, research also shows that such powers are usually exercised within a shared-power context. The US Congress can and often does play a strong role during crises (Kriner 2010; Polsky 2012). Decisions during crisis are not solely made by single individuals such as presidents or prime ministers. Instead crisis decision making typically unfolds in the wider context of group dynamics, advisory systems or institutional settings (Janis 1982; Boin et al. 2005, 64; Rosenthal and 't Hart 2008; 't Hart 2011).

Decision making as we understand it is deeply interrelated with sensemaking, which requires political crisis managers to make judgements about what kind of situation they are in (Weick 1995). During a crisis, these judgments must often be made in contexts characterized by ambiguity and uncertainty. To make decisions in these circumstances, crisis managers have to gain an understanding ("make sense") of the crisis. Decisions made during a crisis are often subsequently evaluated in terms of this understanding and public leaders may ultimately be held accountable for the inferences they draw during the crisis (Weick 1993, 635). Thus, sensemaking and decision making are reciprocal processes with decision making both preceding and following from sensemaking (Maitlis and Christianson 2014, 64).

Meaning making is the task that is concerned with explaining these decisions publicly and offering a convincing interpretation of the crisis.[1] Public leaders have to consider the political implications of their decisions and make sure that the explanation and interpretation of the crisis they offer is accepted by parliaments, courts, public agencies, the media, interest groups and the general public: "Political, bureaucratic, economic and other special interests do not automatically pull together and give up their self-interest just because a crisis has occurred. They engage in a struggle to produce a dominant interpretation of the implications of the crisis" (Boin et al. 2008, 9).

---

[1]   Crisis communication is a critical part of meaning making, using press releases, press conferences and interviews to distribute the "official" interpretation of the crisis and offering explanations for the decisions that are made.

STUDYING CRISIS MANAGEMENT: A FOCUS ON FAILURE

Public crisis management has received a growing amount of academic attention in recent years (e.g., Hillyard 2000; Rosenthal et al. 2001; Boin et al. 2005; Underhill 2008; Moynihan 2009; Helsloot et al. 2012; Lodge and Wegrich 2012; Lodge 2013; Duit 2016; Roe and Schulman 2016). Crisis management is now a distinct and swiftly expanding field in political science and public administration. While studies on political crisis management initially focused on international relations and international conflicts (Lauren 1979), attention to domestic crises have increasingly received more attention, prompting new questions on the political aspect of crisis management ('t Hart et al. 2008, 229–30).

Intriguingly, this growing body of literature is marked by a focus on failed or misguided attempts of crisis management (see Anheier and Moulton 1999; Rosenthal et al. 2001; Howitt and Leonard 2009).[2] These failures may pertain to organizational behavior (disintegration, conflicts, blind corners, and so on) that undermine effective crisis response (Hermann 1963; Turner, 1978) or with stress that affects the performance of leaders during crises (Hermann 1979; Janis 1982; Walker 2009; Dyson and 't Hart 2013). This focus on failure can be found both in the studies on operational crisis management (i.e., crisis responders on the ground) and in the literature on strategic crisis management.

A vast number of case studies have identified failure factors in crisis decision making. Case studies of industrial crises have documented how wrong decisions have led to the catastrophes of Chernobyl and Bhopal (Shrivastava 1987; Czada 1991; Sen and Egelhoff 1991; Ebel 1994) and the accident at the Three Mile Island nuclear power plant (Perrow 1984, 2001). McConnell and Stark have shown how the governmental decision to reduce control measures because of an upcoming election prolonged the foot-and-mouth disease crisis in the UK (McConnell and Stark 2002).

Other scholars have highlighted how the slow response to the heat waves in Chicago and France could be traced to the faulty decisions of local and national governments, which caused many casualties especially among the poor and elderly (Klinenberg 2015; Lagadec 2004). Perrow and Guillen (1990) have described how the personal biases and political ideologies of decision makers hindered an effective response to the early AIDS epidemic in the US. In all these cases, decision makers were not able to identify and make crucial

---

[2]   Anheier and Moulton (1999, 3) argue that this focus on failures and breakdowns stands in a long tradition of social science that dates back to the works of Durkheim, Marx and Weber.

decisions on how to respond to the crisis because the crisis was underestimated, misunderstood or denied.

Scholars find that failures also result from the challenge of quickly and convincingly communicating about the crisis and the crisis response. After the Exxon Valdez oil spill in 1989, the oil company Exxon was heavily criticized for downplaying the effects of the crisis while staging inefficient clean-up operations and distracting media campaigns to improve its public image (Daley and O'Neill 1991; Small 1991; Williams and Treadaway 1992). Forbes has shown how similar failures of communication and conflicting frames intensified the BSE crisis in the UK (Forbes 2004; also see Grönvall 2001; Zwanenberg and Millstone 2005). The Swedish government faced a political crisis for its slow public communications after a tsunami hit Southeast Asia in 2004, leaving 550 Swedish tourists dead (Boin et al. 2005, 80; Strömbäck and Nord 2006). The mishandling of the Hurricane Katrina catastrophe led to the widespread perception that President Bush had not shown enough interest in the crisis and was not personally involved in the crisis response (Fletcher and Morin 2005; Sylves 2006; Spence et al. 2008; Benoit and Henson 2009).

FOCUSING ON SUCCESS?

Taken together, all these cases show that crisis managers may perform poorly—or be perceived to perform poorly—on crisis decision making and meaning making. But there is also research that shows how some crisis managers do better than one might expect.

One particularly well-known example of successful crisis management is NASA's Apollo 13 mission in 1970. After an oxygen tank exploded and damaged the life-support systems of the spacecraft on its way to the moon, the NASA engineers on the ground had to find a way to bring the three astronauts safely back to earth ("Houston we have a problem"). Since the explosion had also affected the energy supply and the navigation system of the spaceship, the NASA engineers could not rely on established routines and procedures. Together with the astronauts of Apollo 13, NASA mission command had to improvise and invent creative solutions. After four days in space the three astronauts finally returned to earth. The safe return boosted NASA's public image and increased public and Congressional support for future manned space missions (Kauffman 2001; Lovell and Kluger 2006).

Research also suggests that some firefighters make better crisis decisions than others. Gary Klein (1998) studied a team of firefighters that entered a building under the assumption that a fire had broken out in the kitchen. Yet, the team commander noticed that several things were at odds with this assumption. The fire was too hot for a small kitchen fire and could not be tamed by spraying water on it. The fire commander quickly ordered his team to evacuate the building. Only seconds after the firefighters had left the house, the ground floor collapsed. The firefighters quickly realized that the fire in the kitchen had only been a small part of a bigger fire that had started in the cellar. If the team commander had not ordered an immediate evacuation, the fire would have killed the entire team (Klein 1998; also see Flin 1996).

The research on so-called High Reliability Organizations (HROs) shows that some organizations such as aircraft carriers or air traffic control centers perform much better in response to unexpected turbulence than other organizations (Roberts 1990; LaPorte and Consolini 1991; Sagan 1994; Weick et al. 2008). These HROs are able to perform almost failure-free despite the complex tasks they have to accomplish in a dynamic and uncontrollable environment. Naval aircraft carriers, for instance, are able to carry out complex tasks because they rely on redundancy and collective monitoring. When a plane lands on an aircraft carrier, the process is controlled and monitored by different people on different parts of the ship. These people are engaged in a constant stream of conversation and verification on several different channels. The landing process is thus continuously evaluated from many different perspectives that allow one to identify any deviations or problems (Rochlin et al. 1987).

Political scientists have shown that some political leaders perform better in times of crises than their peers (Preston 2001; Greenstein 2011; 't Hart 2011; Mitchell 2005; Pious 2008; Walker 2009). President Kennedy's (and Russian leader Khrushchev's) handling of the Cuban Missile Crisis has been lauded as a successful example of crisis management that prevented a nuclear war (Allison and Zelikow 1999; Schwarz 2013). After the Elbe flood hit the eastern part of Germany in 2002, Chancellor Gerhard Schröder was publicly perceived as such an efficient crisis manager that his Social Democratic party won the national elections a few weeks later (Bytzek 2008).

Other public leaders have been less successful in handling major political crises. When several bomb explosions left 192 people dead in Madrid in March 2004 only days before a national election, the conservative Spanish government led by Prime Minister Aznar blamed the Basque ETA for the terrorist attacks. After evidence emerged that the attacks were carried out by Islamist terrorists as a reaction to Spain's participation in the Iraq War, the Conservative Party—which had comfortably led in the polls—lost the elections to the Socialist Party (Olmeda 2008). US President Carter's handling of the Iran Hostage Crisis was marked by internal conflicts between key advisors and ill-advised decisions, which may have contributed to Ronald Reagan's landslide victory in 1980 (Sigelman and Conover 1981; Houghton 2001).

This observation about variance in crisis management performance prompts an important question: Why do some organizations and their leaders seem to cope so much better with crisis threats than others? In other words, how can we explain the variance in crisis management performance?

TOWARDS A THEORY OF EFFECTIVE CRISIS MANAGEMENT: A PRAGMATIST TURN

An overarching theory of effective public crisis management does not exist. Moreover, much of the literature on crisis performance focuses on the operational level and has little to say about the specific challenges that top-level public leaders face during crises. But studies of crisis management performance do offer important cues. Karl Weick has emphasized how improvisation, creativity and the probing of solutions are crucial elements of crisis management (Weick 1988, 1993, 1995). Psychologist Gary Klein has identified similar qualities of effective crisis management in his analyses of how first responders deal with the ambiguous situations. Developing a distinct theory of "naturalistic decision making," he debunks rationalist models that regard decision making as a process of comprehensive comparison of different options (Kahneman and Klein 2009; Klein 2009). Instead Klein highlights how successful decision making during crises is a process based on mental simulations, metaphors, hypothesis testing and experimentation (Klein 1998). Researchers have also highlighted how high reliability organizations employ similar techniques of flexibility and redundancy to reduce the chances of failures and errors (LaPorte and Consolini 1991; LaPorte 1996; Roe and Schulman 2008, 2016).

By investigating successful practices, Weick, Klein and the HRO researchers have developed a different perspective on the management of complex systems and crises, emphasizing distinct terms and concepts in the process. They have analysed effective crisis management as a process of learning-while-doing, as enactment, as adaption, as bricolage, as trial-and-error or as hypothesis testing. These characteristics of effective crisis management closely resemble core concepts of Pragmatist philosophy. Pragmatism is a philosophical approach that originated in the late 19th and early 20th centuries with American philosophers like Charles S. Peirce, William James, Jane Addams, John Dewey and George Herbert Mead. It is a broad school of thought that contributes to ethics, logic, epistemology, psychology, political theory and art (Lovejoy 1908; Posner 2003; Koopman 2009). In the remainder of the book, we capitalize *Pragmatism* when we are referring to the philosophy and use the lower-case *pragmatism* to refer to the more generic, and non-philosophical ordinary meaning of the term.

What is interesting about Pragmatism from the perspective of crisis management is that it offers a model of practical rationality that is particularly well-suited to responding to the conditions of uncertainty that characterize crises. Most philosophical and practical attempts to address uncertainty, according to the Pragmatist philosopher John Dewey, try to negate or remove it (Dewey 1990). By contrast, Pragmatism suggest that humans must learn to live with uncertainty and hence it strives to build a philosophy that enables "successful action under conditions of uncertainty" (Joas 2000, 39).

For Pragmatists, the key to a philosophy of successful action under conditions of uncertainty can be found in human practice (see Joas 1993, 1996; Menand 1997). In practical action, people routinely face situations of uncertainty where they are not sure what to do. Yet people are able to make decisions under such conditions and do not need to wait for conclusive evidence to do so. Although people may rely on fixed beliefs or principles to simply override uncertainty, this requires them to assume the true or right decision a priori (Peirce 1997b). Pragmatists reject this approach as flawed because fixed beliefs and principles override rather than respond to uncertainty. Instead, people can explore a situation of uncertainty and acquire more information about it; they can then try something and see if it "works" and then revise and adapt their strategy based on the feedback they receive. This style of probing and revising was at the heart of Pragmatist Charles Sanders Peirce's conception of the scientific method of hypothesis testing.

We identify and discuss four features of Pragmatist practical rationality that may aid strategic crisis managers in responding effectively to crisis conditions, and particularly to uncertainty: anti-dualism, fallibilism, experimentalism and deliberation. *Anti-dualism* rejects strict black-and-white dichotomies and highlights the continuum between perceived extreme poles. *Fallibilism* reminds us that all knowledge remains potentially fallible and that it might need to be revised when new evidence comes to light. *Experimentalism* probes and tries out hypotheses in order to solve a given problem. Finally, *deliberation* addresses uncertainty through imagination and dialogue.

These Pragmatist concepts of anti-dualism, fallibilism, experimentalism and deliberation are close to what Weick, Klein and the HRO researchers have described as learning-while-doing, enactment, adaption, bricolage, trial-and-error or as hypothesis testing. These researchers share with philosophical Pragmatism a focus on the "primacy of practice" and they share an emphasis on placing successful human practice at the center of their theories. As we will argue, beginning in Chapter 2, the practical rationality illuminated by Pragmatism suggests hidden resources for successful crisis management.

RESEARCH OBJECTIVE AND METHODOLOGICAL APPROACH

In the remainder of this book we build a model of Pragmatist crisis management at the political-strategic level, translating the core concepts of philosophical Pragmatism into a concrete model of what *Pragmatist crisis management* looks like in practice. To clarify the implications of Pragmatist crisis management, we also contrast it with what we will call *principle-guided crisis management*, which mirrors the Pragmatist approach along its four core dimensions (anti-dualism, fallibilism, experimentalism, deliberation). These two contrasting models are meant to apply to political crisis management in a generic and ideal-typical fashion (Weber 1949, 90). That is, they depict Pragmatist and principle-guided political crisis management in their "pure" form, implying that a continuum between both approaches exists and that hybrids of both approaches can be expected in empirical practice.

We then roughly operationalize these two crisis management models by defining a set of empirical specifications that we should expect to see in crisis situations. To explore the usefulness of these empirical specifications, we then analyse two critical decision-making episodes during the US financial crisis of 2008: (1) the decision by the Bush Administration to rescue the investment bank Bear Stearns in March 2008 and (2) the Bush Administration's decision to let the investment bank Lehman Brothers fail in September 2008. In probing these two cases, our goal is to identify which of the model specifications—or which combination—best characterizes decision making and meaning making.

From a methodological perspective, it is also important to note that the two case studies do not aim to provide conclusive evidence for the model of Pragmatist and principle-guided political crisis management. Instead, they are best understood as "plausibility probes" (Eckstein 1992, 147) that are intended to explore if we can find preliminary empirical evidence for the model. The analysis of these cases therefore should not be understood as full-blown case studies but as initial probes of whether Pragmatism offers insight into political crisis management.

As we will demonstrate, these models help us recognize things that we might not otherwise observe. In the study of the Bush Administration's financial crisis management, we identify Pragmatist decision making and meaning making in the Bear Stearns case. We will see how the Bush Administration was guided by Pragmatist political crisis management in departing from its own free-market principles in its attempt to rescue Bear Stearns. However, in the Lehman case, we find mixed results that include evidence for both approaches. After the Bear Stearns rescue, the decision to let Lehman fail can be characterized as principle-guided political crisis management that intended to send a strong message that the Bush government had returned to its free-market principles. After Lehman failed, the Bush Administration again returned to a Pragmatist approach in its decisions to save the insurance company AIG and the money market funds.

In a summarizing chapter (see Chapter 8) we offer hypotheses to explain the shifts between Pragmatist and principle-guided political crisis management for future research. Since part of the research objective is to demonstrate how this model can be used in empirical research, this chapter paves the way for future empirical research by briefly introducing and discussing several hypotheses regarding the causes and combinations of Pragmatist and principle-guided political crisis management. These hypotheses can serve as starting points for future research projects and should demonstrate the possible scope and reach of empirical research that can build on this model.

OUTLINE OF THE STUDY

Chapter 2 provides an overview of Pragmatism, situating its development in wider philosophical debates. In their attempt to break away from the legacy of dualism (e.g., subject versus object; mind versus body) inherited from continental European philosophy, the founding Pragmatists developed a rich conception of practical rationality. This practical rationality is distinctive in its interpretation of intentionality, cognition, meaning, emotion and even values, seeing them as partly arising in the course of action rather than as prior to action. This position allows Pragmatism to more fully embrace the role of uncertainty and the fallibility of knowledge. These general considerations serve as the theoretical foundation for identifying four hidden resources of a Pragmatist conception of crisis management—anti-dualism, fallibilism, experimentalism and deliberation.

Chapter 3 further investigates decision making and meaning making under uncertainty. The chapter begins with a discussion of the meaning of uncertainty and then begins to examine what the crisis management literature and other relevant discussions say about how decisions are made under uncertainty. Naturalistic decision making, case-based reasoning and sensemaking models capture important elements of the Pragmatist practical rationality described in Chapter 2. The chapter then investigates how decision makers communicate uncertainty, drawing on an extensive literature on risk communication. The idea of "blame games" is also discussed. The chapter concludes by discussing the tensions in prior research about the successes and failures of decision making and meaning making under uncertainty.

Chapter 4 takes the theoretical insights from Chapters 2 and 3 and translates them into models of Pragmatist and principle-guided political crisis management. These models are structured according to the four basic building blocks of anti-dualism, fallibilism, experimentalism and deliberation (and their opposites in the case of principle-guided political crisis management). By creating empirical specifications for these building blocks, we provide empirical standards for ascertaining what Pragmatist and principle-guided political crisis management will look like in practice. These specifications guide the empirical research process in Chapters 6 and 7.

Chapter 5 introduces the two episodes of the US financial crisis of 2008 that we use to probe the usefulness of our two models. The first case is the rescue of Bear Stearns in March 2008 and the second is the decision to allow Lehman Brothers' investment bank to fail in September 2008. These two episodes were critical decision-making and meaning-making points in the wider financial crisis. This chapter introduces both episodes in order to prepare the reader for more systematic empirical analysis of our two conceptual models in Chapters 6 and 7.

Chapter 6 analyses the first of the two empirical cases, the Bush Administration's decision to rescue the investment bank Bear Stearns. The chapter finds evidence of Pragmatist political crisis management for all four of the building blocks of Pragmatist political crisis management.

Chapter 7 then analyses the case of the Bush Administration's decision to let the investment bank Lehman Brothers fail. Although our analysis finds evidence for both Pragmatist and principle-guided political crisis management, the outcome primarily reflects a shift back to principle-guided political crisis management.

Chapter 8 summarizes and contrasts the results of the preceding empirical chapters and provides ideas for future research. The chapter focuses on the question of why the Bush Administration switched from Pragmatist to principle-guided political crisis management and then back to Pragmatism again. It offers various hypotheses that formulate answers to this question and discusses them briefly. The concluding part of the chapter deals with combinations of Pragmatist and principle-guided political crisis management and revisits our understanding of both approaches.

Chapter 9, the concluding chapter, briefly summarizes the main insights from this study while also highlighting its limitations and formulating a research agenda for future research.

2.   Pragmatism and the hidden resources of practical rationality

To understand how leaders can engage in strategic crisis management, it is useful to consider how they may think and act under conditions of uncertainty and turbulence. We argue that the philosophical tradition of Pragmatism provides under-appreciated insights into thinking and action under just these circumstances. Our chief interest in Pragmatism, for the purposes of this book, is that it offers a powerful and distinctive model of practical rationality (Garrison 1999, 2000; Frega 2012). This model provides an account of how people act in the face of doubt to solve problems, large and small. Part of the attraction of this model is that it is not a narrow or reductive model of human rationality. It fully appreciates that humans are social beings guided by habit and emotion to make decisions in an imperfectly understood world—social beings who partially make up for their limitations as mental calculating machines through their experience, resourcefulness and creativity.

The tradition of philosophical Pragmatism grew out of the distinctive philosophical and historical milieu of late 19th- and early 20th-century US. Working at the intersection of the dueling traditions of Cartesian and Kantian rationality, on the one hand, and British empiricism, on the other (Thayer 1968; Kloppenberg 1988), Pragmatist philosophers like Charles Peirce, William James, Jane Addams, John Dewey and George Herbert Mead critically probed the relationship between *knowledge, values* and *action*. Shaped to some degree by Emersonian transcendentalism (West 1989), Pragmatism arose at a time when secular, scientific and Darwinian influences were ascendant (Menand 2001) but when the disciplines of psychology and philosophy remained closely intertwined. While these genealogical influences are themselves fascinating, the focus of this chapter is on describing the model of practical rationality that the Pragmatists developed from this heady brew of ideas (Bernstein 1971; Rescher 2004).

By *rationality*, we mean the way that people "critically take hold of their experience" and "control action" (Frega 2012, 1).[1] By *practical* rationality,

---

[1]   Hickman proposes a slightly different view of what Dewey meant by rationality: "He constructed 'rationality' as 'intelligence'—the formulation and testing of ends that are proposed in the context of, and grow from, experimental activities" (1990, 11).

we mean the way that people engage in action to solve everyday problems. To say that Pragmatists had *a* model of practical rationality is certainly an overly heroic claim. It is much more accurate to say that the thinkers that we refer to when we talk about classical Pragmatism engaged in a whole series of investigations to explore the relationship between knowledge, values and action. There was never a convergence on a single theory, nor even agreement on the overarching purpose of these investigations. However, there is a great deal of affinity of thought. Richard Bernstein proposes that we understand Pragmatism as a broad *mentality*—that is, "a general orientation—a cast of mind or way of thinking—that conditions the way in which we approach, understand, and act in the world" (Bernstein 2005, 18). Dewey and his collaborators themselves referred to the Pragmatic "attitude" (Dewey 1917). Nevertheless, we can draw synthetically on this tradition to articulate a Pragmatist model of practical rationality.

Although we use a more limited version in subsequent chapters, the purpose of this chapter is to explore the full richness of Pragmatism's model of practical rationality. Among its virtues, we point to Pragmatism's attention to uncertainty and the fallibility of knowledge, its joining together of habit and creativity and emotion and reason, its focus on inquiry, experimentation and deliberation, and its insightful treatment of temporality, value and inference. While this model of practical rationality offers no straightforward recipe for how to make decisions and meaning under uncertainty, it does suggest *hidden resources* that ordinary citizens and leaders may draw upon in a crisis— hidden, that is, from the perspective of textbook accounts of utilitarian or value rationality.

ANTI-DUALISM AND THE ORIENTATION TO ACTION

Pragmatism's conceptualization of practical action did not grow out of a desire to eschew philosophy for practice, but rather out of a deep engagement with philosophical questions. Most importantly, perhaps, Pragmatists wrestled with a Cartesian philosophical legacy that they saw as dualistic—as creating overly drawn dichotomies such as culture versus nature, thought versus instinct, mind versus body, individual versus society, theory versus practice, fact versus value, and so on (Dewey 1896; Rorty 1979; Colapietro 2006). The founding Pragmatists sought to reconceive these dichotomies as interdependent and continuous rather than independent and oppositional. Although Pragmatists disagree on many points, anti-dualism is a common theme woven through their work, leading to new insights into how people think and act.

Transforming a dualism into a duality, however, is not just a stratagem for philosophers; it may be a hidden resource for all of us (Farjoun 2010). Thinking in anti-dualistic ways may help us to address the kinds of contradictions and paradoxes that pervade everyday life and that are arguably magnified in crisis situations (Ansell 2001; Smith and Graetz 2006; Farjoun 2016).

One of the most fundamental ways in which classical Pragmatists sought to break down dualisms was to adopt a strong orientation towards action (Strauss 1993). They took the perspective of people acting in situ, living their lives, making sense of the world, and confronting challenges (Colapietro 2011). This led them to emphasize the practical nature of rationality, with a focus on experience and problem-solving, an emphasis on process and social interaction, and a view of beliefs as subject to ongoing experimentation (Garrison 1999, 2000). Pragmatism's orientation towards practical action is problem-oriented and emphasizes the importance of situation and context and of process and temporality. This orientation offers a counterpoint to what Dewey called the "spectator theory of knowledge" (Dewey 1990, 19). The central claim is that humans generate knowledge and meaning of the world not through pure observation or reason but through their active engagement with it (Bernstein 1971).

Pragmatism's model of practical rationality diverges in critical ways from models of rationality that start with fixed values, norms, preferences or ends. A Pragmatist version of rationality can be broadly contrasted with two other common versions of rationality—utilitarian and value rationality.[2] The utilitarian model of rationality—typically known as "rational choice"—adopts the perspective that individuals make choices that optimize their preferences, while the model of value rationality assumes that individuals take action that comports with or realizes their ethical principles. While these two models of rationality are quite different in many respects, they share an important common feature: they both regard action as motivated and determined by preferences or values ("ends") established prior to choice or action. As a philosophy, much of what Pragmatism seeks to do is break away from this notion of fixed utilitarian preferences or ethical principles that determine subsequent action. While it is a misconception to interpret Pragmatism as uninterested in meaning or value, Pragmatism does stress that preferences and values are not fixed prior to action but rather are partially discovered through action.

While sharing a purposive conception of action with rational choice theory (Knight and Johnson 1999), Pragmatism departs significantly from the latter's model of utility maximization (Mousavi and Garrison 2003). It also breaks with the conception of intentionality that lies at the core of rational choice theory—a conception that views action as flowing from predetermined ends

---

[2]   We recognize that there are many versions of utilitarian and value rationality and that behavioral models of rationality have added a great deal of nuance and insight in recent years. Our purpose here is not to make a full-blown critique or analysis of these models of rationality. We simply use these contrasts to draw out what is distinctive about the Pragmatist model.

(Joas 1996; Emirbayer and Mische 1998; Whitford 2002; Beckert 2003; Mousavi and Garrison 2003; Gross 2009). Although Pragmatists do imagine that people have future-oriented goals, they are looser and more historically conditioned than imagined by rational choice theory—Dewey referred to them as "ends-in-view." Rather than understanding ends as prior to and distinct from means, Pragmatism understands goals as partially emerging from and being clarified through action and in interaction with means. This view undermines the dualism of ends and means, making Pragmatism sensitive to how the means we employ subsequently shape the ends that we can imagine (Whitford 2002).[3]

Another important implication of this orientation is that Pragmatism understands cognition, meaning, valuation, reflexivity and emotion in relation to action. Pragmatism rejects the idea that cognition forms our intentions and hence stands prior to action (Beckert 2003). Instead, cognition is part of action (Joas 1996) and develops in interaction with the environment. Thus, thinking is not purely "internal" to the mind (Menary 2016), a perspective supported by current research in the "embodied," "situated" and "extended" cognition traditions (Alexander 1990; Johnson and Rohrer 2007; Franks 2010; Engel et al. 2013; Gallagher 2014). Pragmatism takes a particular stance on how people think. It argues against the idea that we necessarily form a mental representation of what we want or believe—and then act. Instead, people often learn what their goals are by trying to do things (Joas 1996).

Pragmatism shares a focus on everyday experience and knowledge with the hermeneutic tradition (Polkinghorne 2000). Both traditions share a concern with "non-deliberative knowledge" or what Dewey called "knowing how." What people know depends on what they have experienced and their skills are conditioned by the environment in which their habits have been formed. Knowledge and skill are therefore partially context-dependent and skills and experiences are expected to vary across individuals (rational choice, by contrast, treats actors as interchangeable). As McGowan writes: "The individual is, in a word, experienced—and carries the way of being in the world that experience has forged" (McGowan 1998, 294).

Despite the focus on concrete experience, the Pragmatist mind is not a passive recipient of sensory data, as it is in the British empiricist tradition (Webb 2007). Rather, it actively engages in interpreting the world and may

---

[3] The Pragmatist perspective on thinking and action breaks, in part, with the teleological conception of action embraced by rational choice theory (Joas 1996; Whitford 2002; Beckert 2003; Mousavi and Garrison 2003). Doing so enables Pragmatism to better fathom the complexity of strategic action (Beckert 2003, 772). However, Pragmatism does not break with a teleological account of rationality altogether. For example, Thomas Alexander writes: "For pragmatists, the meaning of action is determined by futural teleology rather than a priori intention" (1990, 337).

"enact" an environment in which a person then acts (Wiley 2003; Gallagher 2014). Decisions require an interpretation of the situation, which is formed in interaction with the situation as a holistic context (Garrison 1996; Frega 2010). Initial engagement with this situation is guided by experience and feeling, which may guide a "selective interest" in the situation (Garrison 1996). Pragmatism regards meaning as "fixed" in relation to a particular purpose, context or reference point—a point-of-view. As Flaherty and Fine write, "There is an infinite number of stimuli in any particular setting—cognitive overload—but the individual selects those that enable him or her to construct a meaningful and useful line of action ..." (2001, 152).

The conclusion that the reader should draw is not that Pragmatism does not care about ends, cognition, meaning or intentions. Rather, the key point is that they are partially discovered or articulated in and through action (Thayer 1968; Stuhr 2003; Miettenen 2006; Frega 2010; Muniesa 2012).[4] As a result, judgment is situational (Nash 2003). Whether seen through a normative or empirical lens, Pragmatism encourages us to orient ourselves to concrete situations, focusing in particular on the opportunities or demands for action entailed by those situations. We must "start from where we find ourselves" (Misak 2014, e12).

HABIT, CREATIVITY AND IMAGINATION

In contrast with rational choice theory, which associates mind narrowly with rational cognition, Pragmatism understands mind as "multi-tiered"—that is, as encompassing habit, instinct and intelligence (Twomey 1998).[5] Habit is particularly central to Pragmatism's conception of action (Lawlor 2006; Barbalet 2008; Kilpinen 2009, 2013). Habits are repertoires of action deployed in response to inferences that relate the situation-at-hand to past experience.[6]

---

[4]   Perhaps it is worth noting here that while Pragmatism is oriented to particular situations, it does appreciate that there is something "general" that transcends situations. In fact, this is a major point about "habit," which Pragmatists understand to be a general disposition to action.

[5]   We acknowledge here that Kahneman's (2012) distinction between system 1 and system 2 comes very close to this "multi-tiered" concept of mind.

[6]   Peirce had an "associative view" of mind (Massecar 2012). He understood the associations formed by the mind to be guided by attention, which is in turn guided by feelings we have about an association. Attention is a critical act of cognition capable of bringing together feelings under a common sign ("all association is by signs") (Massecar 2012, 196). Attention is the basis of induction, which is a judgment that an association has a certain quality. Peirce spoke of habits as inductively derived rules of action. A habit is a general idea (formed inductively by association) that proves itself useful through repeated use (while formed by induction, they become the basis for

These inferences are themselves habitual and acquired through trial-and-error (Baldwin 1988). Habits develop from transactions with the environment— they are "an interactional product of the encounter of agent with situation" (McGowan 1998, 293). Like the models of bounded rationality elaborated by the Carnegie school of organization theory, Pragmatism emphasizes the habitual and learned basis of action and the importance of attention. Yet unlike the Carnegie school's view of routine, habit is mindful rather than mindless (Cohen 2007).[7]

Both Peirce and Dewey explicitly noted that their conception of habit deviated somewhat from common usage.[8] This is in part because the Pragmatists understood habit as "intelligent" rather than as mindless routine.[9] Habits are analogous to skills—learned techniques for dealing with situations (Dewey 1922, 15; Barbalet 2008). We are to some extent aware of our habits and can to some extent direct them. Indeed, Kilpinen (2009) refers to Pragmatism's distinctive perspective on habit as "reflexive habit" and Peirce emphasized that "self-control" over habit is critical to the subsequent development of habit.

---

hypothesis formation (e.g., abduction; Mullins 2002)). Associations may be incomplete, which leads to vague or abstract thoughts. Habit unites the different modes of inference—it is formed by induction, but makes possible abduction and deduction (Massecar 2012, 203).

[7]   Habits are non-deterministic dispositions to action (Dewey 1922, 26, 42) and are linked directly to emotion and cognition (Baldwin 1988). They shape thought and belief (Dewey 1922, 30, 32; Kilpinen 2013) and Peirce often referred to beliefs as habits of action. As Kilpinen (2009) writes: "motivation, volition and deliberation are situated inside the habitual dimension" and as Hogdson (2004, 27) similarly notes: "Habit is not the negation of deliberation but its necessary foundation."

[8]   The concept of habit takes us deep into the heart of Peirce's complex philosophy. First, an overarching aspect of Peirce's philosophy is its rejection of seeing the world as either random or deterministic. For Peirce, habit represents the "lawful" character of the world. However, as a law, habit is only a general disposition to act in a particular way. In Peirce's tripartite system of categories, habits represent "thirdness" (e.g., law-like). Exhibiting thirdness, habits mediate between firstness (quality, feeling, instinct) and secondness (force, causation, dyadic relation). Habit is also a "general"—an abstraction from particulars. Appreciating this helps us understand why Peirce described habit as a general disposition. Habit is also fundamentally related to his categorization of signs and to his analysis of semiosis. For Peirce, the sign process is triadic, composed of a sign, an object and an "interpretant." Habit is the "interpretant" of symbols (a sign embodying "thirdness"), producing a "law-like" interpretation of the meaning of the sign (Nöth 2010). The habitual interpretation is what makes the sign a symbol. This point helps us understand why Peirce referred to beliefs as "habits of action." Habits link signs and actions.

[9]   Prawat (2000) notes that Dewey self-consciously followed Peirce's conception of habit.

One of the most distinctive features of the Pragmatist model of practical rationality is that it sees human action as *both* habitual and creative (Joas 1996; Berk and Galvan 2009; Kilpinen 2009; Glăveanu 2012). Action is guided by habit until people encounter problems that trigger reflection and inquiry. Failed or blocked habits create an uncertain and problematic situation that triggers doubt, reflexivity, inquiry, deliberation, imagination and experimentation (Kuruvilla and Dorstewitz 2010; Massecar 2011; Miettinen et al. 2012). Problematic situations push people to creatively forge "new and more complex ends" (Dewey 1917, 63) and to reconstruct their own habits (Berk and Galvan 2009). Even in these problematic moments, however, habit may provide important scaffolding for creativity (Dalton 2004; Kupers 2011; Sonenshein 2016).

Pragmatists sometimes talk about creativity in term of play or playfulness, which emphasizes the adaptive or improvisational discovery of new possibilities for action (Joas 1990). From this perspective, creativity emerges out of the process of engaging with problems (Sawyer 2000). It is also associated with the emphasis that Pragmatists place on imagination. In a discussion of Dewey, Thomas Alexander notes that "imagination seeks to understand the actual in light of the possible in a dramatic or experimental way" (1990, 337). As he further notes: "Our capacity to view the present from a number of possible points of view offers the basis from which more fulfilling values may emerge and be implemented in reconstructive activity. By dramatically engaging these options in imagination, we can anticipate the meaning of the situation" (1990, 338). Imagination is thus about grasping the meaningful possibilities in a situation.

PRACTICAL RATIONALITY AND TIME

Pragmatism stresses the temporal aspects of human action, a perspective most fully developed in the work of George Herbert Mead. Mead's view of temporality argues that the past and the future are linked by the present. Although this sounds like a fortune cookie saying, it is consequential for understanding how people behave. Mead argues that the present is related to certain events that lead actors to construct (or reconstruct) the past in relation to a future orientation (Mead 1932, 15). Mead's perspective is nicely summarized by Barbara Simpson: "Actors located between the past and the future are obliged to continuously reconstruct their histories in order to understand their present transactions. At the same time, they project these understandings into the future to infer the likely outcomes of present actions" (2009, 1338; see also Emirbayer and Mische 1998).

Pragmatism is therefore "presentist" in that it focuses on the present. As Thomas Alexander writes: "The rationality of action lies in its acknowledgement of the play of possibility in the present" (1990, 334). Yet, as noted, the present links the past to the future. An important feature of Pragmatism is that while emphasizing experience and habit—legacies of the past—its attention to action lead it to frame problems in future terms (Elkjaer 2009). On the one hand, as Colin Koopman (2009) argues, Pragmatism adopts a historicist view on action, which means that action is understood to be historically situated and conditioned. On the other hand, Pragmatism has a strong future orientation (Barbalet 2004, 343). The Pragmatist focus on the present problem mediates between past and future.

Another important feature of the Pragmatist understanding of temporality is its focus on the continuous flow of activity (Rosenthal 1996; Hookway 2013). Hitlin and Elder summarize an important implication of this point for practical rationality: "We make choices within the flow of situated activity, and emotions and personality traits—along with idiosyncratic personal histories, moral codes, and predispositions—influence the choices we make in emergent situations" (2007, 178).[10] A further implication of this emphasis on continuity is that we can understand action in terms of the narrative flow of individual biography or identity. Until interrupted, action attempts to maintain the continuity of biography or identity (Maines et al. 1983; Ezzy 1998).

The past, however, does not determine the present because continuity is disturbed by events—and as a result, time becomes discontinuous. Mead (1929) argued that it is in these discontinuities that novelty emerges. His perspective on time as eventful leads to a stress on the possibilities of emergent novelty as actors try to construct the past and anticipate the future in order to address the present problems (Hernes et al. 2013). Thus, Mead's conception of temporality parallels Pragmatism's unusual connection of habit (past), creativity (present) and imagination (future).

ACTING IN THE FACE OF UNCERTAINTY: FALLIBILISM, INQUIRY AND EXPERIMENTATION

A concern with uncertainty is baked into classical Pragmatism because it starts with the view that all knowledge is fallible and subject to continuous revision (Dieleman 2017). Peirce's initial development of Pragmatism started with a critique of Cartesian philosophy, and in particular, with its position on

---

[10]   One way to bring together this "presentist" sensibility with the idea of continuous flow between past and future is via the idea of "transitions." Colin Koopman argues that the way to understand Pragmatism's stress on historicism, presentism, continuity and futurity is via the idea of transitions (Koopman 2009, 2010). For instance, in Dewey, judgment takes place in the transition from a problematic situation to its resolution (Frega 2012).

certainty and uncertainty (or in the terms of that debate, on belief and doubt). Cartesian approaches were after something that Peirce regarded as impossible and unnecessary—a final "test of certainty" (Peirce 1992, 29). For Peirce "absolute certainty ... can never be attained by mortals" (Peirce 1992, 158) and the whole Cartesian debate about it is an artificial and counterproductive one.

John Dewey built on this argument and extended it to ethical action, arguing against the attraction of what he regarded as the false certainties of moral philosophy: "[I]n morals a hankering for certainty, born of timidity and nourished by love of authoritative prestige, has led to the idea that absence of immutably fixed and universally applicable ready-made principles is equivalent to moral chaos" (Dewey 1922, 238). Dewey finds moral philosophy's retreat to such universal principles as highly problematic because it tends to ignore "situations into which change and the unexpected enter" (Dewey 1922, 239).

That does not mean that Dewey rejects moral ideas. What he criticizes here is something this study will refer to as *principles*, that is, beliefs that are "immutably fixed and universally applicable" (Dewey 1922, 238). Rather than treating such principles as fixed and universal, Dewey suggests that we treat them as "methods of inquiry and forecast which require verification by the event" and "as hypotheses with which to experiment" (Dewey 1922, 239). Highlighting the centrality of uncertainty in the field of moral philosophy Dewey shows that a Pragmatist position does not come to the conclusion that there are no values at all. Rather, it focuses on how values adapt (see Joas 2000).

In *The Quest for Certainty*, Dewey voices an analogous critique about assuming that knowledge stands in an a priori relationship to action: "The common essence of all these theories, in short, is that what is known is antecedent to the mental act of observation and inquiry, and is totally unaffected by these acts; otherwise it would not be fixed and unchangeable" (1990, 19). This point has powerful implications for how we understand practical rationality, as nicely illustrated by Daniel Bromley (2008) using an example from a famous debate on epistemology between Otto Neurath and Rudolf Carnap:

> The comprehensive inability to write down objective descriptions of the future entailments of available actions puts us in the position of Neurath's Mariner who was forced to repair his ship while at sea. Unable to reach port, the mariner needed to figure out what he must do as he figured out what it was possible for him to do. Each of us must work out (learn about) what is to be done as we work out (learn about) what can be done. (2008, 4)

The powerful implication here is that we must learn about ends and means together. Strategy emerges through action (Simpson 2009), a process Donald Schön (1992) has called "reflection-in-action."

Pragmatists suggest that working under uncertainty—repairing the ship at sea—requires a combination of habit and inquiry. Habits are learned dispositions to respond in certain ways in certain circumstances (Baldwin 1988; Lawlor 2006; Kilpinen 2009).[11] As long as the context is stable and familiar enough, habits are crucial in "selecting" the goals, preferences, outlooks and actions we pursue (or avoid) and the environments where they are likely to flourish (Lawlor 2006). Inquiry is prompted by the need to act in an "objectively precarious but improvable environment" (Festenstein 2001, 732) or as Bromley provocatively puts it, "indeterminacy is the reason we reason" (2008, 4). Local breakdowns, non-routine events or surprises (such as crises) trigger an emotion of doubt, which, in turn, initiates a process of inquiry through reflexivity, deliberation and experimentation (Kuruvilla and Dorstewitz 2010; Massecar 2011; Miettinen et al. 2012).

For Dewey, inquiry is a practice used to "define the specific problem that the situation presents and to re-establish in accordance with human purposes the provisional equilibrium which held" (Festenstein 2001, 732). Inquiry involves the "elucidation of meaning" (Festenstein 2001, 734), including abstraction and concept formation (Webb 2007; Winther 2014) and, critically, self-reflection on one's own beliefs, interests and values (Miettinen 2000). Inquiry brings existing knowledge and prior experience to bear on the situation, while seeking to avoid moralizing "position-taking," on the one hand, or a narrow instrumentalism, on the other. Reflection on and revision of existing habits and values is a central aspect of inquiry.

Although an emphasis on inquiry sounds rationalistic, Pragmatism does not assume that decision makers optimize a single underlying value metric (e.g., utility) or that they know the risk probabilities underlying their decisions. Schön argues that a Deweyian approach uses a mode of inquiry that is like design, though not design in the sense of a heuristic search in a given search space. Instead, he writes, it is a form of design that "emphasizes the construction of coherence through play and appreciative judgment" (1992, 131).

While actors often have feelings and intuitions about problematic situations, these situations have an incomplete and "qualitative" character. Therefore, the first phase of reflexive problem-solving is to articulate the problem (Frega 2012). This articulation leads to a controlled hypothesis about how to address the problem, which through resolution may transform prior beliefs or habits

---

[11] In *Human Nature and Conduct*, Dewey frames this issue using the term *tendency*: "We have to admit the role of accident. We cannot get beyond tendencies … The word 'tendency' is an attempt to combine two facts, one that habits have a certain causal efficacy, the other that their outworking in any particular case is subject to contingencies, to circumstances which are unforeseeable and which carry an act one side of its usual effect" (Dewey 1922, 48–9).

(Festenstein 2001; Frega 2010). This mode of inquiry is experimental and is carefully used to find out more about the world around us and gather new knowledge by actively engaging with and adapting to our surroundings.[12]

PRAGMATISM ON VALUES AND VALUATION

As the previous discussion has stressed, Pragmatism reinterprets intentions, principles, cognition and knowledge as internal to practical action rather than as standing prior to that action. It adopts a similar stance towards values. John Dewey was the Pragmatist who most fully elaborated a Pragmatist position on values, as usefully summarized by Roberto Frega:

> Values and norms do not enter judgment as ready-made criteria requiring only careful application in deductive reasoning. At the beginning of reasoning, they are, instead, underdetermined entities which require to be articulated with reference to the situation. This reflective act, consisting in the selection, determination and interpretation of norms and values, is a specific phase of valuation. (2012, 63)

Valuation is an important aspect of Pragmatism's model of practical rationality. Values emerge through practical action (Peltola and Arpin 2017) and valuation is situational and prompted by problems (Whitford 2002). Value judgments are therefore a kind of practical judgment (Stark 2011; Muniesa 2012; Proulx 2016; Hauge 2017).

In shifting the focus from value to valuation, Dewey breaks away from a linear ends-means model of rationality (Whitford 2002). By understanding values as situational and practice-oriented, we move away from seeing value as an objective quality of things or as embodied in fixed moral rules (Klamer 2003; Stuhr 2003; Muniesa 2011; Stark 2011). By doing this, we break with the rational choice view that "postulates actors with 'values' or 'desires' that serve as ends and in turn as the unique source of all valuations; only the appropriate means is selected" (Whitford 2002, 337). As Klamer puts it, channeling Dewey, "[p]eople do not have values written on their forehead ..." (2003, 197).

As with the more general Pragmatist understanding of judgment, value judgments begin with feelings about an indeterminate situation and proceed to a more refined and reflective understanding of the issues at stake. Dewey distinguishes between "inital valuation" (without reflection), which is shaped by our desires and experiences, and a second stage of evaluation, which is more reflective. Reflexive evaluation requires putting a particular value in relation to other values (Proulx 2016). However, Pragmatism does not assume that values

---

[12]   Bromley (2008) draws an analogy between Bayesian decision making and Pragmatism's emphasis on continuous updating of reasonable beliefs about action.

are commensurable—that is, that they can be represented on a common scale of utility (Klamer 2003). Instead, it assumes that values will often clash and that problem-solving often requires adjudication or integration across values (Hutter and Stark 2015).

Emotion may aid in the process of finding a balanced solution to conflicting imperatives. As William James argued in *The Sentiment of Rationality*, Pragmatism suggests that we discover courses of action that balance our desires, goals, interests in emotionally satisfying ways (James 1896; Barbalet 2004, 2008). Morse summarizes the argument: "It is, rather, an emotional preference for that course of action that promises to actually resolve the original conflict such as it is" (Morse 2010, 226). Moreover, James, the classical Pragmatist theorist who paid the most attention to emotion, viewed emotion as important for coping with the uncertainty of future-oriented action. Emotion is partly driven by conflicting imperatives and social interaction (Denzin 1985), but is also motivational (Barbalet 2004; Zeelenberg and Pieters 2006; Shusterman 2012). As both an aid to judgment and as a motivation for action, emotion is another hidden resource of practical rationality—though by no means an infallible one.

As in his other work, Dewey breaks down the dualism of subject versus object by reinterpreting value as interactional or transactional. He concedes that desire is primal, but as Frank Ryan notes:

> Deliberation directed toward 'appraisal' is a crucial step in valuation activity. Dewey does not deny that desired ends are prized, but for him this marks only an *initial* phase of inquiry. The desired end is not yet a genuine value, but a *value candidate* subject to modification in the hypothetical interplay of means and ends. (2003, 250, emphasis in the original)

Valuation is therefore an experimental process that is only complete once the hypothesis has been tested through action.[13]

PRACTICAL RATIONALITY AND INTERPRETATION-AS-INFERENCE

Like rational choice theory, Pragmatism tends to stress the instrumental character of action, but it differs from a utilitarian perspective in stressing the symbolic and the meaningful dimensions of action. As Gross puts it in his development of a Pragmatist view of "mechanism": "In a pragmatist model, all

---

[13]   "Genuine value is a process of valuation where something desired proves its desirability by being tested in the encountered world" (Ryan 2003, 246). Thus, "[v]alue is a quality that has to be performed" (Hutter and Stark 2015, 2).

social action involves cultural interpretation" (2009, 373). Whether in Charles Peirce's development of semiotics, William James's analysis of religiosity, John Dewey's theories of art, communication, experience or education, or in George Herbert Mead's development of social psychology, human action is symbolic and communicative.[14]

Like hermeneutics and social constructivism, Pragmatism understands action as an interpretive process rooted in a sign process, or semiosis.[15] At the heart of Peirce's development of semiotics is a fundamental concern with inference. Humans use signs as tools to draw inferences—to draw conclusions from information. Peirce was a logician and logic is, of course a highly formalized version of inference. But Peirce was also interested in how this worked in thought in general. As Errki Kilpinen puts it: "all mental movements according to Peirce are of an inferential nature" (2009, 110).[16] For Dewey, inference is central to intelligent thought: "Inference, the use of what happens to anticipate what will—or at least may—happen, makes the difference between directed and undirected participation" (1917, 22).

Distinctively, therefore, Pragmatism understands interpretation as inference, a position that leads to several attractive features. First, it keeps uncertainty, indeterminacy and context at the center of our considerations because an inference is a fallible judgment. Second, it emphasizes the dynamism of the process of interpretation—culture is not a set of rules that we act out mindlessly, but an active process of forming judgments. And third, inference calls attention to the point where meaning and action most clearly intersect. Dewey argued that all inference requires a "leap"—"a jump from the known into the unknown."

---

[14]   The mediating role of symbols is explicitly developed in Peirce's analysis of signs, which he developed into semiotics (Atkin 2013). A distinctive feature of his semiotics is a triadic model of interpretation, which is often contrasted with a dyadic, structuralist (Saussurian) semiotics. Peirce distinguishes three interrelated aspects of the semiotic process—the sign, the object and the interpretant. According to Peirce, the signification of the object is not contained by the relationship between the sign and the object. Rather, the meaning of the sign-object relationships is "fixed" by a third element—the interpretant. An important implication of this triadic process is that meaning tends to be "fixed" in reference to a specific context, social interaction, purpose or question—that is, in relation to a concrete situation. This emphasis on situated and emergent meaning runs throughout Pragmatist thought. Another important implication of Peirce's semiotics is that the meaning of the interpretant is fixed, in turn, by reference to another interpretant. Thus, meaning opens itself to an open web of signification. It is often noted that this open-ended conception of signification anticipates Wittgenstein's concept of language games.

[15]   Shalin (2007) argues that Pragmatist hermeneutics combines a "word-body-action arc" that encompasses symbolic-discursive, somatic-affective and behavioral-performative aspects of the semiotic process.

[16]   If inference is understood in a broad way.

Subsequent action tests that hypothesis (1933, 96). As Flaherty and Fine put it in a discussion of Mead's work: "interpretations are akin to working hypotheses" (2001, 155).[17]

Pragmatism emphasizes this type of hypothesis-forming "exploratory inference" as a mode of action, particularly in its development of the idea of abductive inference (Menary 2016). Peirce was the first to describe a distinctive form of inference that stands alongside induction and deduction, which he called abduction. He argued that abduction is a conjecture that takes the form of a hypothesis. Here is a syllogism that Peirce used to describe an abductive inference:

> The surprising fact, C, is observed
> But if A were true, C would be a matter of course,
> Hence, there is reason to suspect A is true.

As this syllogism suggests, abductive thinking is triggered by surprise (Aliseda 2005; Gonzalez 2005; Nubiola 2005).[18] Surprise is a break from habit that leads to doubt. This doubt encourages the formation of a hypothesis about what is happening under conditions of incomplete information. Abduction is sometimes described as "inference to the best hypothesis." It is a form of "reasoning backwards" from "consequence to antecedent." That is, we start with the surprise and reason backwards to a hypothesis about what explains the surprise. This hypothesis is akin to a "creative leap" or a "guess" and Peirce associated abduction with creativity.[19] He also thought it has an instinctive or experiential basis.

Abduction is understood by the decision maker to be fallible or provisional knowledge and hence it triggers further inquiry and experimentation. Although

---

[17] James and Dewey both believed that conceptual abstraction is important for making sense of concrete situations. However, they also appreciated that conceptual abstraction can lead to reification, making people blind to contextual factors. Therefore, they both advocated an "abstract-concrete interactionsism"—that is, a moving back and forth between the abstract and the concrete. Winther (2014) argues that this abstract-concrete interactionism is essential to processes of reflection.

[18] Aliseda (2005) distinguishes two types of surprise in Peirce's work—anomaly and novelty. Surprise arises when our expectations (as shaped by our previous beliefs) are disrupted. Cooke (2011) argues that surprise is a perceptual judgment of error recognition (rather than doubt). Paavola (2005) argues that there is a tension in Peirce about whether abduction is instinctive or inferential. The distinction depends on whether "clues" are unconsciously apprehended and result merely from association (abductive instinct) or whether they are consciously apprehended and result from reason (abductive inference).

[19] Dewey also saw inference as central to thinking and developed a concept of creative inference similar to Peirce's concept of abduction (Rogers 2007).

abduction may occur through a flash of insight, it can also arise through an iterative process of experimentation that gradually refines the hypothesis. Experimentation here does not necessarily mean randomized controlled experiments (Ansell and Bartenberger 2016b). Rather, Pragmatism gives a lot of attention to the use of imagination or mental simulation to conduct thought experiments—it is an "imaginative form of understanding" (Alexander 1990, 329).

As this discussion suggests, abduction fits into the wider conceptual scheme of Pragmatist practical rationality as discussed in previous sections. As Peirce's syllogism suggests, we start with a surprise, which is analogous to temporal discontinuity or a problematic situation. An abduction is a fallible hypothesis that draws on habit, experience and feeling, but also creatively draws on imagination in order to respond to uncertainty. Abduction is also a starting point for further inquiry and experimentation. As Bromley writes, pragmatism "grounds human action in abduction" (2010, 137). It is an important hidden resource of Pragmatist practical rationality.

PRACTICAL RATIONALITY THROUGH DELIBERATION

Finally, we come to a discussion of the role played by deliberation in judgment. In *Human Nature and Conduct*, Dewey defines deliberation as follows:

> ... [D]eliberation is a dramatic rehearsal (in imagination) of various competing possible lines of action ... Deliberation is an experiment in finding out what the various lines of possible action are really like. (1922, 190)

As Dewey's description of deliberation attests, he associates deliberation with imagination, experimentation and creativity. For rational choice, deliberation is "introspective," while for Pragmatism, deliberation is partly about experimentation with different courses of action (Whitford 2002, 339).

Deliberation is a central aspect of Pragmatism's distinctive model of practical rationality because it takes the place of the optimization of commensurable values in rational choice theory (Mousavi and Garrison 2003). As Dewey puts it: "[t]he office of deliberation is not to supply an inducement to act by figuring out where the most advantage is to be procured. It is to resolve entanglements in existing activity, restore continuity, recover harmony, utilize loose impulse and redirect habit" (1922, 199). Pragmatist actors do make tradeoffs across values, but these tradeoffs are typically not determined by a clear, a priori hierarchy of preferences. The action-oriented, problem-solving inclination of Pragmatism leads it to place more emphasis on the attempt to discover ways to coordinate, unify, integrate or reconstruct incommensurable values rather than to "optimize" across commensurable values (Garrison 1999, 301; Mousavi and Garrison 2003; Morse 2010, 226). Pragmatist decision makers use deliberation to adjudicate and reconstruct value conflicts and to balance desires, goals and interests in emotionally satisfying ways (James 1896; Mousavi and Garrison 2003; Barbalet 2004, 2008).[20]

A distinctive feature of the Pragmatist model of deliberation is that it is linked to inquiry (Bohman 2004). Problem-solving calls for an inquiry into the problematic situation. As Hans Joas writes in an essay on Mead: "a pragmatist ethics places itself in the situation of the actor, who has been set the practical problem of mediating between the values he holds and the givens of a particular situation" (1990, 183). Pragmatist inquiry does not somehow magically dissolve conflicting desires, interests and beliefs, but rather helps to illuminate and deepen our understanding of them through "situated problem-solving" (Holmwood 2011, 2014). For Dewey, inquiry and deliberation can lead to a *transformation* or *reconstruction* of the situation in order to try to "functionally coordinate" incommensurable values (Frega 2010). Ends and means are partially discovered in the process of inquiry, which then provide a "stimulus" for a particular course of action (Garrison 1999, 296; Mousavi and Garrison 2003).[21] The concept of deliberation is thus a necessary complement to Pragmatism's rejection of starting with fixed beliefs, values or preferences.

Although deliberation may be an internal, individual process, a distinctive feature of Pragmatism's deliberation-as-inquiry perspective is that inquiry is also understood to be a communal process. Peirce famously referred to "communities of inquiry" and Dewey used the term "public" to convey the communal nature of inquiry. To understand this perspective, we must appreciate that Pragmatism understands human action to be both social and communicative. For Pragmatism, action is fundamentally social (Kilpinen 2013, 4023) and therefore understood in terms of social *interaction* (McGowan 1998, 296).[22] As Beckert puts it: "[s]trategies of action … are formed in social interaction

---

[20] By dropping the presumption of utility maximization (Garrison 1999; Mousavi and Garrison 2003; Frega 2010; Morse 2010), Pragmatism greatly reduces information-processing demands on decision makers, directing their attention instead to the creative resolution of conflict.

[21] Purposes are partially discovered in the course of action in order to work out conflicting desires and values in the face of constraints. William James speaks eloquently on this topic. For instance, in his *Talks to Teachers and Students*, James discusses "the Will" as a matter of finding an idea or conception, through deliberation, that resolves conflicting impulses and inhibitions in a way that elicits action (1900, 169–98).

[22] See McGowan (1998, 296) on Pragmatism's "interactionism"; on interactionism in Pragmatist-inspired symbolic interactionism, see McCall (2013) among many others. As Simpson (2009) points out, however, the term "interaction" can be confusing because Pragmatism stressed the triadic nature of action and Dewey clearly distin-

through the interpretation of the attitude of relevant others" (2003, 777). This process of interaction is itself a semiotic process, in which the behavior of others is treated as a sign from which meaning can be inferred. Thus, people draw inferences about the intentions, motivations and identity of others with whom they interact, which leads to an appreciation for "role-taking" as a way of comprehending the perspective of others (McCall 2013).

Communication is also a central theme in Pragmatism's view of human action (Russill 2005, 2008; Bergman 2009) and at the heart of this interest in communication is a conception of dialogue (Wiley 1994). One of Mead's key ideas was that role-taking is a dialogue between perspectives. By adopting the perspective of an alter, an ego becomes capable not only of communicating with others, but also of developing a critical vantage point for self-reflection. The capacity for reflexivity—the ability to reflect on your own behavior— emerges from our ability to engage in an inner dialogue between different roles or perspectives. Even more profoundly, Mead argued that the "social self" emerges from the ability of people to view themselves from the perspective of others (Mead 1925; Wiley 1994; Simpson 2009; Bakker 2011). Thus, while deliberation may be internal dialogue about different courses of action, it may also be part of a wider process of social communication and communal inquiry.

THE HIDDEN RESOURCES OF PRACTICAL RATIONALITY

As this chapter has elaborated, the Pragmatists' philosophical commitment to anti-dualism led them to a focus on action. To break down Cartesian dualisms—like subject versus object or mind versus body—they focused on how people experience the world and how they engage with it in practical ways. If we draw on the rich legacy of ideas they developed together, we find a model of action that stresses how goals, cognition and meaning are shaped and iteratively refined through practical problem-solving and social interaction. Past experience and habitual skills guide action until they confront a situation that blocks their successful consummation. Uncertainty, doubt and emotion then triggers reflection and inquiry, leading ultimately to an interpretation of the situation. Interpretation is inferential and leads to the formation of working hypotheses that guide subsequent action. Through experimentation and deliberation, problem-solvers seek to align or coordinate incommensurable values, both by imagining fruitful courses of action and/or by reconstructing habits or situations. Emotion guides this process.

---

guished a "transaction" from an "interaction." Note that there is a Pragmatist tradition in social psychology (Fiske 1993).

This model of practical rationality suggests a distinctive view of how people act as they go about the business of living. However, this model also suggests *hidden resources* that people may draw upon as they make decisions and make meaning in both everyday problem-solving and under crisis conditions. By *hidden*, we are referring to aspects of practical rationality that are not fully appreciated or even imagined when decision making is viewed through the lens of utilitarian or value rationality; by *resources*, we mean aspects of practical rationality that people can draw upon to make difficult tradeoffs in the context of complexity, time constraint and uncertainty.

A first hidden resource comes from Pragmatism's *anti-dualism*. As a philosophical starting point, anti-dualism offers many novel insights into human behavior. However, anti-dualism is not simply a philosophical starting point. Anti-dualism may also shape our everyday strategies for addressing the contradictions and paradoxes we encounter in problematic situations. While real tradeoffs must be made in the world, decision makers are also confronted with false oppositions. Anti-dualism encourages decision makers to explore problem-solving strategies that bridge the gap between these false oppositions. More generally, Pragmatism encourages decision makers to look for creative ways to address the dilemmas that arise in a given situation, including a reconstruction of one's own habits and beliefs.

A second hidden resource comes from Pragmatism's emphasis on *fallibility* and the acceptance of uncertainty. Decision makers are often pressured to assume they are right and to vigorously defend their position, or they are encouraged to delay decisions until uncertainty has been vanquished. Pragmatism's stance on fallibility, by contrast, encourages decision makers to adopt an attitude of humility towards what they know, but also to avoid delaying action until they have all the information. Pragmatism suggests that to learn more, we must often take action. Most importantly, appreciation for the fallibility of knowledge encourages decision makers to reflect on their own assumptions and to engage in inquiry about what the problem is. Embracing an attitude of fallibility encourages reflexive action.

A third hidden resource of Pragmatist practical rationality is its emphasis on *experimentation*, which is a way of engaging in reflexive action. By moving away from a model of action that starts with clearly formed preferences or principles, Pragmatism encourages decision makers to appreciate the importance of testing one's assumptions and revising them continuously. An experimental stance suggests that decision makers can and should act in an improvisational way and that they can learn-from-doing. This stance is also related to Pragmatism's appreciation for abductive inference, which points to the hypothetical nature of our judgments and the need to further evaluate these working hypotheses.

A fourth hidden resource is Pragmatism's emphasis on *deliberation*. For Pragmatism, deliberation is linked to inquiry and it helps us to define the situation and what is at stake. Through deliberation, decision makers interrogate the potential impact of their decisions and the values that will be lost or gained in the process. Deliberation takes the form of both internal and external communication and is an imaginative process that triangulates between past, present and future. A particularly important aspect of deliberation is that it encourages decision makers to view the world from different perspectives and to be aware of how emotion may help us to evaluate the meaning of potential decisions.

To be completely clear, our argument is not that Pragmatic actors will necessarily "get it right." On the contrary, Pragmatism's stress on the fallibility of knowledge clearly implies that people can and do get it wrong. We would also grant that both rational choice theory and value rationality have normatively attractive features. When preferences are well defined and values are commensurable, rational choice theory provides a powerful utilitarian account of how individuals and groups arrive at efficient tradeoffs between competing values. Likewise, where a clear hierarchy of ethical values exists, value rationality points to how individuals and groups act upon and uphold cherished social values in a principled way. Under conditions of uncertainty, urgency and complexity, however, the assumptions that utilitarian and value rationality build upon are likely to be quite problematic.

Under these challenging conditions, we would say that Pragmatist practical rationality is more likely to lead to desirable outcomes than utilitarian or value rationality. Obviously, this is a difficult claim to uphold because it depends on how we value the ultimate outcome of a situation as it unfolds over time. However, the hidden resources of anti-dualism, fallibilism, experimentation and deliberation are responsive to the uncertainty, urgency and complexity of crisis situations. We think this is particularly true in contrast to value rationality, which we will call *principle-guided crisis management* in subsequent chapters.

The founding Pragmatists left us with a rich and complex account of practical rationality. We draw on a simpler version of practical rationality in subsequent chapters in order to develop an operational model of *Pragmatist crisis management*. This model builds on the four hidden resources of anti-dualism, fallibilism, experimentation and deliberation described above. Before doing this, however, we first explore what we can learn from the literature on crisis management and strategic management about decision making and meaning making under uncertainty.

3. Decision making and meaning making in the face of uncertainty

How do strategic crisis managers make decisions in the fog of uncertainty? How do they make sense of what is happening and communicate that to the public? Strategic uncertainty in a crisis is a bit like what Winston Churchill said about forecasting the Soviet Union's actions at the beginning of World War II: "It is a riddle wrapped in a mystery inside an enigma ..."[1] Or, to paraphrase Timothy Geithner, what happens when the options look dismal but we still have to choose? As we shall argue in later chapters, humility is probably not a bad place to begin, because it models the attitude of fallibility that characterizes Pragmatist practical rationality.

The model of Pragmatist practical rationality set out in the previous chapter is not, of course, the first or last word on decision making or meaning making under uncertainty and during crises. Therefore, before further specifying our model of Pragmatist crisis management in Chapter 4, we first investigate what we can learn about decision making and meaning making under uncertainty from the wider literatures on crisis management and decision making, while calling attention to the relationship to Pragmatist practical rationality as appropriate.

Surprisingly, relatively few studies on crisis decision making and meaning making focus specifically and explicitly on uncertainty, particularly at the strategic crisis management level (Mumford et al. 2007). Therefore, we canvass a body of literature that goes beyond crisis management per se. Indeed, the challenges of decision making and meaning making under uncertainty are generic to many circumstances—environmental problems, medical diagnosis, military conflicts, political negotiations, mega-projects, high-tech start-ups, and so on. To varying degrees, these and many other problem-solving situations confront the uncertainty, urgency and threat that we associate with crises. Funtowicz and Ravetz, for instance, write that environmental problems are situations "where facts are uncertain, values are in dispute, stakes are high, and decisions urgent" (1994, 1882). While our focus in this chapter is on crisis

---

[1] http://www.churchill-society-london.org.uk/RusnEnig.html (accessed June 19, 2019).

decision making and meaning making, we draw on this wider body of literature where we find it useful to do so.

WHAT IS UNCERTAINTY?

While the concept of uncertainty is perhaps one of those ideas where you "know it when you see it"[2] (or perhaps more accurately, "know it where you feel it"), many different conceptions of uncertainty have been suggested. In their review of decision making under uncertainty, Lipshitz and Strauss propose a useful framing for our purposes: "Uncertainty in the context of action is a sense of doubt that blocks or delays action" (1997, 150), a definition that they note is consistent with Pragmatism. They identify three different foci of uncertainty confronting decision makers—uncertainty about situation, alternatives and outcome (1997, 151).[3] They also observe that uncertainty can arise from imperfect information, inadequate understanding, or conflict between or lack of differentiation of alternatives.

In the early 20th century, the economist Frank Knight (1921) drew a still used—and still debated—distinction between risk and uncertainty.[4] With risk, he argued, we can quantify the probabilities that underlie our decisions, while probabilities are unknown or impossible to quantify for uncertainty. As Hertwig nicely explains it: "Many of our behaviors—falling in love, job interviews, marital arguments, crossing the street—come without a package-insert detailing possible outcomes and their probabilities" (2015, 241). Building on this Knightian distinction between risk and uncertainty, Faucheux and Froger (1995) argue that the difference between certainty and ignorance has two dimensions—one, the precision of the underlying probabilities; and two, the

---

2   US Supreme Court Justice Potter Stewart famously used the standard "I know it when I see it" in reference to the regulation of pornography.

3   In organization theory, Milliken (1987) has developed a similar classification of perceived uncertainty, which he defines "as an individual's perceived inability to predict something accurately" (1987, 136). "State uncertainty," he argues is when organization decision makers perceive the organizational environment or its components to be hard to predict. This also implies not understanding how the different components of the organization's environment are changing. Environments are perceived to be uncertain when they are volatile, complex or heterogeneous. Milliken also distinguishes "effect uncertainty," which he describes as the inability to predict the effect of a future of the environment on the future. Effect uncertainty is uncertainty about cause and effect. A third type of uncertainty is "response uncertainty," which is a lack of knowledge about how to respond to the environment. As Milliken points out, these three different kinds of uncertainty imply the absence or weakness of different kinds of knowledge or information.

4   There is a complex historiographical debate about whether and how Knight's distinction drew on Pragmatism—see Nash (2003) and Hands (2006).

reliability of these probability distributions. From this perspective, high uncertainty occurs where the underlying probabilities are imprecise and unreliable. A somewhat different perspective is provided by Mousavi and Gigerenzer, who define "fundamental uncertainty" as a situation where "some of the alternatives and outcomes, in addition to probabilities, can be unknown" (2014, 1672).[5] When events are rare or novel, as they often are in crisis situations, probabilities are difficult to evaluate and uncertainty is magnified (Starbuck 2009).

The concept of uncertainty is sometimes used interchangeably with concepts like complexity or turbulence. This is because complexity and turbulence are often drivers of uncertainty, and vice versa. In a study of how firms engage in foresight in uncertain environments, Vecchiato (2012) distinguishes between "complexity" and "dynamism" as drivers of uncertainty. Complexity refers to a situation in which the environment has a large number of diverse components with many relationships or interactions between them; dynamism refers to the speed of change of components and frequent disruptive changes.

Uncertainties often arise or are linked to the complexity of underlying social, political, natural or technological systems (Perrow 1984; Beckert 2003; Berkes 2007).[6] Funtowicz and Ravetz refer to "system uncertainties" to suggest that the "problem is concerned not with the discovery of a particular fact (as in traditional research), but with the comprehension or management of a reality that has irreducible complexities and uncertainties" (1994, 1882). One of the critical implications of this relationship between uncertainty and complexity is that more information can actually increase uncertainty, since more information can reveal the complexity of a system (Walker et al. 2003; Koppenjan and Klijn 2004; Walker et al. 2013).

---

[5]   For other relevant distinctions related to conceptualizing uncertainty, see Walker et al. (2003) and Dequech (2000, 2003, 2006). Rather than draw a distinction between risk and uncertainty, Dequech draws an initial distinction between weak and strong uncertainty, where the latter refers to the absence of a "unique, additive, and fully reliable probability distribution" (2003, 519). He then distinguishes two types of strong uncertainty—fundamental uncertainty and ambiguity. Under ambiguity, the decision maker does not know the probability distribution, but does know all possible events. By contrast, fundamental uncertainty is where "some relevant information cannot be known, not even in principle, at the time of making many important decisions" (2003, 520).

[6]   Page argues that it is important to distinguish uncertainty, difficulty and complexity: "uncertainty refers to the absence of information about some relevant variable or what some call the state of the world," while "[d]ifficulty refers to problems that have many interacting variables" and "[c]omplexity refers to dynamic environments that contain multiple actors who interact with one another" (2008, 117).

Uncertainty is also frequently connected to change. As conditions change—particularly when they change rapidly or unexpectedly—decision makers face a challenge of understanding cause and effect relationships and anticipating the ultimate course of change. A long tradition in the organization theory and strategic management literatures suggests that "turbulent" conditions produce uncertainty (Cameron et al. 1987; Ansell and Trondal 2017). Anticipating the future in turbulent situations is often challenging at best because the "ground is in motion" (Emery and Trist 1965, 26). In fact, change and complexity often interact to produce what Sommer and Loch (2004, 1343) call "unforeseeable uncertainty," which Sommer et al. suggest "refers to the presence of influence variables that are relevant to the venture's success, but cannot be recognized by the management team at the outset, and cannot, therefore, be included in initial planning and risk analysis" (2009, 120).

The endogenous nature of the relationship between action and uncertainty must also be appreciated.[7] Faucheux and Froger note that decision making becomes complex because "the option set can change endogenously owing to the effects of past decisions, as well as through time as a consequence of the multidimensional interactions between the economic system and the environment" (1995, 31). The endogenous nature of uncertainty is often closely related to strategic uncertainty, which refers to how others will behave in response to your actions (Huff 1978; Koopenjan and Klijn 2004). Uncertainty may also arise from the institutional conditions inherent to the response. The loosely coupled "networked" nature of crisis response systems, for instance, often creates its own uncertainty (Koopenjan and Klijn 2004; Moynihan 2008), as does the multi-jurisdictional or transboundary nature of crisis (Ansell et al. 2010). Institutions often induce uncertainty about who is in charge and who is responsible, which can generate "structurally induced inaction" (Snook and Connor 2005).

The terms "ambiguity" and "uncertainty" are often used interchangeably. Here, we adopt the understanding of ambiguity developed in the organization theory literature, which equates ambiguity to equivocality, or the inability to distinguish between two interpretations.[8] Combe and Carrington (2015) suggest that during a crisis, ambiguity can lead to too many interpretations

---

[7]   Sigel et al. (2010) distinguish between phenomenological and epistemic uncertainty, with the former referring to the state of the world and the latter referring to our knowledge of that world. The organization theory and strategic management literatures draw a similar distinction between objective and perceived uncertainty (Jauch and Kraft 1986). In the cognitive science tradition, Kahneman and Tversky (1982) distinguish between ignorance and external uncertainty.

[8]   James March defined ambiguity as a situation where "goals are vague, problematic, inconsistent, or unstable" (1978, 590). However, Dequech (2000) defines ambigu-

because in ambiguous situations there are often several plausible interpretations of the situation. A final distinction that is now widely discussed is between *known* and *unknown* unknowns. In some areas—for instance in the area of natural hazards—we know that certain events may occur, but not precisely when or how (Berkes 2007). These are sometimes called *known unknowns* to distinguish them from novel "black swan" events that could not have been imagined or anticipated (Taleb 2007; Aven 2013; Feduzi and Runde 2014).

The term "surprise" is also a cousin of the term "uncertainty." Surprise illuminates or triggers uncertainty because it is at variance with what we know or expect (Kahneman and Tversky 1982; Gross 2010). Thus, Schneider et al. define surprise as "[t]he condition in which the event, process or outcome is not known or expected (1998, 172). Surprise is therefore linked to the many psychological and institutional factors that shape our expectations (Bar-Joseph and Sheaffer 1998; Parker and Stern 2002). As a departure from what is expected, surprise is also closely related to the concept of "anomaly."

One implication that might be drawn from this brief characterization of uncertainty is that when we say that decision makers face uncertainty, it is typically a shorthand for saying they face a rather differentiated situation where they know some things with relative certainty, while remaining uncertain about other specific aspects of the situation. For Pragmatism, doubt is important, but an equally important point is that it is not possible to doubt everything at once. Indeed, this argument against "universal doubt" is part of the basic anti-Cartesian position of Pragmatism (Peirce 1868). Thus, although crisis decision making is clearly characterized by uncertainty, we should not forget that the decision maker knows many things, though some better than others. To move forward in life, we must act based on what we know in the face of uncertainty. Or, as Timothy Geithner put it, "in a fog of uncertainty when our options all look dismal ... we still had to choose" (Geithner 2014, 19).

UNCERTAINTY AND DECISION MAKING

Many scholars have pointed out the limits of "classical" or "linear" models of rational decision making in the face of uncertainty or ambiguity (Lindblom 1959; March 1978; Lipshitz and Strauss 1997; Polasky et al. 2011; Huff et al. 2016; Flach et al. 2017). One somewhat overlooked article that makes this argument in the context of crisis decision making is Anderson's (1983) analysis of the Cuban Missile Crisis. Anderson argues that crisis decision making

---

ity as lack of information about probabilities, which is essentially the description that Knight gave to uncertainty.

departs from the standard "linear" model, which begins with established goals and preferences, moves to identify and evaluate alternatives, and then makes the optimal choice between these alternatives. By contrast, Anderson argues that goals are partially discovered through action and via deliberation, a point similar to that made in our discussion of Pragmatist practical rationality in the last chapter.

Anderson's argument is not that actors do not have goals, but rather that they have global goals that have to be specified through action—a point analogous to John Dewey's view that actors have "ends-in-view" (1922, 225). For example, Anderson observes that the goals retrospectively articulated by the ExComm (the key decision-making body during the Cuban Missile Crisis) to explain American actions during the crisis were, with one exception, not even mentioned in its initial meetings. Instead, Anderson argues that goals emerged during ExComm meetings via argument and dialogue (see also Allison 1971). Although Anderson acknowledges that goals may arise from previous choices, he suggests that the most important goals during the missile crisis were discovered during debate—or as the Pragmatist tradition would say, deliberation. The sensemaking perspective that will be explored later in this chapter also argues that "action precedes cognition" (Maitlis and Christianson 2014, 84).

In a number of respects, the "naturalistic decision-making" model (Lipshitz and Strauss 1997; Klein 1998) is close in spirit to Pragmatist practical rationality. The model was developed by observing experienced decision makers—like firefighters—operating in situations characterized by uncertainty and time urgency. At the heart of the naturalistic decision-making model is the idea of *matching*. For example, when expert firefighters enter a burning building, they draw on prior experience to appraise the situation and decide how to act—in other words, they match the current situation to prior situations by analogy. Decisions take the form of following simple decision rules that draw on past experience—that is, if the situation is X, then do Y.[9] The naturalistic decision-making model stresses that action is "recognition primed," which means that classification of the situation in terms of prior experience is critical (Klein 1998). This perspective is very similar to Pragmatism's account of habit as described in the previous chapter. Like Pragmatism, the model notes

---

[9]   Consistent with the idea of simple decision rules, there is an extensive psychological literature on the heuristics used by actors in making decisions (the keystone article is Tversky and Kahneman 1974). Most of this literature focuses on distortions of rationality (Montibeller and Von Winterfeldt 2015) or on how heuristics lead us to underestimate threats (Meyer and Kunreuther 2017). Mousavi and Gigerenzer (2014), however, argue that simple decision rules can outperform more sophisticated rational analysis in the context of uncertainty *if* the decision rules fit the situation in question (which they refer to as ecological rationality).

that when decision makers confront novel situations or constraints that prevent this matching, they may utilize their imagination to try out various possible scenarios.

As stressed by Pragmatism, experience matters in crisis decision making (Mumford et al. 2007; Weick and Sutcliffe 2011; Combe and Carrington 2015). One way that experience plays a role is via "analogical reasoning," which works by drawing analogies between present and past situations (Brändström et al. 2004; Jervis 2017). A closely related way to think about experience is in terms of "case-based reasoning," which is knowledge drawn from past experience (Mumford et al. 2007). In his memoir of the financial crisis of 2009, for example, Timothy Geithner wrote that "I had spent much of my career dealing with financial crises—in Mexico, Thailand, Indonesia, Korea, and beyond ..." (2014, 2). Based on these experiences, Geithner had a particular sense of what the problem was. "Every financial crisis," he writes "is a crisis of confidence" (2014, 7). His experience told him that government must intervene to stem the panic that arises from this crisis of confidence.

Although analogical reasoning and case-based reasoning might appear to be simply "rote" forms of reasoning useful only in routine decision making, they have also been found to apply to novel situations as well (Houghton 1996) and to the development of creative solutions (Hunter et al. 2008). As Mumford et al. write: "Not only do the leaders of creative ventures appear to rely on their experience with prior related incidents in generating solutions, they also seem to apply the kind of heuristics used in case-based reasoning when working through various problems" (2003, 421). Drawing on knowledge from past cases can be quite a complex process, but also speedy (Sayegh et al. 2004).

Some assumptions and analogies in case-based reasoning, of course, can be wrong and may lead to error.[10] For example, despite repeated warnings, Dutch decision makers erroneously assumed that Germans would respect their neutrality, as they had (analogously) in World War I (Rosenthal and 't Hart 1991). Eric Stern argues that in the time-pressured context of crisis decision making, decision makers often rely on "pre-existing schemas" that can lead to errors as well as skillful performance. For example, when Swedish decision makers encountered unexpected radioactivity, they reasonably but incorrectly concluded that the local nuclear power plant was the source. In fact, the source of the radiation was the Russian nuclear accident at Chernobyl. Stern describes the schema adopted in this case as "the cognitive path of least resistance" (1999, 203). The mistaken schema persisted until enough anomalies had developed in the account to drive a reinterpretation of the situation.

---

[10]   For an example of a mistaken analogy in the BSE ("mad cow") crisis, see Ansell and Gingrich (2007).

In a study of crisis decision makers, Hermann and Dayton (2009) found that surprise and time urgency can lead decision makers to quickly resolve uncertainties by adopting a "dominant frame"—leading to the somewhat counterintuitive result that decision makers experienced more uncertainty where they had more time to reflect (i.e., when they were less time-pressured). They suggest that this may lock decision makers into a particular way of responding, with the result that it becomes more difficult for decision makers to update their assumptions as situations change. This argument is also similar to what is known as the 'threat-rigidity" response, which finds that a decision maker may respond to threats by becoming more rigid, sometimes escalating commitment to a particular course of action (Stern and Sundelius 1997). Thus, while case-based reasoning, heuristics and schemas may lead to speedy decisions that draw on skilled experience, they may also lead to inertia, lock-in and slow response to changing circumstances (Mumford et al. 2007).

Information Processing

How do decision makers handle information uncertainty in fast-paced situations? Lipshitz and Strauss (2014) argue that decision makers can do so by collecting more information, waiting until more information is available (forestalling), or by suppressing the uncertainty through denial, disguise or rationalization. They use the acronym RAWFS to describe such coping strategies: decision makers reduce uncertainty by collecting more information (R), fill in gaps in understanding with assumptions (A), weigh the alternatives (W), forestall action in anticipation of better information (F), and use suppression if all else fails (S).[11] In a study of strategic-level police response to simulated high uncertainty situations, van den Heuvel et al. (2014) add "reflection-in-action" to the RAWFS heuristic. Building on the work of Donald Schön, they describe reflection-in-action as "a reflective approach taken by decision-makers at a meta-cognitive level, where professionals reduce uncertainty by drawing on their previous experiences and continuously engaging with information and by critiquing, restructuring, and testing their understanding of a situation and their actions" (2014, 27). Recall that this kind of reflexivity is a central feature of Pragmatist practical rationality.

As the RAWFS acronym suggests, decision makers in a crisis may weigh alternatives, but they may also investigate courses of action more sequentially.

---

[11] Assumption-based reasoning is a particularly interesting feature of this model from a Pragmatist perspective, because it is close to what Pragmatism calls abduction. Recall that abduction is the formation of hypotheses, typically based on prior experience.

In Anderson's (1983) analysis of the Cuban Missile Crisis, discussed above, he found that decision makers evaluate courses of action one at a time (sequentially), rather than as competing alternatives. Others note that time pressures truncate the consideration of alternatives (Smart and Vertinsky 1977).

Another strategy of avoiding information overload during a crisis is to limit who participates in decision making (Smart and Vertinsky 1977; Dutton 1986; Hermann and Dayton 2009; van den Heuvel and Power 2014). One way this can develop during crises is to centralize decision making and to constrain the number of people involved in the decision. Various decision-making pathologies can develop in such circumstances because group think tends to occur under conditions of hierarchy or group insularity (Janis 1982; 't Hart 2011). As fewer decision makers become responsible for decisions, stress can also increase, which in turn can narrow cognition, making decision makers less receptive to new information (van den Heuvel and Power 2014).

Strategic decision-making teams are not always insular and, in fact, they might not always cohere as groups. Drnevich et al. (2009) find that strategic decision-making groups are often assembled from multiple units, and their home affiliations may be decisive influences on decision making, particularly in the early phases of decision making and where uncertainty is high. Other research shows that where decision-making teams are diverse, better outcomes can occur if participants appreciate and understand one another's mental models (Huber and Lewis 2010).

Another perspective on "uncertainty avoidance" argues that crisis decision makers tend to fall back on routines and standard operating procedures (Drnevich et al. 2009, 219). Nelson and Katzenstein argue that decision makers use convention to "simplify uncertain situations" (2014, 362). Research has found that policymakers facing both urgency and uncertainty are more likely to fall back on prior strategies and less likely to weigh options. As Hermann and Dayton find: "[p]olicymakers who perceive short time (sic) and have been caught by surprise are the most path dependent. Even though they do develop options, these alternatives grow out of decisions that have been taken before" (2009, 238). Other research finds that moderate stress can be beneficial, but highly stressed decision makers can become rigid in their perception and cognition (Weisæth et al. 2002). Anticipation of the negative consequences of decisions can also lead to decision inertia (Power and Alison 2017).

While rationality is often understood to be "cold" (free of emotion) and emotion is understood to distort rationality, some research suggests that emotion can help to us to make decisions in uncertain situations because emotions alert us to ethical concerns and other warning signs and assist decision makers to anticipate the meaning of different outcomes (Damasio 1994; Li et al. 2014). Emotion can also help to speed decision making, helping "the manager to quickly eliminate some options, retain others, permitting them to focus on fewer alternatives" (Sayegh et al. 2004, 193). Moreover:

> The emotions experienced under conditions of crisis and uncertainty—fear, anxiety, hope, and regret—force the decider to move away from traditional decision-making paradigms to alternative models of choice. Time simply does not permit a carefully thought-out rational approach. Emotions seem to have an adaptive function in times of high uncertainty: people tend to minimize past fears, but exaggerate the fear they may experience in the future. (Sayegh et al. 2004, 193)

While decision makers may revert to routine, research also suggests that they may be capable of recombining and reorganizing existing perceptions and experience in an adaptive and creative way. Mumford et al. (2003) argue that creative leaders often use idea evaluation to stimulate idea generation. They suggest that idea evaluation "involves forecasting or projecting the outcomes of idea implementation within the setting at hand" and then "these forecasted outcomes are ... used to appraise the idea with respect to a set of a priori standards held to apply in the setting under consideration" (2003, 415). This account is very similar to Dewey's notion of valuation and imagination, as described in the last chapter.[12]

Planning versus Adaptation

Aaron Wildavsky (1988) drew a now classic distinction between "anticipation" and "resilience," arguing that planning is possible when we can anticipate the future but that "resilience"—or what we might call real-time adaptation—is more useful and realistic when we cannot. In the strategic management literature, this distinction is represented by two different schools of thought—one that emphasizes the importance of planning as a response to uncertainty and another that stresses the importance of adaptation (Vecchiato 2012). Scholars of environmental policy have also contributed to this discussion, arguing that where the dynamics of the ecological systems are non-linear (and hence more uncertain) and the consequences of human action are irreversible (and hence, weightier), policy should foster ecosystem resilience (Polasky et al. 2011; Seidl 2014). Fast-moving and turbulent crises are generally thought to be surprising and difficult to anticipate and thus to necessarily rely more on

---

[12] Mumford et al. find that case-based knowledge is more important than principle-based knowledge for innovation: "Among leaders, however, principle-based knowledge appears less important to idea generation than case-based knowledge. Case-based knowledge structures are used by people to represent incidents of prior performance and are less abstract than principle-based structures including information about actions, procedures, goals, and restrictions" (2003, 416).

resilience and adaptation than planning. However, the tradeoff between these options may not be as sharp as these accounts imply and it may be possible, to some degree, to combine elements of both anticipation and resilience in crisis response (Comfort et al. 2001).

We identify two strategies discussed in the literature on strategic management that stand somewhere on the spectrum between planning and resilience. The first is attention to *weak signals*. "Weak signals" are understood to be "information on potential change of a system toward an unknown direction" (Mendonça et al. 2004, 205) and viewed as early indicators of strategic discontinuity—where the future is not a linear extrapolation from the past (Holopainen and Toivonen 2012). In a retrospective study of communications leading up to the Enron crisis, for example, Klein and Eckhaus (2017) found that there were many cues of an impending crisis before the crisis actually materialized. Weak signal detection can be viewed as a form of "real-time anticipation" or early warning that may help decision makers anticipate, if not to fully plan for, a crisis situation. Conversely, inattention to weak signals can lead to slow response to the emerging seriousness of problems (Vendelo and Rerup 2009).

To advise decision makers to attend to weak signals is, of course, a tricky business because weak signals are like the proverbial needle-in-a-haystack. Moreover, when a signal is weak, it is difficult to mobilize organizational commitments to take action on them (Wohlstetter 1962; Vaughan 1997; Zegart 2009). Rerup (2009) proposes a strategy of "attentional triangulation" to deal with recognition of weak signals. This method acknowledges that decision makers often face environments with a lot going on where it is not easy to adaptively respond to weak signals. It advises decision makers to move between attention to the stability, vividness and coherence of cues in order to identify and focus on critical issues. This focus fits with the Pragmatist account of practical rationality in the sense that decision makers engaged in reflection-in-action can come to appreciate the selectivity of their own attention.

Some strategic management scholars have distinguished between *predictable* and *unpredictable* surprises (Watkins and Bazerman 2003). Where surprises are predictable, scenario planning has been advanced as one strategy for dealing with uncertainty. A scenario is "a set of plausible stories, supported with data and simulations, about how the future might unfold from current conditions under alternative human choices" (Polasky et al. 2011, 401). Full-fledged scenario planning may not be possible during a crisis, but imagination and deliberation—as stressed by Pragmatism—represent a quick and low-cost alternative.

Feduzi and Runde (2014) suggest a model of "Baconian eliminative induction" to grapple with "unknown unknowns." They stress that this approach combines hypothesis generation with hypothesis testing. *Induction* is often understood to be a generalization from multiple reinforcing demonstrations of a pattern—for example, if we can show an outcome to be true in cases 1, 2 and 3, we can inductively infer that it will also hold true in case 4). Baconian eliminative induction works in a different fashion. It seeks out variety, in the form of alternative hypotheses, and then tests (eliminates) these alternatives. Feduzi and Runde argue that this approach is more likely to identify the "black swans" that surprise us because it seeks out information that might reveal unexpected states of the world and might counteract confirmation bias. This approach is similar in spirit to the ideas about the importance of abduction discussed in the previous chapter.

On the adaptive side of responding to uncertainty, there is a considerable literature on the role of experimentation as a mode of real-time adaptation. In the context of product development, for example, Lynn et al. (1996) argue that discontinuous innovation demands a "probe-and-learn" strategy. Elsewhere, we have argued that this probe-and-learn strategy is very useful where situations are poorly understood, turbulent and unruly (Ansell and Bartenberger 2016a). Edmondson et al. have generalized this argument, proposing what they call an "exploratory response" to uncertainty and ambiguity that "involves constant challenging and testing of existing assumptions and experimentation with new behaviors and possibilities" (2005, 235). The literature on coping with information gaps in risk analysis makes a similar point: "[A] decisionmaker's ability to adapt—to revise, reverse, or correct earlier actions—is a plausible proxy for robustness against surprise and ignorance" (Smithson and Ben Haim 2015, 1914).

Different strategies for probing and learning have not received much attention, but work by Sommer and Loch (2004) and Sommer et al. (2009) provide some useful insights. Using both simulation modeling (Sommer and Loch 2004) and an empirical study of start-up firms (Sommer et al. 2009), these authors explore whether parallel experimentation (conducting many experiments and then selecting the best *ex post* outcome) or trial-and-error experimentation (try something, learn from the results, and then revise your strategy and try again) performs better as a decision-making style when confronted with unforeseeable uncertainties (unknown unknowns). They find that trial-and-error is generally the more robust strategy.

SENSEMAKING

In the organization theory literature, sensemaking is an important theoretical perspective on decision making under conditions of uncertainty and ambiguity. As the name implies, sensemaking focuses on how individuals and groups make sense of novel or ambiguous situations (Weick 1995; Weick et al. 2005; Maitlis and Sonenshein 2010; Maitlis and Christianson 2014; Sandberg and Tsoukas 2015). The sensemaking perspective—which Maitlis and Christianson (2014) suggest has roots in Pragmatism—points out that surprising events can disrupt the flow of action, triggering an attempt by decision makers to "extract cues" from their environment in order to make sense of what is happening. Crises are thus important situations in which processes of sensemaking occur (Maitlis and Sonenshein 2010).

Consider how the sensemaking perspective relates to the "recognition-primed" decision-making model described earlier in this chapter. Building on experience and case-knowledge, experts encountering new situations can invoke heuristics or analogies to apply decision rules to the situation—if x then do y. However, in sensemaking situations, prior assumptions are often disrupted, or, in the case of ambiguity, difficult to differentiate. For example, in the case of the collapse of the roof of a museum, which caused significant damage to the museum's artifacts, decision makers faced deep ambiguity about how to interpret the meaning of the event—did it mean the end of the institution or did the disaster signal an opportunity for renewal (Christianson et al. 2009)?

From a sensemaking perspective, extracted cues are typically assembled into a narrative—a story that interprets the events. This argument is somewhat different from the schema-driven accounts of crisis management suggested above. In those accounts, decision makers bring prior schemas or conventions to bear on current situations. From the sensemaking perspective, by contrast, the narrative—which may eventually become a cognitive schema—is at least partly assembled from cues extracted from the situation. Moreover, the sensemaking perspective suggests that decision makers actively engage with uncertainty through the interaction of "action" and "cognition." As Maitlis and Christianson note: "actions are important because they create more raw ingredients for sensemaking by generating stimuli or cues: people can quickly learn more about a situation by taking action and paying attention to the cues generated by that action (2014, 84).

Action is also experimental and helps to yield knowledge to fill in narrative accounts, which can in turn be further tested through subsequent action. In other words, sensemaking is a probe-and-learn strategy. However, Weick emphasizes that sensemaking is not simply interpretive—once a narrative is formed, decision makers "enact" that schema. Thus, sensemaking is not a linear process where "schema" or "conventions" or "rules" precede action in a linear sense. Rather, decision makers form schemas (narratives) in the course of action and then project those schemas on to the world. In the sensemaking (and Pragmatist) account, cognition and action interact in a recursive loop (not in a linear schema-action fashion). Moreover, in sensemaking (as in

Pragmatism), this interaction between cognition and action is triggered when prior assumptions (or rules or habits) are disrupted or indecisive.

Taking action has consequences that affect the situation in which the decision maker is acting. Weick provides a useful account:

> Bateson's description of exploring illustrates the key point about sensemaking. The explorer cannot know what he is facing until he faces it, and then looks back over the episode to sort out what happened, a sequence that involves retrospective sensemaking. But the act of exploring itself has an impact on what is being explored, which means that parts of what the explorer discovers retrospectively are consequences of his own making. Furthermore, the exploring itself is guided by preconceptions of some kind ... (1988, 305–6)

This implication of sensemaking is central to Pragmatism as well: the decision maker is not outside of and looking in to the crisis, but a part of the situation with ongoing sensemaking shaped by prior action. Probe-and-learn actions can lead to error, but the sensemaking perspective also leads to an alternative view—that the failure to take action in an uncertain situation can lead to error because inaction produces no useful information feedback (Weick 1988).[13]

Recursive feedback loops between cognition and action can produce both good and bad results in crises. On the one hand, the loop can reinforce commitment to a particular course of action, leading to what Weick calls a "tenacious justification" (Weick 1988; Cornelissen et al. 2014). Groups often develop a joint "frame" or "narrative" to help them respond to crisis situations (Abolafia 2010) and commitment to one single frame or narrative can become problematic (Cornelissen et al. 2014).[14] For example, Fligstein et al. (2014)

---

[13]   It is interesting that Weick describes this point in terms that are reminiscent of Dewey's (1896) famous reflex arc paper: "All crises have an enacted quality once a person takes the first action. Suppose that a gauge shows an unexpected increase in temperature. That is not enactment. Suppose further that in response to the unexpected temperature increase people tap the gauge or call the supervisor or proceed with a tea break or walk out to look at the tank whose temperature is being measured. That still is not enactment, because all that exists so far is a simple stimulus and response. But the response of tapping, calling, drinking, or walking produces a new stimulus that would not have been there had the first been ignored. The 'second stimulus' is now a partial human construction. The assumptions that underlie the choice of that first response contribute to enactment and the second stimulus. As action continues through more cycles, the human responses which stimulate further action become increasingly important components of the crisis" (1988, 309).

[14]   Cornelissen et al. (2014) identify three types of enabling conditions that may produce overcommitment to a single frame: linguistic framing, reinforcement over time and joint orientation development. They argue that when a provisional framing of a situation receives repeated reinforcement through use, it may become a taken-for-granted frame. Social interaction, emotions and communication can further reinforce this frame

found that the Federal Reserve's decision-making body, the Federal Open Market Committee, was unable to update its understanding of the emerging financial crisis because of its commitment to a particular macroeconomic policy perspective.[15] Frames and cues may also interact in ways that reinforce erroneous sensemaking (Colville et al. 2013). Overly optimistic commitments are another source of error during crises (Maitlis and Sonenshein 2010). On the other hand, recursive feedback loops can also produce richer accounts of a situation (Weick 2007). From a sensemaking perspective, groups can develop rich interpretations of situations by engaging in what Weick and Roberts have called "heedful interrelating," by which they mean "dispositions to act with attentiveness, alertness, and care" (1993, 374). In contrast with group think, Weick and Roberts understand heedful interrelating to be a form of distributed and continuously revised group-level cognition that builds rich interpretations: "Heedful interrelating of activities constructs a substrate that is more complex and, therefore, better able to comprehend complex events than is true for smart but isolated individuals" (Weick and Roberts 1993, 373).[16]

Rather than converging on a single frame, heedful interrelating attempts to reduce ambiguity by taking different perspectives into account. In their study of firefighting, Baran and Scott (2010) found that firefighters stressed the importance of remaining open to their environments and alive to the importance of reevaluating the situation. Firefighters were vigilant for shifts in action (recall the earlier point about how strategic discontinuities can be detected via weak signals). This awareness and attentiveness to possible shifts in assumptions is akin to Schön's (1983) model of reflection-in-action, whose affinity with Pragmatism we have noted (see Schön 1992). Baran and Scott (2010) describe this as "organizing ambiguity" through a combination of framing, heedful interrelating and adjusting. Their analysis of firefighters in dangerous and ambiguous circumstances finds that firefighting groups engage in these processes to cope with the ambiguity they face.

Team deliberation can also help to reduce decision-making errors by bringing multiple perspectives to bear on an issue (Combe and Carrington 2015). Faraj and Xiao (2006) demonstrate how open and frequent dialogue among team members improves coordination in hospital trauma units. Deliberation can enable groups to explore various future-oriented scenarios (Gibson 2011). However, deliberation is not a foolproof method of improved decision making.

---

and social commitments may get built up around it, making departure from it difficult. Thus, interactive social processes may lead to an escalation of commitment over time.

[15] For another sensemaking account of how the Fed and the European Central Bank (ECB) interpreted the financial crisis, see Rosenhek (2013).

[16] We should, however, keep in mind Huff's (1978) concept of "consensual uncertainty," where multiple interpretations of a situation create their own uncertainty.

Deliberations may "tip" towards making the wrong call in a situation (e.g., Dunbar and Garud 2009). Or deliberation may have trouble reaching a decision. Van den Heuvel et al. point to the problem of "redundant deliberation" which they describe as "pointlessly deliberating between options without actively reducing uncertainty" (2014, 30).

CRISIS AND MEANING MAKING: COMMUNICATING UNCERTAINTY

A crisis is not only a sensemaking situation; it is also a situation of *sensegiving* (Gioia and Chittipeddi 1991). Strategic crisis managers are inevitably called upon to interpret the crisis and give it meaning. A growing body of literature focuses on how strategic leaders engage in meaning making during crises (Boin et al. 2005; Masters and 't Hart 2012; Jong et al. 2016). It finds that effective crisis management requires leaders to do much more than simply interpret and act upon a situation; they must also persuade others to take certain actions and defend those actions after the fact (Boin et al. 2005). Here we focus on identifying the implications of strategic meaning making in the face of uncertainty. To do so, we also draw upon an extensive literature on risk communication. According to this literature, effective public communication about risk is essential for getting people to comply with protective advice, to dampen rumors and fear, to encourage crisis coordination and to maintain public trust (Rogers et al. 2007).

Although uncertainty is a prominent theme in the literatures on crisis and risk communication, there is a limited amount of research that addresses uncertainty per se (Frewer 2004; Markon and Lemyre 2013; Liu et al. 2016). What is clear from these literatures is that communicating uncertainty is far from straightforward and rests on a tense relationship between crisis or risk communicators and the public. The public understands uncertainty in relation to how they experience it in everyday life (Rogers et al. 2007). But scientists are often skeptical about whether the public can understand uncertainty and they often believe that expressions of uncertainty intensify public distrust (Frewer et al. 2003). Moreover, the "public" is not monolithic. Some people prefer to be told categorically whether something is safe or unsafe, while others prefer to learn about the range of risk (Johnson and Slovic 1998). Different public preferences for receiving information, in turn, affect perceptions of the honesty and competence of those communicating the risk.

A common fear in risk communication, particularly by scientists or other experts, is that the expression of uncertainty will encourage panic or reduce trust (Doyle et al. 2014). However, Frewer et al.'s (2002) research on the communication of uncertainty about food safety risks reaches a different conclusion:

> People are more accepting of uncertainty associated with the scientific process of risk management than a lack of action or lack of interest on the part of the government. The results indicate that the focus of communication should be on "what is being done to reduce the uncertainty." It is suggested that people want transparency in risk management and to be able to make informed choices about exposure to food risks. (2002, 371)

An experimental study on government advisory warnings found that public reactions may depend on the kind of uncertainty in question. Markon and Lemyre (2013) draw a distinction between: (a) the lack of knowledge about a risk—epistemic uncertainty, (b) contradictions in the data, and (c) the contradiction between experts concerning the existence of a risk for human health—ambiguity (2013, 1103). Ambiguity, they found, reduced respondents' adherence to government advice, but epistemic uncertainty did not. As these distinctions suggest, risk and uncertainty have multiple dimensions (Liu et al. 2016).

When public officials hide uncertainty, they may increase public skepticism (Wynne 1989, 1992). The risk communication literature now largely supports the view that it is better for public officials to communicate the uncertainty in their decisions (Seeger 2006; Rogers et al. 2007; Markon and Lemyre 2013). As Rogers et al. conclude: "communicators must acknowledge the ability of the public to understand and accept uncertainty in risk communication. When communicating about a specific risk, or a situation involving risk, it is better to say 'I don't know', rather than provide false reassurances before all of the facts are known" (2007, 283–4). Beginning with a model of communication stressing the simple transmission of knowledge and information from experts to the lay public, the risk communication literature gradually moved to a perspective that emphasized deficits of public information or understanding and that stressed the role of individual and societal factors in amplifying or attenuating the perception of risk (Kasperson et al. 1988). Criticism of this model—which emphasized the gap between knowledgeable experts who had access to true knowledge and the limited knowledge and understanding of the lay public—has been partially modified by a recognition of how risk is socially constructed (Slovic 1999). The risk communication literature has also become more appreciative of the context in which risk is communicated, and in the trust in and credibility of who communicates the risk (Wynne 1992). Trust is a critical factor in risk communication, with risk communication being more effective when the receiver of the communication trusts the sender (Slovic 1993, 1999; Poortinga and Pidgeon 2003; McComas 2006; Rogers et al. 2007; Engdahl and Lidskog 2014). In short, the model of risk communication has moved towards a more social, relational and contextual model of interacting with the public (Wynne 1992), one that emphasizes that risk communicators need to have better contextual understanding of risk perception if they are to effectively communicate risk (Rogers et al. 2007; Krieger et al. 2014). This emphasis on context is consistent with the importance that Pragmatism places on situational reasoning.

Crises can also create strong emotions that affect how people process information and how they respond to risk communications (McComas 2006; Kim and Cameron 2011). However, it is important to recognize that emotions are rarely just shaped by authoritative communications from strategic crisis managers. They are also widely shaped by the communication strategies of different groups, particularly the media. Thus, it is probably a mistake for decision makers to understand the communication of uncertainty in terms of the public's cognitive processing of information—that is, merely by relating the "facts." When the public is experiencing feelings of anger, for example, they are more likely to seek to attribute blame. Expressions of empathy and concern for the well-being of crisis victims have been found to be important in responding to emotion-laden crisis situations (Kim and Cameron 2011).

The success of risk communication partly depends on how audiences process and react to communications. One prominent line of analysis is the so-called Risk Information Seeking and Processing (RISP) model, which tries to bring together two different models of how people find and use information to deal with risk—a "systemic" (rational-analytic) and a "heuristic" (application of simple rules) models.[17] In their review of research on the RISP model, Dunwoody and Griffin conclude:

> Tests of the RISP model over time and across risks indicate that individuals will indeed engage in more effortful information seeking and processing of risk information when they feel social pressures to know about the risk or sense that they have insufficient information for decision making. This is good news for policymakers and for communication professionals who emphasize the importance of providing information as an important catalyst to learning and possible behavior change. (2015, 112)

The risk perception literature has also come to advocate a "dual processing" perspective that people process risk both in terms of feelings and in terms of rational analysis (Slovic et al. 2004).

---

[17]   Uncertainty reduction, uncertainty management and problematic integration theories focus on how people are motivated to reduce or manage uncertainty and might be relevant here, but Liu et al. (2016) note that these ideas have not been developed for crisis situations.

A lack of information can often amplify fears, as it did in the Fukishima nuclear crisis (Cleveland 2014). Negative emotions like fear and anger have also been found to be correlated with perceptions of greater uncertainty (Powell et al. 2007). Stress, anxiety and various biases in information processing can accentuate gaps between the risk perceptions of risk communicators and the lay public (Krieger et al. 2014). If the source is credible, fear can decrease as more information is reported (Rogers et al. 2007). However, attempting to reassure citizens while providing them with limited information can accentuate their skepticism—again, as it did in the Fukushima crisis (Krieger et al. 2014). Overly reassuring communications can undermine credibility and produce more alarm (Seeger 2006; Klein and Eckhaus 2017). However, messages that provide information on what people can do to protect themselves may help them reduce their anxiety.

Although it is important to be honest about uncertainty, Rogers et al. point out that it is not enough to simply report uncertainty. One way of understanding the importance of context is that risk communicators must "test" for trust in their communication process and consult with and engage the public to find out if information is being properly conveyed (Rogers et al. 2007). An appraisal of best practices in risk communication emphasizes that the public should be engaged in a "dialogical" fashion (Seeger 2006). Consistent with the Pragmatist model of deliberation, this dialogical view suggests that engaging publics prior to crisis events is often a good strategy for building up credibility and trust. While admittedly difficult to achieve during a crisis, open, honest and candid communications with the public can discourage the public from looking to alternative sources of information.

During a crisis, meaning is often shaped through processes of framing, storytelling or narrative construction. The private-sector literature on crisis management, for example, stresses that firms facing a crisis can protect their reputations by managing perceptions and by controlling the framing of the crisis (Coombs 2007). However, a key point to recognize is that crisis framing is rarely a unilateral phenomenon. Although a "crisis frame" may be used to close down debate (Van Buuren et al. 2016), many different actors are typically engaged in framing processes, particularly in the era of social media (Mirbabaie and Youn 2018). In the 2008 financial crisis, for example, many different stakeholders influenced the framing of the crisis, and not just the government (Schultz and Raupp 2010). Crises create opportunities for some stakeholders to reframe the status quo, creating battles to define the situation ('t Hart and Tindall 2009).

Another important point is that crisis communications often revolve around attributions of responsibility—or what are called "blame games" (Hood 2011; Masters and 't Hart 2012; Schultz et al. 2012; Resodihardjo et al. 2016). As the expression "blame game" implies, attributions of blame occur through strategic interactions, or "framing contests" (Boin et al. 2009; 't Hart and Tindall 2009). Boin et al. capture the dilemma that blame games create for strategic crisis managers:

> They must navigate a difficult pathway between an open, reflective, responsibility-accepting stance that encourages policy-oriented learning but may leave them politically vulnerable, and a defensive, responsibility-denying stance that may deflect blame at the price of undermining learning and eroding a leader's long-term legitimacy. (2010, 708)

Not only are government authorities and partisan players involved in blame games, but the wider public—through social media—may actively contribute to framing contests and blame games (Schultz and Raupp 2010; Schwarz 2012).

From our perspective on uncertainty, one of the important implications of crisis framing contests and blame games is that they are likely to increase uncertainty and ambiguity. A crisis often disrupts routine organizational narratives (Willihngaz et al. 2004) and heightens the challenge to the credibility of those charged with communicating risk and uncertainty. A second implication is there will be a strong tendency to "fill the vacuum" created by uncertainty with the certitude of ideological framings and preexisting political agendas. As Van Buuren et al. nicely put it: "Frames mobilize the values against which 'risks' and policy 'problems' are judged to exist" (2016, 74).

CONCLUSION

This review suggests that the wider body of literature reviewed in this chapter is partially but not wholly consistent with Pragmatist practical rationality. On the one hand, work on naturalistic decision making and case-based reasoning is very close in spirit to Pragmatism's model of habitual action. Decision makers draw on simple rules (habits, or in contemporary lingo, heuristics) to make decisions. However, when this action is disrupted or blocked by doubt, decision makers engage in reflection-in-action, deliberation and imagination to draw on past knowledge and experience in creative ways. Although decision makers may weigh alternatives during this phase of doubt, they do not necessarily fully engage in rational-analytic decision making. Rather, decision making looks more like sensemaking and exploratory "probe-and-learn" action in which goals and values are partially discovered through action. In this exploratory action, decision makers act in an experimental fashion, evaluating not only different courses of action, but also their own assumptions, goals and values. Emotions help to focus their attention, alert them to potential negative consequences, and clarify their values. These decision makers deliberate with others in ways that may bring a diversity of perspectives to bear on the situation.

On the other hand, there is a less productive version of this account that can be drawn from the literature reviewed in this chapter: decision makers may lock-in to prior "frames" or "mental schemas" or "conventions" in response to conditions of uncertainty or urgency. Rather than updating their assumptions through experimental action, they persist in their initial judgment and ignore information at variance with their expectations. They fail to reflect on their own assumptions in a critical fashion and the pressures of threat, urgency and time may lead them to exclude different perspectives on the situation.

A similar contrast can be drawn for meaning making. On the one hand, strategic crisis managers may communicate uncertainty to the public and to stakeholders, appreciating that the perception of risk and uncertainty are shaped by contextual factors. Moreover, these managers appreciate that emotions—and not just cold cognition—are important in how people process information during crisis situations. They also recognize the need to deliberate with the broader public and a wide array of stakeholders in order to understand how the situation is being defined and perceived. As in the discussion of decision making, they may engage in deliberation in a reflective and exploratory fashion, seeking to evaluate their preconceptions about the attitudes of the public and of stakeholders.

On the other hand, to prevent panic and ensure compliance with expert decisions, strategic crisis managers may try to reassure the public and stakeholders of the certitude of their position. They may regard public emotion as an expression of irrationality and regard it as something to be quelled or manipulated rather than learned from. Most importantly, a crisis may be framed in ways that advance ideological agendas or that avoid or allocate blame for the crisis, filling in the vacuum of uncertainty with the certitude of a fixed position. In this way, meaning making can reinforce the tendency of crisis decision making to lock-in to fixed crisis frames that are resistant to updating and exploratory action.

These two different images of how leaders grapple with uncertainty, urgency and threat reappear in the following chapters as a distinction between *Pragmatist* and *principle-guided* political crisis management.[18]

---

[18] We note that the contrast we draw here is similar though not identical to the one drawn earlier by Stern (1997) and Stern and Sundelius (1997).

4.   Pragmatist political crisis management

In the preceding chapters we have seen how Pragmatism can be understood as a philosophy that is both analytical and prescriptive. From these analytical and prescriptive claims an ideal type of Pragmatist crisis management can be derived. This ideal type embodies what strategic crisis management might look like from a Pragmatist perspective. Building on the four hidden resources of practical rationality described in Chapter 2—anti-dualism, fallibilism, experimentalism and deliberation—this chapter develops a model of Pragmatist political crisis management, further elaborating it by contrasting it with principle-guided political crisis management.

The chapter proceeds as follows. The first section builds on the theoretical discussions of the preceding chapters and identifies two possible approaches to strategic crisis management: a Pragmatist and a principle-guided one. The four key concepts of Pragmatism—anti-dualism, fallibilism, experimentalism and deliberation—are briefly recounted as the building blocks of the model. We then show how our two distinct theoretical approaches (Pragmatist and principle-guided) are linked to two core tasks of political crisis management: decision making and meaning making. The final section provides an empirical specification of the two models, which guides the empirical analysis in Chapters 6 and 7.

PRAGMATISM'S CRITIQUE OF PRINCIPLE-GUIDED APPROACHES TO UNCERTAINTY

We have already discussed how Pragmatism embraces uncertainty. In this section, we further explore how Pragmatism challenges a principle-guided approach towards uncertainty. This challenge begins with the view that doubt is a valuable asset. Charles Peirce argued that humans want to reach a state of belief since doubt is uncomfortable. When beliefs are taken for granted—that is, when they have become a fixed *principle*—doubt is forestalled.[1] A principle

---

[1]   We use the term principle-guided to describe a state where doubt has been ultimately ruled out and absolute certainty prevails. Another term that might come to mind to describe such a "belief held unquestioningly and with undefended certainty" (Blackburn 2005a, 109) is dogma. Because of the pejorative connotation of the term dogma, we prefer the term principle.

is defined as a fixed belief (or set of beliefs) that is closed to new experiences or arguments and that leaves little space for doubt. Peirce argued vigorously against those who become entangled in a net of certainty:

> They do not waste time in trying to make up their minds what they want, but, fastening like lightning upon whatever alternative comes first, they hold to it to the end, whatever happens, without an instant's irresolution. This is one of the splendid qualities which generally accompany brilliant, unlasting success. It is impossible not to envy the man who can dismiss reason, although we know how it must turn out at last. (Peirce 1992, 122)

For Pragmatism, by contrast, the "irritation of doubt" (Peirce 1992, 114) triggers inquiry, which produces new knowledge. Doubt is therefore productive and leads to reason (or what Peirce called the *method of science*).

In *The Quest for Certainty* John Dewey took up this topic in more general terms, criticizing the tendency to fix belief by striving for absolute certainty.[2] In "Pragmatic America" Dewey reinforced this position and contrasted this false certainty with Pragmatist experimentalism. For him Pragmatism "discourages dogmatism and its child, intolerance. It arouses and heartens an experimental spirit which wants to know how systems and theories work before giving complete adhesion" (Dewey 1998b, 30). While Peirce and Dewey discussed this topic theoretically, their arguments have practical implications. From a political perspective, for instance, it follows that Pragmatism advises politicians not to build their decisions on the false certainty of fixed principles and ideologies but instead to adopt a fallibilist and experimentalist spirit towards new problems.

A prominent contemporary Pragmatist, Richard Bernstein criticized the political reaction after 9/11 along these lines. In 2005, when Bernstein published his book *The Abuse of Evil*, President George W. Bush had just led the US in two wars in Afghanistan and Iraq after constantly evoking the need for a broad "war against terror" and warning about the dangers of Islamic terrorism. Bernstein finds Bush's statements and actions highly problematic. They exemplify for him an approach that has been based on *false certainty* guided by *principle*. Bernstein develops the following critique:

> "Certainty" is used to express our *certitude*, our subjective personal conviction that something is so-and-so. But all too frequently there is a slide from this subjective sense of *certitude* to an objective sense of certainty—where we act as if the *strength* of our personal conviction is sufficient to justify the objective truth of what we are claiming. (2005, 13, emphasis in the original)

---

[2]   See also Dewey's analysis of orthodox Marxism as a political form of such a quest for certainty (Dewey 1979; Zeldin 1991).

For Bernstein, the Bush Administration fell prey to this false certainty through its evocation of a "radical evil"[3] that leaves no space for discussion or critique.

In striking contrast to the Bush Administration after 9/11, Abraham Lincoln's reaction to the end of the Civil War might be regarded as a good example of a Pragmatist rejection of principle-guided action. Lincoln's approach is most explicitly encapsulated in his Second Inaugural Address from 1865. As historian Garry Wills summarizes, Lincoln's speech was a profoundly Pragmatist document:

> The Second Inaugural was meant, with great daring, to spell out a principle of not acting on principle. In the nation's murky situation all principles—except this one of forgoing principle—were compromised. He was giving a basis for the pragmatic position he had taken in the Proclamation of Amnesty, which was deliberately short-sighted, looking only a step at a time down the long, hard road ahead. (Wills 1999; for a related although slightly different discussion, see Siemers 2004)

Facing a deeply divided nation, Lincoln struggled to reconcile the two parties of conflict, both of them relying on strong convictions and principles.

Lincoln was not inviting moral relativism here, just as Pragmatism is not a relativist "anything goes" attitude. LaFollette nicely summarizes Pragmatism's attitude towards ethics:

> A pragmatic ethic is not based on principles, but it is not unprincipled. Deliberation plays a significant role, albeit a different role than that given it on most accounts. Morality does not seek final absolute answers, yet it is not perniciously relativistic. (LaFollette 2000, 418; also see Joas 2000)

From the Civil War, Lincoln took the lesson that principle-guided behavior leads to a false certitude and an unbridgeable clash of different beliefs.

TWO FORMS OF POLITICAL CRISIS MANAGEMENT: PRAGMATIST AND PRINCIPLE-GUIDED

As explained in the Introduction, crisis management can be analysed on both an operational and a strategic level. This study will focus on the strategic level and—more precisely—on the role that political crisis managers (elected or appointed officials at the very top of a polity) play in crisis management.[4] To understand what a Pragmatist form of political crisis management looks

---

[3]   A term which he discusses by mainly drawing on the work of Hannah Arendt.

[4]   Operational crisis management is mostly implicit in its usage of Pragmatism, with Karl Weick's work coming the closest to a Pragmatist approach to crisis management. While Weick has explicitly linked his ideas to Pragmatist thinkers such as

Table 4.1   Summary of key Pragmatist concepts

	Core Thesis/Prescription	Important Works
Anti-Dualism	Dichotomous (on-off) concepts blind us to the complexities of our environment and should be avoided.	(Dewey 1990; Peirce 1992, ch. 7, 8)
Fallibilism	All our knowledge remains fallible and needs to be adapted once substantiated doubt emerges.	(Peirce 1992, ch. 7, 8; James 1997; Bernstein 2005, 2010)
Experimentalism	Since we can never be sure about our knowledge we constantly need to assess it in practice by trial-and-error and learning-while-doing.	(Dewey 1911b; Dorf and Sabel 1998; Ansell 2012; Ansell and Bartenberger 2016b)
Deliberation	The best way to solve (social) problems is to create dialogical processes among communities of inquirers.	(Dewey 1998c; Misak 2004; Bacon 2010)

like, we build on the four main building blocks identified in Chapter 2: anti-dualism, fallibilism, experimentalism and deliberation. Table 4.1 briefly summarizes the core theses of the four building blocks and lists some of the most important sources from the Pragmatist literature.

These ideas can be contrasted with an ideal-typical approach to principle-guided political crisis management. In the context of political crisis management such a principle-guided approach seems to be especially prevalent. When confronted with crises, politicians routinely invoke values and principles—at least to explain and justify their behavior. In his public remarks after 9/11, President Bush and his cabinet invoked strong values and principles by contrasting the importance of "freedom" with the dangers of "absolute evil," and advocating for an uncompromising "war on terror" (Bernstein 2005). In a similar vein French President Hollande declared after the Paris attacks of 2015 that France would lead a "pitiless" war against the attackers who had committed an "act of war … against the values we uphold" (Sharma 2015).

We recognize that such statements may simply be a public relations veneer layered on a hard core of political pragmatism. But to the extent that such principles guide, rather than merely justify strategic crisis management, they can be shown to differ in important ways from a Pragmatist-inspired crisis management. William James drew the contrast in his typically lucid fashion when he defined Pragmatism as an "attitude of looking away from first

James, Dewey and Rorty (Weick 2006), Pragmatism is just one of the many intellectual sources that have inspired his work.

things, principles, 'categories', supposed necessities; and of looking towards last things, fruits, consequences, facts" (James 2000, 29). As noted earlier, Pragmatists are highly skeptical about strict principles since they lead to a false sense of certainty that blocks any further inquiry.

Since principle-guided action delivers an a priori answer to the problem, there is no place left for Pragmatist anti-dualism, fallibilism, experimentalism or deliberation. Instead, we see elements at work in principle-guided political crisis management that are often in opposition to the Pragmatist version. In place of anti-dualism and fallibilism, principle-guided crisis management tends to rely on dualist dilemmas and infallible claims. And whereas Pragmatist political crisis management relies on experimentalism and deliberation, a principle-guided approach to political crisis management postulates that there is one best way to do things and that there is no need for broad deliberation.

We recognize the danger here of adopting a dualist position ourselves by contrasting principle-guided political crisis management as an *ex negativo* in contrast to Pragmatist political crisis management. It is important therefore to clearly state that we do not believe that "principle" and "Pragmatism" are antithetical—both certainly play a role in crisis management. Nor, as we have stressed in Chapter 2, can Pragmatism be understood as endorsing a narrow instrumentalism unconcerned about values. Pragmatism is a value-based philosophy that inquires and deliberates about the practical consequences of values (see Joas 2000; Ansell 2016). Moreover, Pragmatism is comfortable understanding principles as habituated beliefs that guide action until problems are encountered. Pragmatism becomes critical of principle-guided action only when it discourages reflexive inquiry, experimentation and deliberation in problematic circumstances.

We have identified a *perceived urgent threat to core values, beliefs or life-sustaining functions of a community* to be a key characteristic of crisis. One way or the other, therefore, crisis management has to deal with these core values and beliefs, either by trying to reconstruct or restore them. Boin and 't Hart (2003) discuss the inherent tension between a "reform imperative" and "crisis-management imperative." For principle-guided political crisis management the second imperative is crucial. Its main goal is to "[m]inimize the damage, alleviate the pain, and restore order. Doing this requires the reaffirmation of existing values and structures" (Boin and 't Hart 2003, 549). For public leaders who rely on principle-guided political crisis management "[c]ore values and proven methods become anchors in stormy seas" (Boin and 't Hart 2003, 549), guiding their behavior when it comes to the critical tasks of political crisis management.

From a legal standpoint, a principle-guided approach might be labeled *rule-based*. In legal terms, Pragmatism advocates against a positivist and narrow interpretation of legal rules. Instead, it advises judges to also take into account the practical consequences of their decision, a position that has been labeled "anti-formalism." Such a Pragmatist, anti-formalist legal stance is most prominently personified by Richard Posner, a legal scholar at the University of Chicago and former judge at the United States Court of Appeals for the Seventh Circuit (see Scheuerman 1999; Strauss 2007). As Posner has written in his dissent in *United States v Marshall*:

> It is the disagreement between the severely positivistic view that the content of law is exhausted in clear, explicit, and definite enactments by or under express delegation from legislatures, and the natural lawyer's or legal pragmatist's view that the practice of interpretation ... authorize judges to enrich positive law with the moral values and practical concerns of civilized society. (*United States v Marshall*)

In the analysis of the Lehman Brothers decision we will see how the strict and narrow interpretation of legal rules prevailed against a more flexible and Pragmatist interpretation that took the practical consequences on the financial markets into account.

We use the term *principle-guided* instead of *rule-based* to contrast with Pragmatist political crisis management. While an emphasis on legal rules might make sense from a legal perspective, the term *principle* is better suited to a political analysis. The term *principle* is also a more general term that encompasses legal rules as well as political ideologies and values.

MODELS OF PRAGMATIST AND PRINCIPLE-GUIDED POLITICAL CRISIS MANAGEMENT

In developing our models of Pragmatist and principle-guided political crisis management we build on Gary Goertz's work (Goertz 2006), which stresses how the *structure* of scientific models matters. We make use of Goertz's recommendations in designing, structuring and illustrating the two models.

We use the term *model* not to refer to a mathematical model but rather to indicate the construction of a systematic yet simplified perspective on the complex empirical world. As Rebecca Morton has put it:

> [W]hen we wish to investigate the DGP [data generating process, i.e., the empirical world] we have to simplify it in some ways. That is, we would only be able to describe what we can observe and measure in words that are available to us. Whenever we engage in such description we abstract from the DGP. We ignore details, we simplify, we assume that things we cannot observe or measure will not change our description if they change. This is the essence of modeling and everyone who tries to talk about the DGP engages in modeling. (Morton 2009, 28)

Ontologically, such a definition entails a realist assumption that assumes that the empirical reality we investigate and the models we construct about it are distinct. Language plays a crucial role from this perspective since it is through verbal terms and concepts that we have to describe and explain the empirical world that we confront (Sayer 2010, ch. 2). In other words, models are "conceptual lenses" (Allison and Zelikow 1999, 2) through which we look at the empirical world and which help us to analyse and explain it. Through models we try to filter the essential characteristics from the less relevant "noise."

What then makes a "good" model? First, we can make use of some general rules of model construction such as logical consistency, clarification of underlying assumptions and a proper balance between complexity and simplicity (Bendor and Hammond 1992). Goertz (2006) has added other specific recommendations to this list which will be used and elaborated in more detail in the following sections. Yet, despite the existence of these useful guidelines the proof of the pudding is in the eating. The value and quality of a model therefore must ultimately be judged according to its usefulness and appropriateness in the process of empirical research and the results the model yields.

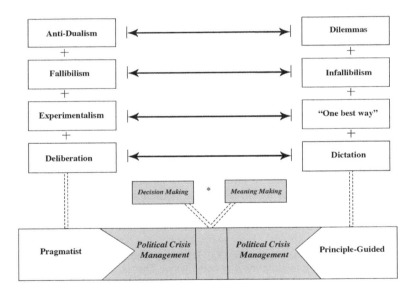

Figure 4.1   Pragmatist and principle-guided crisis management

Figure 4.1 illustrates the elements of Pragmatist and principle-guided political crisis management proposed in this study. The left side lists the main elements of Pragmatism that would be present in a pure Pragmatist form of political crisis management. These are the four elements that have been introduced in Chapter 2 as the hidden resources of Pragmatist practical rationality—anti-dualism, fallibilism, experimentalism and deliberation. Here we treat them as the key building blocks of Pragmatist political crisis management. The right side of the figure contrasts this Pragmatist approach with the elements of principle-guided behavior, which are construed as opposites of the building blocks of Pragmatism: they have been labeled dilemmas, infallibilism, "one best way" and dictation. As we will see in much more detail later, the two approaches can be regarded as the ideal-typical extreme poles of a continuous scale. This study explores how each of them plays out when it comes to two major tasks of strategic crisis management: decision making and meaning making.

This distinction between Pragmatist and principle-guided crisis management refers back to another one of Goertz's recommendations for robust concept building. He advises (2006, 30) that it helps to illuminate the concrete meaning and reach of concepts and their elements by examining (1) the negative pole of a concept, (2) the substantive content of the continuum between the two poles, and (3) the type of continuum (dichotomous or continuous). Pragmatist and principle-guided crisis management are not dichotomous constructs. Instead, there is a continuum and a large "gray zone" between the two poles (Goertz 2006, 34). They can be regarded as ideal types in a Weberian sense that marks the two extreme poles on a continuous scale. In the empirical world, many cases will be hybrids that draw on both approaches.[5]

The Meaning of Pragmatism and Principle-Guided Political Crisis Management

It is important to note here that the relationship between Pragmatism and its four building blocks is a *constitutional* (or *ontological* as Goertz also calls it), not a *causal* one. Just as elections are an essential building block of democracy and constitute this broader concept, anti-dualism, fallibilism, experimentalism and deliberation together *constitute* the concept of Pragmatism, which is not a neatly defined toolkit but rather a general approach that can be expressed and realized in various forms.

---

[5]   See Weber's original definition of such ideal types: "An ideal type is formed by the one-sided accentuation of one or more points of view and by the synthesis of a great many diffuse, discrete, more or less present and occasionally absent concrete individual phenomena, which are arranged according to those one-sidedly emphasized viewpoints into a unified analytical construct. In its conceptual purity, this mental construct cannot be found empirically anywhere in reality" (Weber 1949, 90).

Using these secondary-level building blocks makes the model more concrete. As Goertz sees it, two different modes of structuration exist: sufficient and necessary conditions and family resemblance: "If one takes the necessary and sufficient condition approach to be expressed as '*if and only if n* characteristics are present' then the family resemblance approach takes the sufficiency-only form of '*if m* of *n* characteristics are present'" (Goertz 2006, 36). In other words, a structure of family resemblance requires *no* necessary conditions for a case to meet its criteria. Instead, there are several sufficient criteria that subsume a case under the concept.

We suggest that the secondary-level elements of Pragmatist (left side of the figure) and principle-guided action (right side of the figure) are linked with a logical OR (as indicated by the + in Figure 4.1) instead of an AND (which is symbolized by *). This means that to count as Pragmatist crisis management, not *all* of the four secondary-level elements have to be fully present (anti-dualism AND fallibilism AND experimentalism AND deliberation). Rather, Pragmatist and principle-guided political crisis management are ideal types in a Weberian sense, with the empirical reality of crisis management populated by many hybrid forms of these two approaches.

Our approach tries to find a middle ground between two extreme positions. The first position regards Pragmatist crisis management as a narrowly defined toolkit that includes a specific set of elements. Only if these elements are all present are we allowed to speak of "Pragmatism." The alternative position treats "pragmatism" as a broad and vague catch-all phrase that merely describes a practical and opportunistic attitude that is impossible to define a priori. Our description of Pragmatism as constituted by a set of broad building blocks suggests an alternative to these two extreme positions.

TWO TASKS OF POLITICAL CRISIS MANAGEMENT: DECISION MAKING AND MEANING MAKING

As discussed in Chapter 1, the core tasks of political crisis management include sensemaking, decision making, meaning making, crisis termination and learning after crises. We focus here on two tasks that play an important role in the hot phase of a crisis: decision making and meaning making.

Decision Making

In hindsight, situations of crisis are often reduced to the big decisions they involved: the blockade decision during the Cuban Missile Crisis, the decision to invade Afghanistan after 9/11 or the decision to bail out Greece in the eurozone crisis. Decision making is accordingly perceived as one of the central tasks of political crisis management. Yet, it also remains one of the most mysterious parts of crisis management, as President Kennedy made clear in a quote that provided the title for Graham Allison's well-known study of the Cuban Missile Crisis:

> [T]he presidential office is the vortex into which all the elements of national decision are irresistibly drawn. And it is mysterious because the essence of ultimate decision remains impenetrable to the observer—often, indeed, to the decider himself. (Kennedy 1964, 701)

The study of decision making during crises therefore does not merely concentrate on single leaders but instead focuses on the broader institutional environment in which decisions are made. As Pfiffner has put it in the context of American presidents:

> Both practitioners and scholars begin from the premises that no one individual can hope to understand all of the ramifications of the decisions facing the president and that staff structures and processes are thus necessary to enable the president to make informed decisions. (Pfiffner 2009, 365)

From such a perspective the wider context of advisory systems and group dynamics is as relevant as the personal characteristics and the leadership style of individual leaders.

The specifications offered in the following section will spell out the differences between a Pragmatist and a principle-guided approach in greater detail. Whereas principle-guided decision making regards decision criteria as fixed, Pragmatist decision making proceeds in a probing and exploring manner, revising and adapting its decisions along the way.

Meaning Making

During crises, leaders must formulate a convincing narrative frame and communicate it to the broad public in order to gather support for their agenda. This is not only a matter of communicating the larger meaning of the crisis to a broader public via mass media and communication channels. Since there are different groups competing on the question of how to frame and interpret the crisis, meaning making is also an inherently political process (see Edelman 1985; 't Hart 2008). In such an environment the main challenge for public leaders is to offer a convincing frame for the crisis and show that they are in control. This seemingly easy task of signifying control is immensely complicated in times of crises, since if leaders "really were in control, there would presumably be no crisis" (Boin et al. 2005, 78).

What is crucial from our perspective is that by publicly offering frames and interpretations, leaders also emphasize and communicate core values. Based on our two approaches to political crisis management these values can either be linked to absolute and strict principles or emphasize the Pragmatist elements as developed in this and preceding chapters. The specifications offered in the following section will provide us with a framework for exploring these two different forms of meaning making. The specifications will clarify how Pragmatist meaning making relies on much more ambiguous and humble frames, whereas principle-guided meaning making constructs frames in more definite and stronger terms.

SPECIFICATIONS FOR PRAGMATIST AND PRINCIPLE-GUIDED POLITICAL CRISIS MANAGEMENT

Figure 4.2 introduces a set of specifications of Pragmatist and principle-guided political crisis management. The specifications are structured along four dimensions that were introduced in the model above (Figure 4.1) and that are based on the building blocks of, respectively, a Pragmatist and principle-guided theory of crisis management (anti-dualism versus dualism; fallibilism versus infallibilism; experimentalism versus "one best way"; and deliberation versus dictation). It is crucial to note that the two poles should not be thought of as a strict dualist dichotomy but as ideal types located on a continuous scale that allows for gray zones and hybrid types.

These specifications suggest what we expect to see in Pragmatist and principle-guided political crisis management. As an exploratory study, we cannot provide a definite list of empirical indicators of what Pragmatist and principle-guided political crisis management look like in practice. Such concrete indicators cannot be easily derived from the Pragmatist literature. What the Pragmatist philosophy allows, however, is to translate its building blocks into a set of more concrete specifications for decision making and meaning making. These theory-based specifications will guide our empirical analysis. Through this empirical analysis we identify and assemble an initial list of empirical indicators. These indicators will be presented and discussed in the concluding chapter and can serve as a starting point for future research.

Anti-Dualism and Dilemmas

Chapter 2 described how anti-dualism is a central characteristic of Pragmatist thinking. As the sociologist Anselm Strauss has explained, the struggle against dualism has been a leitmotif of Pragmatism since the beginning:

> In the writings of the Pragmatists we can see a constant battle against the separating, dichotomizing, or opposition of what Pragmatists argued should be joined together:

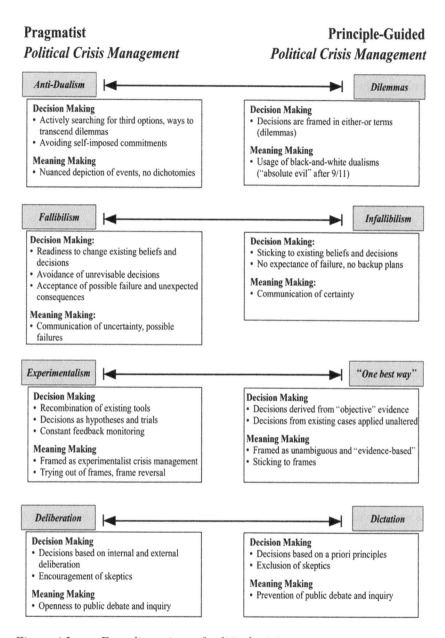

Figure 4.2   Four dimensions of political crisis management

knowledge and practice, environment and actor, biology and culture, means and ends, body and mind, matter and mind, object and subject, logic and inquiry, lay thought and scientific thought, necessity and chance, cognitive and noncognitive, art and science, values and action. (Strauss 1993, 45)

In place of dualism, Dewey recommended the idea of continuity. According to Dewey knowing is a continuous act: "What makes it continuous, consecutive, or concentrated is that each earlier act prepares the way for later acts, while these take account of or reckon with the results already attained ..." (Dewey 1980, 347).

Overcoming dualism is also a matter of concentrating on practical consequences. Recalling William James's example of the camping party that debated about a squirrel going around a tree, we see that Pragmatism seeks to overcome false dualisms by pointing to practical consequences. James proposed to resolve the hunting party dispute by making it clear that the two opposing positions simply had different practical conceptions of the term "going round." This also encapsulates the meaning of the Pragmatist method: By moving beyond fixed principles to concentrate on practical consequences, the absolute juxtapositions of dualisms collapse.[6]

While the Pragmatist emphasis on practical consequences points to the continuity (common ground, shared assumptions, and so on) of dualisms, principle-guided crisis management invites the construction of dualist dilemmas. Following the *Cambridge Dictionary* here, a dilemma is defined as "a situation in which a difficult choice has to be made between two different things you could do" (Cambridge Dictionary n.d.). McConnell (2003), for instance, describes how the Thatcher government was trapped between two principles when British envoy Terry Waite was taken hostage in Lebanon in 1987: "The dilemma facing the Thatcher government was that it had one objective of releasing Terry Waite and another of refusing to bargain with terrorists" (McConnell 2003, 407). Thinking in such strong dualist dilemmas is a key feature of principle-guided political crisis management.

Pragmatists argue that such dualisms unnecessarily limit our options and paralyse decision makers rather than enabling action. This anti-dualist rationale can also be found in the Pragmatist approach to tragedies. In the face of a tragedy, Sidney Hook has advocated the use of the *method of creative intelligence* to deal with tragic dilemmas: "Its categorical imperative is to inquire, to reason together, to seek in every crisis the creative devices and inventions that will not only make life fuller and richer but tragedy bearable" (Hook

---

[6]   Eugenie Gatens-Robinson (1999) has demonstrated the relevance and capability of the Pragmatic method by identifying common ground even between pro-life and pro-choice groups in the highly contested issue of abortion.

2002, 84–5). It is an approach that tries to overcome tragic dualist dilemmas via an approach of mediation and continuity and enables action with its deep *meliorist* optimism (Glaude 2004). As Hook writes, the Pragmatist approach to tragedy "does not conceive of tragedy as a preordained doom, but as one in which the plot to some extent depends upon us, so that we become the creators of our own tragic history" (Hook 2002, 85).

The following specifications enable us to explore Pragmatist anti-dualism in the field of political crisis management and contrast it with a dualist principled-oriented approach.

Decision making

As we have seen in the Terry Waite example mentioned before, decision making during crises is often described as dealing with dilemmas, framing decisions in either-or terms. Anti-dualist decision making tries to overcome these dualistic dilemmas by offering a mediating concept (see Ansell 2011, 10). The Cuban Missile Crisis provides an example. There, the dualism of invasion and non-invasion was overcome by introducing a blockade as a mediating third option (Allison and Zelikow 1999). Anti-dualism also encompasses the way that urgency is handled. As Rosenthal et al. have pointed out, urgency is about "the perception of decision makers rather than some set of predefined circumstances" (Rosenthal et al. 2001, 8). Self-imposed commitments such as arbitrary deadlines can promote such a dualist approach ("now or never") and are therefore best avoided in Pragmatist political crisis management.

Meaning making

How a crisis is framed and which interpretation is communicated to the public is the concern of meaning making. Following an anti-dualist approach to meaning making we would expect to see a nuanced depiction of events and the avoidance of dichotomies. Lincoln's Second Inaugural Address at the end of the Civil War is probably the classical example. By carefully balancing out the different positions and by grasping the interests of the conflicting parties, Lincoln was avoiding dualist meaning making by framing the war in an ambiguous and complex way. A dualist approach to meaning making, by contrast, will employ a strategy heavily relying on dichotomies. Since meaning making is chiefly concerned with identifying core values that relate to the crisis, a principle-guided approach is expected to put these values at the center of meaning making. A prime example for such a principle-guided dualism in meaning making can be found in George W. Bush's framing of the 9/11 attacks as an act of "absolute evil," or Hollande's strategy of "we are at war" after the Paris attacks of 2015. According to Richard Bernstein, such responses can be described as textbook examples of dualist meaning making: "Suddenly the world was divided in a simple (and simplistic) duality—the evil ones seeking to destroy us and those committed to the war against evil" (Bernstein 2005, 10).

Fallibilism and Infallibilism

Fallibilism is the second building block of Pragmatist political crisis management. As Hilary Putnam has put it, Pragmatist fallibilism is the insight "that there is never a metaphysical guarantee to be had that such and such a belief will never need revision" (Putnam 1995, 152). In other words, we can never be sure that our beliefs are correct and will not need to be adapted once we have substantial reason to doubt them. As we have seen, this position has been developed against all attempts to establish a position of absolute certainty, whether they are built on religious doctrines, formal authorities or rationalist analysis. Dewey (1990) has called such attempts a futile "quest for certainty."

Against this quest for absolute certainty, Pragmatism highlights the centrality of uncertainty. This is in line with the general literature on crisis management which has highlighted how crises are situations of "irreducible uncertainty and imperfect knowledge" (Weick et al. 2008, 47). For Pragmatists, this deep uncertainty is not limited to situations of crisis (although it is heightened and becomes more visible during a crisis) but an inevitable human condition: since we cannot avoid it we better work with it. As Glaude has summarized Dewey's position, Pragmatism states

> that uncertainty pervades our lives and involves us in the perils of evils, that there are dimensions of life that are far beyond our control ..., and that this uncertainty defines our moral life in the sense that we don't have recourse to fixed, universal rules that resolve our moral dilemmas. (Glaude 2004, 90)

The recourse to universal rules and principles that provide ultimate guidance for dealing with tragic dilemmas is a core element of a principle-guided approach to political crisis management. Pragmatism rejects this infallibilism of principle-guided approaches and promotes the importance of flexibility and continuous revision. For the political sphere this means "that decisions of policy and value are open to critical revision and that their *justification* is a matter of inquiry—not the sheer tenacity of belief or closed conviction" (Thayer 1968, 351, emphasis in the original).

William James advanced a Pragmatist fallibilism in its most radical form through his conception of truth. As James saw it, a true idea is "[a]ny idea that helps us to *deal*, whether practically or intellectually, with either the reality or its belongings, that doesn't entangle our progress in frustrations, that *fits*, in fact, and adapts our life to the whole setting ... It will hold true of that reality" (James 2000, 94, emphases in the original).

In other words, from a Pragmatist standpoint an idea is true if it helps us to *deal* with reality, that is, to act in an effective way. Such an idea "fits" reality just as a map fits the area we have to navigate through. What is essential to understand here, however, is that the true idea is not thought of as an exact copy of reality. Such an understanding would suspend any further process of inquiry and truth-making. As James writes: "When you've got your true idea of anything, there's an end of the matter. You're in possession; you *know*; you have fulfilled your thinking destiny" (James 2000, 88, emphasis in the original). Such is the case for fixed principle and ideologies that are thought to be true without feeling the necessity for further exploration and verification.

For Pragmatism, on the other hand, finding truth is a never-ending process that calls for constant adaption and revision, just as the maps of the world have to be continuously refined. In the literature on crisis management, an empirical example for such a fallibilist approach has been found in the mindfulness of High Reliability Organizations (HROs). As Weick et al. have described it, this fallibilist mindfulness is a "persistent mindset that admits the possibility that any 'familiar' event is known imperfectly and is capable of novelty. This ongoing wariness is expressed in active, continuous revisiting and revision of assumptions, rather than in hesitant action" (2008, 28). Likewise, fallibilism is an attitude that does not give in to the quest for absolute certainty but constantly tests the truth value of ideas and beliefs when confronted with novel situations. This emphasis on fallibilism is reflected in the specifications of Pragmatist political crisis management.

Decision making

One key specification of fallibilist decision making is the ability to change and overcome existing beliefs and decisions. From a fallibilist standpoint, the right solution is not obvious a priori. Thus, fallibilist decision making avoids decisions that are unrevisable. Because the truth-value of an idea has to be continuously explored, it is essential that decisions that turn out to be wrong can be revoked and adapted. A principle-guided approach, on the other hand, does not bother with revisability. Since its integral infallibilism ensures it of the correctness of its decision, potential failures are ignored. In the political psychology literature such a phenomenon is associated with "group think," which is described as "a mode of thinking that people engage in when they are deeply involved in a cohesive in-group, when the members' strivings for unanimity override their motivation to realistically appraise alternative courses of action" ('t Hart 2011, 297; also see Janis 1989, 59). Such a conception of invulnerability also leads to a situation where the necessity of backup plans is neglected.

Meaning making

The fallibilist insight that deep uncertainty can never be completely eliminated also appears in the meaning-making process of Pragmatist political crisis management. Richard Bernstein offers a concrete example of what such fallibilist meaning making can look like and how it goes together—as we will later see—with an appreciation for deliberation:

> A fallibilistic orientation requires a genuine willingness to test one's ideas in public, and to listen carefully to those who criticize them. It requires the imagination to formulate new hypotheses and conjectures, and to subject them to rigorous public testing and critique by the community of inquirers. (Bernstein 2005, 29)

Fallibilism implies that uncertainty is openly communicated during crises and that possible failures are anticipated ("we are not totally sure what to do and while we think that this solution will work it could also fail"). For the infallibilism of a principle-guided approach to meaning making, on the other hand, a strong sense of certainty in the framing of the crisis can be expected. The remarks delivered by France's President Hollande after the terrorist attacks in Paris in November 2015 illustrate this infallibilism. With the attacks still going on as he spoke, Hollande tried to communicate a strong sense of infallibilist certainty: "This is a terrible ordeal which once again assails us. We know where it comes from, who these criminals are, who these terrorists are" (Sharma 2015).

Experimentalism and the "One Best Way"

If our beliefs and ideas are always potentially wrong and need to stay open for revision and adaptation, Pragmatist experimentalism offers a way to proceed. While we do not know the correct answer in many situations, experimentalism offers a way out by allowing us to try out different ideas to see how they work. This strategy is particularly relevant in the context of crisis management where actors are confronted with an increased level of uncertainty.

Donald Schön has described Pragmatist experimentalism as the approach of being "open to the situation's back-talk" (Schön 1983, 164). Peirce formulated the same principle in his method of abduction or hypothesis testing, in which he also described this method as making a "fair guess" (Peirce 1932, 374). He described abduction as a method of inference that allows us to generate new knowledge and deal with situations of uncertainty.

Through its emphasis on experimentation, Pragmatism further highlights how meaning is not constructed and determined *prior* to action but discovered, employed and adapted *through* action. Donald Schön put it like this: "In the most generic sense, to experiment is to act in order to see what action leads to" (Schön 1983, 145). Karl Weick has highlighted a similar point in his concept of "enactment." He uses the term "to preserve the central point that when people act, they bring events and structures into existence and set them in motion" (Weick 1988, 306). This dynamic action is a delicate point during crises because "action that is instrumental to understanding the crisis often intensifies the crisis" (Weick 1988, 305). Under such conditions, proceeding in an experimentalist manner, while necessary, might also include significant risks and costs that only become visible in hindsight.

By resting on the solid ground of (false) certainty, a principle-guided approach to political crisis management rejects experimentalism and assumes instead that there is one best way to react to the crisis. Since a solution can be derived from a fixed principle (e.g., "financial crises can only be tamed by reducing debt immediately") there is no need for experiments in an (ideal-typical) principle-guided approach. Even more, experimenting during times of crisis might be undesirable given the risk and uncertain outcome they involve. This has been found especially for so-called High Reliability Organizations such as nuclear power plants or airport control towers, where the "scale of consequences precludes learning through experimentation" (Weick et al. 2008, 32; also see Sagan 1994, 237).

A Pragmatist argument for experimentalism counters that we can never escape this problem of enactment during crises: we need to act in order to understand the crisis better, but at the same time our actions might make the crisis worse. To minimize the risks (or ethical implications) of experimentation, Pragmatist experimentalism promotes the usage of small-scale experiments and thought experiments such as simulations (Ansell and Bartenberger 2016a). In the literature on crisis management, simulation plays a similar role:

> Simulations improve the disaster and crisis management capacity of an organization or society. They provide a cost-efficient, controlled environment in which individuals and teams can safely experiment with procedures, protocols, and strategies—while testing suggested improvements of the coping repertoire. (Boin et al. 2004, 390)

This contrast of different approaches to experimentation is present in our two tasks of political crisis management:

Decision making

Following an experimentalist logic, Pragmatist decisions made during crises are regarded as hypotheses that are put into action and if necessary adapted and revised. Decisions are accordingly regarded as experimentalist trials that often are creative recombinations of existing tools that deliver important insights into the nature of a crisis and help to improve decisions through the feedback they provide. In other words, and as also suggested by Weick's enactment perspective, decision making is characterized as a constant feedback loop with decisions providing the actions necessary to better understand the crisis. In order to reduce the potential risks and costs of such an experimentalist approach, techniques such as thought experiments (simulations) and small-scale experiments might also be employed in this context.

Principle-guided decision making does not rely on experimentalism. Instead, a best possible solution is derived from a fixed principle and implemented decisively. The decision will be based on supposedly "objective" evidence (derived from the principle and cases that support it) or based on prior decisions from existing cases that are applied unaltered.

Meaning making

For the level of meaning making, there are at least two different aspects of an experimentalist approach. First, the experimentalist response to the crisis can be part of the frame that is used and communicated to the public. In other words, the government openly describes its reaction as based on the experimentalist maxim of "trial-and-error." When oil flowed into the Gulf of Mexico for almost 90 days during the Deepwater Horizon oil spill in 2010, attempts to fix the leak necessarily resembled a "trial-and-error" approach (Wheaton 2010). In a speech in June 2010, with the oil leaking for almost two months, President Obama more or less openly admitted this fact:

> Because there has never been a leak of this size at this depth, stopping it has tested the limits of human technology. That is why just after the rig sank, I assembled a team of our nation's best scientists and engineers to tackle this challenge ... Scientists at our national labs and experts from academia and other oil companies have also provided ideas and advice. (Reuters 2010)

Second, an experimentalist variant of meaning making might try out different frames and test them to see how they work (e.g., if they raise public support for the response). In the most extreme form this can also result in frame revisions where a frame that has been shown not to work is revised or even replaced. A principle-guided approach, on the other hand, would have the opposite appearance. A crisis framing would signal "unambiguous" knowledge based on solid and undisputed evidence. Procedurally, different frames would not be tried and we would see no or limited frame revision. Instead, the one best frame would be identified and the government would stick to it throughout the crisis.

Deliberation and Dictation

The call for debate and inclusiveness pops up at many different occasions in Pragmatist writings, making deliberation a central feature of Pragmatism. For Peirce it is embodied in the community of inquirers that advance our knowledge through the method of science (Peirce 1997b). Dewey gives this idea a political spin and makes it the foundation of his theory of democracy, connecting democracy and deliberation with Peirce's *method of science* (Dewey 1998a, 343). In a setting of creative democracy, where deliberation, collective inquiry and experimentalism flourish, decision making does not need to rely on what Peirce (1997b) rejected as the methods of *tenacity*, *authority* and *a priori reasoning*.

We have discussed how Pragmatism rejects the notion that the wise leader, acting unilaterally, should determine the answer to a crisis. Instead, effective solutions should rely on collective intelligence. However, Pragmatism is not necessarily opposed to centralization or limited participation, but can recognize that deliberation may have to be limited in certain regards, both when it comes to the number of participants and the time available (Bernstein 2005, 57). Still, Pragmatism does reject an approach that can be labeled *dictation*. In such a scenario, deliberation is suspended and replaced by an authoritarian principle that gives orders categorically and without discussion. Needless to say, in such an atmosphere, the concepts of fallibilism or experimentalism can play no role. Weick has summarized this concern of intellectual contraction in times of crises explicitly: "The person in authority is not necessarily the most competent person to deal with a crisis, so a contraction of authority leads either to less action or more confusion" (Weick 1988, 312).

These contrasting ideal types of deliberation and dictation are reflected in the following specifications:

Decision making

For decision making, the Pragmatist approach heavily relies on the results from collective deliberation, both from internal deliberation but also from deliberation with external stakeholders. There is encouragement of dissenting voices and internal or external skeptics. From a Pragmatist perspective this is necessary "to maintain the state of doubt and to carry on systematic and protracted inquiry" (Dewey 1910, 13). This is also known as *devil's advocate* or *multiple advocacy* (George and Stern 2002). In the Obama Administration, for example, Vice President Joe Biden was widely identified as playing the role of devil's advocate in the foreign policy team (Bailey 2009; Colvin 2009; Woodward 2010; Pfiffner 2011).

A principle-guided approach to decision making would strongly rely on principles established prior to the crisis. This approach would exclude dissenting voices. An often-cited example for this principle-guided decision making is the ability of neo-conservative proponents in the Bush Administration to use the crisis of 9/11 to push an agenda that evoked and implemented long-held principles but had little to do with the crisis itself (see Halper and Clarke 2004).

Meaning making

A deliberative approach to meaning making implies a general openness to collective debate and inquiry that is then reflected in the framing and public communication of the crisis. Accordingly, it would prescribe the general encouragement of public debate and inquiry. This is clearly an ideal-typical assumption and under conditions of high urgency such attempts have, of course, to be limited. Yet, Pragmatist political crisis management would allow as much room as possible for these practices. A principle-guided approach, however, would include a general tendency that tries to prevent and suppress such public debate and inquiry. Instead, we would find a strong public evocation of fixed principle that can also spill over to the dimension of decision making and limit it further.

CONCLUSION

This chapter marks the shift from the theoretical considerations of Chapter 2 to our more empirical-oriented work in subsequent chapters. It has tried to articulate the knowledge and arguments from our philosophical investigations into Pragmatist practical rationality into a model useful for empirical research.

While its content tries to incorporate the key contributions from Chapter 2, the model follows the modeling guidelines and recommendations offered by Gary Goertz (2006). The model has integrated the comprehensive understanding of Pragmatism and its four main building blocks (anti-dualism, fallibilism, experimentalism and deliberation) and has contrasted them with a principle-guided approach to political crisis management. As emphasized, these two conceptions of political crisis management should not be thought of in a strictly dualist manner, but should instead be regarded as ideal types that help us to span the space of possibilities.

This chapter mapped the two ideal types on two key tasks of political crisis management: decision making and meaning making. A set of specifications has been developed that we will apply to the key episodes of the Great Recession in Chapters 6 and 7. Before we begin that analysis, Chapter 5 first introduces the historical context.

5. An "unprecedented crisis": the US financial crisis of 2008

This chapter provides a brief overview of the financial crisis in the US in order to provide context for the two decisions (Bear Stearns and Lehman Brothers) that will be analysed in more depth in the next chapters. We select August 9, 2007 as the beginning of the financial crisis. It was the day that BNP Paribas, France's largest bank, halted withdrawals from its three mortgage funds (Paulson 2010, 61; Blinder 2013, 90). The bank's action is now widely seen as the first major sign of the bursting bubble of the American housing market—a bubble that especially affected subprime mortgages that were bundled into complex financial derivatives held by almost all financial institutions (Shiller 2008). When the bubble did burst, the value of these derivatives quickly evaporated and posed a serious threat to many financial institutions who held them on their books.

The really "hot" phase of the crisis began when these troubles reached the heart of American capitalism in March 2008, represented by the investment bank Bear Stearns. This bank was the smallest of the five big investment banks on Wall Street. As Blinder (2013, 102) has noted, amidst the growing economic turmoil on the subprime markets, Bear Stearns was being "widely viewed as that slow antelope" that would be hit first by the approaching storm. When rumors about the liquidity of Bear started in March 2008, trust in the company decreased dramatically and a run on Bear began (Kolb 2011, 95–6). In a matter of days, the cash reserves of Bear vanished and the investment bank faced bankruptcy. Even though Bear Stearns had been on the radar of the Fed and the Treasury for a while the sudden crisis surprised most actors. As the Treasury Secretary Henry Paulson recalls: "it was unclear what we could do to stop that disaster. This was a dangerous situation and there weren't any obvious answers" (Paulson 2010, 97). Ultimately, and after intense discussions, the Bush government decided to intervene and enabled a merger between Bear Stearns and banking giant J.P. Morgan, supporting it with a $30 billion loan (Schaefer 2013).

Even after this perceived "bailout" of Bear Stearns by the government, the markets did not calm down. The next financial institutions that ran into trouble were the two government-sponsored enterprises (GSEs), Fannie Mae and Freddie Mac, who were strongly entangled in the turbulent mortgage markets.

With pressure from the Bush Administration (especially Treasury Secretary Paulson), Congress passed a law that granted the Treasury broad authority to support the two GSEs. Soon after that the government made use of this authority and put both enterprises under conservatorship, essentially taking them over. At this point in time, this was, as Paulson has put it, "the biggest financial rescue in history," leaving the Bush Administration confident that they had "just saved the country—and the world—from financial catastrophe" (Paulson 2010, 18). But bigger problems were yet to come.

In September 2008, the investment bank Lehman Brothers found itself in roughly the same position that Bear Stearns had been in a few months earlier and it became increasingly clear that the company could not survive on its own. Lehman's troubles were not as surprising as Bear Stearns. Treasury Secretary Paulson began worrying about the firm shortly after the Bear Stearns rescue and contingency planning had started immediately (Paulson 2010, 123, 138). Following the Bear rescue, Lehman had tried to raise additional capital but could increase its position only marginally. Various other financial actors such as the Bank of America and Barclays Capital explored the opportunity of taking over Lehman, but the negotiations went nowhere. The Treasury Department and the Federal Reserve Bank supported Lehman's search for a buyer but made it clear that they would not put public money on the line this time. Ultimately, when no buyer for Lehman could be found and with the Bush Administration sticking to its decision to let the investment bank fail, Lehman Brothers had to file for bankruptcy on September 15, 2008.

Blinder (2013, 128) has called the downfall of Lehman Brothers "the watershed event of the entire financial crisis." With Lehman strongly connected to other financial institutions and the markets expecting another bailout by the government, the downfall of Lehman sent shock waves across the globe. Under conditions of growing uncertainty, with nobody knowing which bank or company would be next, trust among market participants plummeted, leaving banks increasingly unwilling to lend to other banks or companies (Financial Crisis Inquiry Commission 2011, 339).

The first major company to experience this decline in trust was the insurance giant AIG. Heavily invested in the risky mortgage business, AIG found it increasingly hard to obtain money via the credit markets. AIG was "larger, more interconnected, and more 'consumer facing'" (Swagel 2009, 42) than Lehman and it soon became clear that letting AIG fail would create even bigger turmoil than the Lehman decision and could even lead to a meltdown of the world economy. Confronted with this gloomy perspective, the Bush Administration essentially decided to nationalize the insurance company. But the panic on the markets continued. Blinder summarizes the dramatic events that followed the nationalization of AIG:

> Merrill Lynch, America's best-known stock broker, avoided oblivion only by selling itself hastily to Bank of America. Goldman Sachs and Morgan Stanley were saved when the Fed declared them to be bank holding companies ... America's largest thrift institution, Washington Mutual, and the nation's fourth-largest bank, Wachovia, crashed and burned. (Blinder 2013, 128; also see Financial Crisis Inquiry Commission 2011, ch. 20)

After seeing one prominent financial institution after the other stumble, the Bush Administration finally decided that after having tackled these incidents with a case-by-case approach (Bush 2010, 459) a more comprehensive response was needed. On September 18, 2008, President Bush, Treasury Secretary Paulson and Federal Reserve Chairman Ben Bernanke went to Congress to ask the policymakers for a $700 billion program, later known as the Troubled Asset Relief Program (TARP), to strengthen the financial sector.

At first, propelled by the strong opposition from the left-wing of the Democratic Party and the Republican right, the bill was voted down in Congress. But on October 3, 2008, the bill for a $700 billion program to support the financial sector by buying its "troubled assets" finally passed Congress. TARP ultimately allowed the government to inject large amounts of capital into banks and other financial institutions in order to stabilize the financial markets. It was the last major action of the Bush Administration in its fight against the financial crisis. In November 2008, Barack Obama was elected the new President of the United States, inheriting an economy in deep distress.

WAS THE US FINANCIAL CRISIS A "CRISIS"?

In the Introduction, we defined a crisis as a *perceived urgent threat to core values, beliefs or life-sustaining functions of a community, which must be dealt with under conditions of uncertainty.* The three elements of urgency, threat and uncertainty have been identified as the key characteristics of situations of crisis. This section will briefly outline how the case discussed here, the financial crisis in the US, can be understood as crisis that involved (perceived) *urgency*, a *threat* to core values and life-sustaining functions of a community and an elevated level of *uncertainty*.

Urgency

Perceived urgency is an aspect that repeatedly pops up in the portrayals of the two decision points analysed in this study. Both the decisions on Bear Stearns and on Lehman Brothers were taken over a weekend, with the opening of the markets on Monday perceived as the hard deadline for finding a solution. In both cases the financial situation of complex and interconnected investment banks had to be assessed in a short amount of time and negotiations with potential buyers facilitated. Treasury Secretary Paulson therefore has called the rescue of Bear Stearns a "race against time" (Paulson 2010, 121) and New York Fed President Geithner commented: "With limited time and limited sleep, we would be making a momentous decision ..." (Geithner 2014, 152). Fed Chairman Bernanke has noted how this persistent urgency took its toll on government actors: "The urgency to act on so many fronts, together with the complexity of the problems we faced, exhausted all of us" (Bernanke 2015, 310).

Threat

The most striking indication that the financial crisis was perceived as a fundamental threat in the US is the fact that a Democratic Congress granted extraordinary powers to a Republican President in order to fight the crisis. Making this bipartisan move even more unusual was the fact that all of this happened during a presidential election season. As Barney Frank, Democratic Congressman and Chairman of the House Financial Services Committee at the time, has written in a foreword to Henry Paulson's memoirs, Democratic support for a Republican government was justified by "the threat of an economic meltdown that would have been worse than anything since the Great Depression and might conceivably have equaled that event in its economic devastation" (Paulson 2010, xv).

This evaluation has been shared by other important policymakers involved. For President Bush the financial crisis was an "economic calamity that could be worse than the Great Depression" (Bush 2010, 440), a fact underlined by Treasury Secretary Paulson who called it "the economic equivalent of war" (Paulson 2010, 254) and who noted:

> Had it not been for unprecedented interventions by the US and other governments, many more financial institutions would have gone under. The economic damage could easily have equaled or even exceeded that of the Great Depression, with 25 percent unemployment, or worse. (Paulson 2010, 436)

This sense of threat was intensified by the extremely complex and interdependent character of financial markets. As Timothy Geithner, President of the New York Fed and Treasury Secretary under Obama, has put it: "There hadn't been a crisis this severe in seventy-five years, and never in a financial system this complex" (Geithner 2014, 5).

Uncertainty

One of the most powerful characteristics of a crisis is that it comes out of the blue and increases the level of perceived uncertainty dramatically. This was the case at the beginning of the US financial crisis. Treasury Secretary Paulson has called the financial crisis "unprecedented" (Paulson 2010, 265) and Bush openly concedes: "I was surprised by the sudden crisis" (Bush 2010, 453). Similarly, Alan Greenspan, the influential Chairman of the Federal Reserve from 1987 to 2006, has underlined how most economists failed to foresee it:

> leading up to the almost universally unanticipated crisis of September 2008, macromodeling unequivocally failed when it was needed most, much to the chagrin of the economics profession. The Federal Reserve Board's highly sophisticated forecasting system did not foresee a recession until the crisis hit. Nor did the model developed by the prestigious International Monetary Fund ... (Greenspan 2013, 7)

And even Robert J. Shiller, an economist and Nobel Laureate widely credited as one of the few who saw the crisis coming, has stated: "The subprime crisis was not on the list of possible scenarios for which we might have made plans" (Shiller 2008, 104).

After the first shock of surprise, uncertainty remained high during the US financial crisis, continuously producing new and vexing challenges for governments. Making matters worse, the crisis affected financial markets, highly complex and interdependent systems. This made it difficult even for such experienced actors as US Treasury Secretary and former Goldman Sachs CEO Henry Paulson to make sense of what was going on (Paulson 2010, 47). The key decisions throughout the crises—the rescue programs for companies like Bear Stearns or AIG or the decision to let Lehman Brothers fail—were therefore clouded by uncertainty, leaving decision makers unsure of how they could improve the situation.

KEY ACTORS

The analysis will concentrate on the actions of the four most important decision makers in the hot phase of the US financial crisis—President George W. Bush, Treasury Secretary Henry Paulson, Chairman of the Federal Reserve Bank Ben Bernanke and President of the Federal Reserve Bank of New York Timothy Geithner. The trio of Paulson, Bernanke and Geithner, in particular, were the most important strategic crisis managers of the Bush government's response to the financial crisis. As the *Washington Post* has found:

> From the rescue of Bear Stearns to the takeovers of Fannie Mae, Freddie Mac and American International Group, all the key decisions have been made by Treasury

Secretary Henry M. Paulson Jr., Federal Reserve Chairman Ben S. Bernanke and Timothy F. Geithner, the President of the Federal Reserve Bank of New York. (Cho and Irwin 2008)

This account has been confirmed by Wessel who has noted: "When Paulson arrived, the pendulum of power swung all the way from the White House to the Treasury next door. During the Great Panic, he, Bernanke, and Geithner called the shots ..." (Wessel 2009, 201). The key institutions at the center of our analysis are therefore the US Department of the Treasury and the central bank of the US, the Federal Reserve. President Bush plays a prominent role in the analysis but remains in the background in both cases (especially in the decision-making process but also in publicly framing these decisions). Our analysis therefore concentrates on Paulson, Bernanke and Geithner and their teams.

TIMEFRAME

In analysing the financial crisis in the US, we will concentrate on two decision points: the bailout of Bear Stearns (March 2008) and the bankruptcy of Lehman Brothers (September 2008). The case studies will therefore focus on the political crisis management of the Bush Administration and will not deal with the events that occurred during President Obama's term.

Our focus will also be limited to the peak of the financial crisis in 2008, with the tasks of decision making and meaning making at the center of our interest. The analysis will not examine the exact causes and mechanisms of the financial crisis. Instead, our focus is on how the Bush Administration (especially the Department of Treasury and the Federal Reserve Bank) handled the evolving crisis. Also, because we limit our attention to the "hot phase" of the crisis, we do not investigate the question of whether the Bush government did a good job of anticipating the crisis.

In the next two sections, we introduce the dynamic context surrounding each of our two decision points. We also provide a preliminary account of the conclusions that we reach through more systematic analysis in Chapters 6 and 7: decision making in the Bear Stearns case represented an instance of Pragmatist crisis management, while the Lehman Brothers decision comes closer to a case of principle-guided crisis management.

The Rescue of Bear Stearns

The first decision we analyse in greater depth is the rescue of the investment bank Bear Stearns. The question we pose is a relatively simple one: Why did

President Bush and his administration rescue the investment bank Bear Stearns even though it clearly violated their free market principles?

On February 8, 2008, only weeks before the rescue of Bear Stearns, President Bush emphasized these economic principles in a public speech at the Conservative Political Action Conference: "Our views are grounded in timeless truths ... We believe that the most reliable guide for our country is the collective wisdom of ordinary citizens ... We believe in personal responsibility ... We applied our philosophy on issues relating to economic prosperity" (Bush 2008d).

A former CEO of the investment bank Goldman Sachs, Henry Paulson shared Bush's philosophy, calling himself "an advocate of free markets" (Paulson 2010, 438). But Paulson also noted: "The interventions we undertook I would have found abhorrent at any other time. I make no apology for them, however. As first responders to an unprecedented crisis ... we had little choice" (Paulson 2010, 438). It is this fallibilist change from a position that favored free markets and skepticism about government interventions to a decision to support a private investment bank with public money that is at the center of our interest here. How did this occur?

In March 2008, Bear Stearns was the smallest of the five big investment banks on Wall Street. Two of Bear Stearns' hedge funds had already failed in summer 2007 because of their strong investments in collateralized debt obligations (CDOs) that were linked to subprime mortgages. In March 2008, Bear Stearns still held many investments in the housing market (Bland 2007; Creswell and Bajaj 2007). On March 10, the rating agency Moody's downgraded 15 mortgage-backed securities issued by Bear Stearns, leading to a run on the firm (Financial Crisis Inquiry Commission 2011, 286). Bear's transaction partners or "counterparties" lost confidence and "refused to believe that the firm was solvent and refused to continue to extend credit" (Kolb 2011, 95). Additionally, counterparties demanded more securities from Bear Stearns (margin calls) which quickly decreased the financial liquidity of Bear Stearns (Financial Crisis Inquiry Commission 2011, 288). While on the morning of March 10, Bear Stearns' liquidity pool stood at around $18 billion, it dropped to $12.5 billion by the end of the day (Financial Crisis Inquiry Commission 2011, 286; Blinder 2013, 103).

On the morning of March 13, Alan Schwartz, CEO of Bear Stearns, called Timothy Geithner at the New York Federal Reserve and Bob Steele at the US Treasury, telling them that his company faced serious liquidity problems (Kelly 2009, 17; Paulson 2010, 93). Treasury Secretary Paulson subsequently called President Bush to inform him about the situation (Bush 2010, 452; Paulson 2010, 96). During the day of March 13, the liquidity reserves of Bear Stearns declined further to $2 billion, leading to a conference call at 7:30 p.m. between representatives of Bear Stearns and its regulator, the Securities and

Exchange Commission (SEC) (Financial Crisis Inquiry Commission 2011, 289). During this conference call Bear Stearns stated that it would have to file for bankruptcy on the following day, a message that was also delivered to Treasury Secretary Paulson and New York Fed President Geithner (Paulson 2010, 97; Geithner 2014, 149). Overnight, a team from the New York Federal Reserve analysed the situation and assessed possible consequences of a bankruptcy of Bear Stearns (Sidel et al. 2008).

During a conference call on early Friday morning, March 14, 2008, members of the Federal Reserve Bank (led by Chairman Ben Bernanke and New York Fed President Timothy Geithner), the US Treasury (led by Secretary Henry Paulson) and the SEC assessed the situation. The short amount of time made it impossible to find a buyer for Bear Stearns or to build a consortium of other financial institutions that would lend to the investment bank (Kelly 2009, 63).[1] Anticipating severe consequences for financial markets and the general economy in case of a Bear Stearns' bankruptcy, Timothy Geithner proposed that the Federal Reserve could lend money to Bear Stearns via the bank J.P. Morgan (Kelly 2009, 66; Geithner 2014, 152). After Treasury Secretary Paulson had agreed to protect the Federal Reserve Bank from any losses of the loan (Paulson 2010, 101), Fed Chairman Ben Bernanke supported the idea and assembled the available Fed governors to approve the loan (Sidel et al. 2008).

With the indirect $12.9 billion loan by the Federal Reserve Bank via J.P. Morgan on Friday morning, Bear Stearns made it through the day (Federal Reserve Bank 2008a) but the rating agencies continued to downgrade the investment bank and the stock of Bear Stearns had fallen by 47 percent by the end of the day (Financial Crisis Inquiry Commission 2011, 289). For the government, this was a clear sign that trust in Bear Stearns had not been restored by the indirect loan. While initially the loan was supposed to be available for up to 28 days, Geithner and Paulson now pushed Bear Stearns to find a buyer over the weekend (Kelly 2009, 100). J.P. Morgan signaled interest to buy Bear Stearns and began to work on a deal with the investment bank over the weekend. On Sunday, however, J.P. Morgan told Geithner and Paulson that it would not be able to take over Bear Stearns without additional financial support (Paulson 2010, 109; Financial Crisis Inquiry Commission 2011, 289). With the backing of President Bush and Treasury Secretary Paulson, Bernanke and Geithner decided to invoke the emergency clause of the Federal Reserve Bank, section 13(3) of the Federal Reserve Act, that authorizes the central bank to lend to any institution under "unusual and exigent circumstances"

---

[1]   The template of a consortium solution was based on the case of the hedge fund Long Term Capital Management, which was bailed out by a consortium of banks and other financial institutions in 1998 (Blinder 2013, 113).

(Federal Reserve Bank 2013). Under this provision the Fed purchased $30 billion of Bear Stearns assets with the special condition that J.P. Morgan would cover the first $1 billion of eventual losses from these assets (Financial Crisis Inquiry Commission 2011, 290). Enabled by the support from the Federal Reserve Bank, J.P. Morgan and Bear Stearns announced on Sunday that J.P. Morgan would take over Bear Stearns, paying $2 per share (Kelly 2009, 219). The takeover by J.P. Morgan prevented a bankruptcy of Bear Stearns and the financial markets calmed down in the weeks that followed (Blinder 2013, 114). The timeline in Figure 5.1 summarizes the events of this case.

Commentaries have noted the unusual character of the steps taken by the government in order to save Bear Stearns. The *Wall Street Journal* concluded that the Bush Administration "more or less threw its rule book out the window" (Sidel et al. 2008). And the *New York Times* quoted an economic historian saying: "Traditionally regulators have helped commercial banks in financial panics, but not investment banks, which do not hold customer deposits … I don't remember a Fed action aimed at a noncommercial bank" (Landon 2008b). Our analysis in Chapter 6 will show how the actions by the government were not only unprecedented but can also be regarded as an example of Pragmatist political crisis management.

The Collapse of Lehman Brothers and the Rescue of AIG

After Bear Stearns had been rescued in March 2008, Lehman Brothers quickly moved to the center of government concern. Paulson, Bernanke and Geithner were worried about the stability of the investment bank (Paulson 2010, 123, 138; Financial Crisis Inquiry Commission 2011, 325; Blinder 2013, 121). Lehman Brothers held large investments in the commercial real estate market and its business model employed high leverage, relying heavily on borrowed money (Financial Crisis Inquiry Commission 2011, 326; Blinder 2013, 120). After March 2008, Lehman tried to raise its capital and liquidity level but had to report a $2.8 billion loss for its second quarter in June 2008 (Lehman Brothers 2008b; Financial Crisis Inquiry Commission 2011, 326). Following reports that other banks were getting increasingly worried about Lehman, the Federal Reserve Bank and the US Treasury began their contingency planning, thinking about a potential Lehman bankruptcy and developing different ways to deal with such a scenario (Financial Crisis Inquiry Commission 2010, 3, 2011, 328).

On September 7, the US Treasury—in collaboration with the Federal Reserve Bank and the Federal Housing Finance Agency (FHFA)—put the two government-sponsored enterprises Fannie Mae and Freddie Mac into conservatorship, a form of temporary nationalization (US Department of Treasury 2008b). The FHFA served as conservator of Fannie Mae and Freddie Mac.

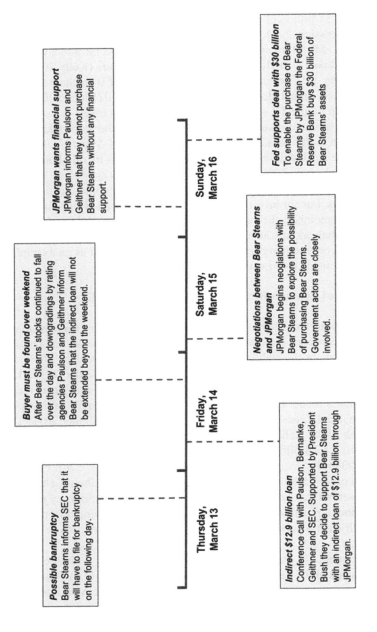

Figure 5.1   Timeline of the Bear Stearns case

Together with the Treasury the FHFA replaced the CEOs of both companies and provided $200 billion in loans (Financial Crisis Inquiry Commission 2011, 320; Blinder 2013, 118). As summarized by the *New York Times*, by putting Fannie Mae and Freddie Mac under conservatorship the "Bush administration seized control of the nation's two largest mortgage finance companies," which the *Times* called "an extraordinary federal intervention in private enterprise" (Labaton and Andrews 2008).

On September 9, 2008, news that the Korea Development Bank would not invest in Lehman Brothers caused the price of Lehman's stock to fall by 55 percent (Financial Crisis Inquiry Commission 2011, 331). The next day, Lehman reported a $3.9 billion loss for the third quarter. Banks and other financial institutions immediately demanded more collateral from Lehman under the threat of halting lending to the investment bank (Financial Crisis Inquiry Commission 2011, 331; Wiggins et al. 2014, 9). As concerns over Lehman continued to grow, the Federal Reserve Bank began to develop a plan that would bring together other major financial institutions in order to prevent a Lehman bankruptcy (Financial Crisis Inquiry Commission 2008d). Treasury Secretary Paulson contacted Bank of America and asked them to consider a takeover of Lehman Brothers while New York Fed President Geithner established contact with the British bank Barclays, another potential buyer (Sorkin 2009, 130; Stewart 2009; Paulson 2010, 173). After further assessing the situation Geithner called Paulson and Fed Chairman Ben Bernanke on Thursday, September 11 and informed them that Lehman would probably not be able to open for business after the weekend (Stewart 2009).

While Lehman Brothers started negotiations with Bank of America and Barclays, Paulson and Geithner convened the most important Wall Street bankers at the New York Federal Reserve Bank (Stewart 2009; Financial Crisis Inquiry Commission 2011, 334). Paulson stated that there would be no public support for Lehman and asked the bankers to help assess the situation and to think about ways to support a Lehman purchase (Paulson 2010, 192; Financial Crisis Inquiry Commission 2011, 334). On the next day (September 13), the negotiations between Lehman, Bank of America and Barclays continued but it became increasingly clear that both potential buyers would not purchase all of Lehman's assets and therefore would need financial support for a takeover (Sorkin 2009, 178; Financial Crisis Inquiry Commission 2011, 335).

On the evening of September 13, the group of assembled bankers informed Paulson and Geithner that they had agreed to support a takeover of Lehman with $10 billion but as no potential buyer could be found this offer was not used in the end (Paulson 2010, 206). Bank of America had already dropped out as a potential buyer (purchasing the investment bank Merrill Lynch instead) but on September 14, Barclays indicated its interest in buying Lehman Brothers. Since Barclays is a British bank, however, it needed the approval of the British regulator, the Financial Services Authority (FSA), which refused to authorize the purchase (Financial Crisis Inquiry Commission 2011, 335; Blinder 2013, 124). Geithner and Paulson tried to persuade their British counterparts but the British Finance Minister Alistair Darling vetoed the purchase of Lehman by Barclays (Evening Standard 2010; Financial Crisis Inquiry Commission 2011, 336). On September 15, 2008, Lehman Brothers filed for bankruptcy (Lehman Brothers 2008a).

Unlike in the Bear Stearns case, Paulson was particularly concerned about the problem of "moral hazard" in the Lehman case—that is, the concern that bailing out the bank in a crisis would encourage banks in the future to take greater risks. As we will demonstrate in Chapter 6, this principled stance reflected political shifts inside the Bush Administration. Overall, we will show that in contrast with the Bear Stearns case, decision making in the Lehman case was characterized by principle-guided, rather than Pragmatist, crisis management.

Lehman's bankruptcy had critical knock-on effects. Over the weekend, the Federal Reserve Bank and the Treasury had also learned that AIG, the world's largest insurance company, had serious liquidity problems (Stewart 2009; Paulson 2010, 200; Federal Reserve Bank of New York 2012). AIG had guaranteed a large number of credits through Credit Default Swaps (CDS) without holding enough capital reserves to cover these risks. Following the heightened nervousness on the financial markets, AIG was unable to meet the calls for higher collaterals (Blinder 2013, 130–4). Faced with these serious liquidity problems, AIG was downgraded by the rating agencies after Lehman Brothers filed for bankruptcy on September 15 (Financial Crisis Inquiry Commission 2011, 349). After internal discussions between Paulson, Bernanke and Geithner, the Federal Reserve Bank announced on September 16 that it would loan $85 billion to AIG, invoking its emergency section 13(3) (Federal Reserve Bank of New York 2012).

Lehman was also strongly interconnected with the money market mutual fund Reserve Primary Fund (Sorkin 2009, 258; Blinder 2013, 143). Money market funds were used by many businesses in a similar way to bank accounts (Bernanke 2013, 79). After the Reserve Primary Fund announced on September 16 that it would be unable to pay out the full value of its deposits, panic spread to other money funds and affected the liquidity of non-financial firms such as General Electric and IBM (Blinder 2013, 145). To stabilize the money market funds, Treasury Secretary Paulson announced on September 19 that the Treasury would guarantee the value of money market funds with $50 billion from its Exchange Stability Fund (ESF) (US Department of Treasury 2008c; Financial Crisis Inquiry Commission 2011, 359). The timeline in Figure 5.2 summarizes the events of this case.

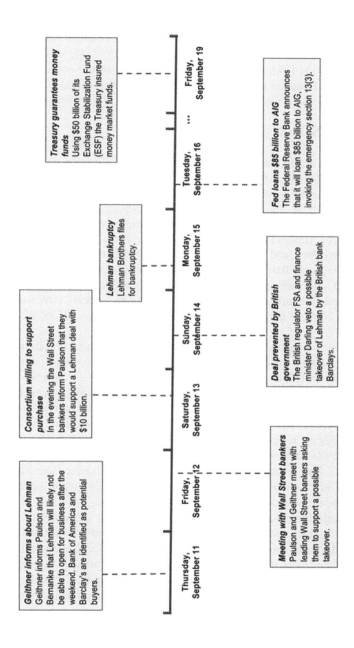

Figure 5.2   Timeline of the Lehman Brothers case

The days around the Lehman decision have been described as one of the most decisive periods of the financial crisis of 2008. For the Financial Crisis Inquiry Commission, it was the time where the crisis reached "cataclysmic proportions" (Financial Crisis Inquiry Commission 2011, 343); for economist Alan Blinder (2013, 128), it was "the watershed event of the entire financial crisis" while the financial journalist James Stewart (2009) called it the "most important week in American financial history since the Great Depression."

A NOTE ON SOURCES

To investigate strategic crisis management at these two decision points (Bear Stearns and Lehman Brothers), we systematically reviewed a wide array of sources, analysing the two decision points and coding for the specifications of the model of political crisis management. These sources included the following: the report of the Financial Crisis Inquiry Commission and its numerous primary sources (internal government materials, mails, reports, briefings, interview transcripts, and so on), the memoirs of the main actors involved (Bush 2010; Paulson 2010; Cheney 2011; Geithner 2014; Bernanke 2015), the transcripts of Congressional hearings (US Congress 2008a, 2008b, 2008c) and journalistic and scientific accounts of the events (e.g., Sorkin 2009; Stewart 2009; Wessel 2009; Stiglitz 2010; Blinder 2013; Conti-Brown 2015b; Wallach 2015a).

Additionally, we engaged in an in-depth analysis by setting a timeframe for both decision points that covered one week before and after each decision. For these time periods (March 9–23, 2008 and September 7–21, 2008) we have further analysed all official documents (press releases, statements, press briefings, and so on) released by the White House, the US Treasury and the Federal Reserve Bank and examined the public speeches of the main actors. For these two time periods we have also analysed the articles published in the *New York Times* and the *Wall Street Journal* that included the keywords "Bear Stearns" and "Lehman." This search returned a list of 170 articles for the Bear Stearns case and 357 articles for the Lehman case. These articles were especially useful in analysing how decisions were publicly framed.

In reviewing this source material, we searched for evidence of both Pragmatist and principle-guided crisis management. When relevant evidence was identified, it was crosschecked with other sources. Evidence specifying our two political crisis management models is only reported in subsequent chapters if we found support from at least one other source. For decision making, we concentrated on internal materials (reports, emails, memos, and so on), memoirs, journalistic and scientific accounts, reports from Congressional hearings and press articles that provided an "inside" view of the decision-making process. For the analysis of meaning making we focused on press releases, official statements, press conferences, Congressional hearings, public speeches and the press articles from the *New York Times* and the *Wall Street Journal*.

We added no novel material by conducting own interviews and so on but built on the corpus of already existing sources. This methodological approach relates to the main empirical objective of this study: re-analysing two well-known cases of political crisis management that have received extensive attention from politicians, scientists and journalists in order to evaluate whether the theoretical framework we have set out can offer a novel perspective on these cases and if preliminary empirical evidence for this framework can be found through these "plausibility probes." The empirical results from this systematic analysis will be presented in Chapters 6 and 7.

6. The rescue of the investment bank Bear Stearns

This chapter provides a systematic analysis of the Bear Stearns case in terms of decision making and meaning making. Our analysis begins with a brief explanation of the main ideological principle from which Bush and Paulson departed: the doctrine of *moral hazard*. President Bush recalls in his memoirs that when he first heard about the liquidity troubles at Bear Stearns:

> My first instinct was not to save Bear. In a free market economy, firms that fail should go out of business. If the government stepped in, we would create a problem known as moral hazard: Other firms would assume they would be bailed out, too, which would embolden them to take more risks. (Bush 2010, 453)

The discussion of whether moral hazard is indeed a problem is a highly ideologized one, a discussion that runs right through economics departments and government agencies (see Bair 2012, 41). While conservative-libertarians emphasize the danger of moral hazard to criticize public regulation and government interventions, liberals argue that such interventions are sometimes necessary in order to fix the deficiencies of free markets (Krugman 1999; Stiglitz 2012).

New York Fed director Timothy Geithner, for instance, has described a group of hawkish regional Fed presidents "whose main concerns were preserving the Fed's inflation-fighting and avoiding moral hazard. They did not expect a downturn, so they generally did not believe the upheaval in mortgages and capital markets justified lower interest rates" (Geithner 2014, 130). Blinder paints the picture in even starker colors and speaks of "moral hazards ayatollahs" (Blinder 2013, 110) while, before the crisis, Lawrence Summers warned of "moral hazard fundamentalists" (Summers 2007).

On the one hand, these three remarks were all issued by persons regarded as close to the Democratic Party. Timothy Geithner built his career during the Clinton Administration and later became the first Treasury Secretary of the Obama Administration. Alan Blinder was a member of Bill Clinton's Council of Economic Advisers while Lawrence Summers served as Treasury Secretary under Clinton before becoming director of the National Economic Council in the Obama Administration.

On the other hand, Kevin Dowd defended the idea of moral hazard in the journal of the conservative Cato Institute, noting that "moral hazard played a central role in the events leading up to the crisis, and we need to appreciate this role if future reforms are to be well designed and prevent further disasters down the line" (Dowd 2009, 142). This notion has been further supported by the libertarian Mises Institute (Hülsmann 2008) and by Anna Schwartz, one of Milton Friedman's former co-authors, who called the Bear Stearns' bailout a "rogue operation" (Torres 2008).

Whether or not decision making in the Bear Stearns case is Pragmatist or principle-guided depends on whether those who deeply believed in the principle of moral hazard—namely, President Bush and Treasury Secretary Paulson—reevaluated it in light of the crisis.

THE FALLIBILISM OF GEORGE W. BUSH AND HENRY PAULSON

Specifications of Pragmatist political crisis management: *Readiness to change existing beliefs and decisions; avoidance of unrevisable decisions*

Fallibilism, as we have seen in the preceding chapters, is one of the building blocks of Pragmatism. As understood by Pragmatism, fallibilism is an approach that is "anti-dogmatic and anti-ideological" (Bernstein 2005, 51) and rejects absolutes and "moral certainties" (Bernstein 2005, 42). Pragmatist fallibilism argues for the revision of existing beliefs and habits when confronted with reasonable doubt.

In the case of the Bear Stearns rescue, fallibilism is illuminated by the decision-making behavior of two of the main actors: President George W. Bush and Treasury Secretary Henry Paulson. Although Bernanke and Geithner also modeled fallibilist behavior, Bush and Paulson are useful for illuminating fallibilism precisely because they expressed the strongest adherence to free-market principles prior to the decision.[1] Thus they can serve as prime examples of fallibilism. In the pre-crisis period, both Bush and Paulson were vocal free-market advocates and they both expressed skepticism about government intervention. From this perspective, their support for a government-backed bailout of Bear Stearns seemed highly unlikely. But as we will see in this section, in deciding to save the investment bank Bear Stearns, both men broke with their preexisting beliefs grounded in free-market ideology. We argue that in this case, their action reflected Pragmatist fallibilism.

---

[1]   Ben Bernanke and Timothy Geithner are interesting but less pronounced examples in this regard (for Bernanke, see Andrews 2008b).

At first, Bush rejected the notion of preventing the Bear bankruptcy, citing the danger of moral hazard as the main reason (Bush 2010, 453). As Bush remembers it, this view was supported by Treasury Secretary Paulson as well, but with a decisive shift: "Hank shared my strong inclination against government intervention. But he explained that a collapse of Bear Stearns would have widespread repercussions ... While I was concerned about creating moral hazard, I worried more about a financial collapse" (Bush 2010, 453). This shift from prioritizing the moral hazard doctrine to highlighting concerns about financial and economic stability lies at the center of fallibilist decision making in the Bear Stearns case. It is a shift that can be traced back to the analysis conducted by the Federal Reserve Bank on the question of what a bankruptcy of Bear Stearns would mean for the financial and economic system. This analysis was carried out by New York Federal Reserve President Timothy Geithner and his team on the night of March 13, 2008.

After Bear Stearns' CEO Alan Schwartz had informed the SEC, the Federal Reserve and the Treasury on the evening of March 13 that without any support his firm would have to file for bankruptcy the next day, the three involved public agencies had different opinions on how to proceed. SEC officials, the main regulators of Bear Stearns, saw little they could do to prevent a bankruptcy and went home after receiving the message from Schwartz (US Congress 2008c, 106; Kelly 2009, 35; Geithner 2014, 149). But Geithner called his team back to the New York Federal Reserve Bank and spent the night exploring what consequences a bankruptcy of Bear Stearns would have for the financial system (Sidel et al. 2008; Kelly 2009, 48; Geithner 2014, 149). The analysis quickly revealed that Bear Stearns was linked to many of the other main financial institutions and that its bankruptcy would have broad and severe consequences (see Ip 2008):

> The closer Fed officials looked at Bear's connections with the broader financial system, the more they feared its sudden failure would unleash utter chaos. Bear was not that big—only the seventeenth largest U.S. financial institution at the time—but it was completely enmeshed in the fabric of the system. (Geithner 2014, 150)

It was this interconnectivity and the risk of contagion that raised concerns about the general stability of the financial and economic system. As a report by the Federal Reserve Bank has put it:

> Market participants were likely to respond to the failure of Bear Stearns by withdrawing generally from short-term collateralized funding markets, resulting in a dramatic drop in the overall availability of short-term financing, and threats to the liquidity and possibly the solvency of other large and highly leveraged financial institutions. (Federal Reserve Bank 2008g, 2)

Around 5 a.m., the main government actors convened a conference call to make a decision on how to proceed. The participants were Timothy Geithner, Ben Bernanke and members of their team from the Federal Reserve Bank, Treasury Secretary Henry Paulson and his aides and Eric Sirri from SEC (Kelly 2009, 61). Timothy Geithner presented the results of the Fed's analysis and introduced three options: letting Bear Stearns file for bankruptcy, finding other financial institutions which could support or take over Bear Stearns or lending public money to Bear Stearns (Sidel et al. 2008; Kelly 2009, 64). Given the interconnectedness of Bear Stearns and the potentially severe consequences of its bankruptcy, Bernanke and Geithner concluded that a Bear Stearns' bankruptcy could potentially be catastrophic (Kelly 2009, 64; Geithner 2014, 151; Bernanke 2015, 217).

Initially, Paulson had doubts but after thinking through the potential consequences of a Bear Stearns' failure, he supported the decision to rescue the investment bank: "Perhaps if Bear had been a one-off situation we would have let it go down. But we realized that Bear's failure would call into question the fate of the other financial institutions ..." (Paulson 2010, 102). Since there was not enough time to find institutions willing to support Bear Stearns,[2] the only option that remained was to lend public money to Bear Stearns. In the night before the conference call, Tom Baxter, the general counsel of the New York Fed had come up with the idea of an indirect loan and during the conference call Timothy Geithner proposed the idea as a way to lend to Bear Stearns (Geithner 2014, 151; Bernanke 2015, 214). Through this indirect loan the Federal Reserve Bank would lend $12.9 billion to the bank J.P. Morgan, which would then "on-lend" it to Bear Stearns (US Congress 2008c, 116; Financial Crisis Inquiry Commission 2011, 289).[3] Paulson and Bernanke supported Geithner's plan, and Paulson called President Bush to get his support.

At first, Bush was opposed to supporting Bear Stearns with public money, but Paulson convinced him that financial stability was more important than moral hazard in this situation (Kelly 2009, 68; Bush 2010, 453; Paulson 2010, 101; Bernanke 2015, 216). However, Bush had political concerns. He had to give a speech at the Economic Club in New York the same day and Paulson advised him not to promise that there would be no bailouts (Kelly 2009, 68;

---

[2] Geithner and his team were in contact with J.P. Morgan during the night, and while the bank was interested in a takeover of Bear Stearns it needed more time (Geithner 2014, 149).

[3] The idea of an *indirect* loan was developed because the New York Fed's general counsel initially thought that it would not require the invocation of the Fed's emergency clause section 13(3). But after extended legal discussions, Fed Chairman Ben Bernanke decided that the indirect loan would also require the invocation of section 13(3) (Bernanke 2015, 214).

Paulson 2010, 93).[4] But Bush was also worried about a meeting with the editors of the *Wall Street Journal* the same day. So Paulson sent Bob Steele, one of his aides, to brief Bush on the rescue of Bear Stearns and to prepare him for the meeting with the editors (Kelly 2009, 71; Wessel 2009, 163; Paulson 2010, 102).

After Bernanke, Geithner and Paulson had discussed several options, consensually agreed on the indirect loan and President Bush had supported the plan, Fed Chairman Bernanke decided to implement the plan at 7 a.m. (US Congress 2008c, 116; Kelly 2009, 69; Geithner 2014, 152; Bernanke 2015, 217). Bernanke assembled the available Fed governors who unanimously approved the indirect $12.9 billion loan from the Federal Reserve Bank to Bear Stearns at 9:15 a.m. (Financial Crisis Inquiry Commission 2011, 289; Bernanke 2015).

Bush's and Paulson's Shift as Pragmatist Fallibilism

The readiness of Bush and Paulson to change their existing beliefs under these circumstances and support a decision that contradicted these beliefs qualifies as fallibilist decision making. It is, in this sense, an example of Pragmatist decision making. This change of existing beliefs was something that both Bush and Paulson seemed to have been aware of. Bush quipped that his friends back in Texas "are going to ask what happened to the free-market guy they knew" (Bush 2010, 460). And Paulson has spoken about the instances during the financial crisis "where I found myself forced to do the opposite of what I had believed for my entire career" (Paulson 2010, 246).

More evidence for fallibilist decision making can be found in Paulson's insistence that Bush should not promise that there would be no bailouts in his speech at the Economic Club on March 14, 2008 (Bush 2008a; Kelly 2009, 68; Paulson 2010, 93). As Paulson remembers it, the reason why he wanted to avoid such a public commitment was the profound uncertainty of the situation: "Mr. President, the fact is, the whole system is so fragile we don't know what we might have to do if a financial institution is about to go down" (Paulson 2010, 92). Paulson's behavior qualifies as "Avoidance of unrevisable decisions" as listed in the specifications for fallibilist decision making. Given the high level of uncertainty Paulson insisted that it was important to avoid the unrevisable commitment of promising no bailouts and instead "preserve

---

[4]   In the final version of the speech, delivered on March 14, 2008, Bush did not mention his commitment against bailouts anymore but promised more vaguely that the "Chairman of the Federal Reserve and the Secretary of the Treasury ... will take the appropriate steps to promote stability in our markets" (Bush 2008a).

optionality" as Timothy Geithner later called it (Geithner 2014, 179). Bush followed Paulson's advice and in the final version of the speech did not promise that there would be no further bailouts.

Accepting Possible Failure as Pragmatist Decision Making

Specification of Pragmatist political crisis management: *Acceptance of possible failure and unexpected consequences*

When Timothy Geithner, President of the Federal Reserve Bank of New York, initially learned about the serious liquidity problems at Bear Stearns on March 13, he stated that his initial goals were humble: "Even if we couldn't prevent an ugly crash, I wanted to explore ways to put 'foam on the runway'—anything to mitigate the damage" (Geithner 2014, 149). Geithner's acceptance of possible failure remained present throughout the weekend in parallel to the negotiations between Bear Stearns and J.P. Morgan. As Geithner testified before Congress:

> As J. P. Morgan and other institutions conducted due diligence, my colleagues in New York and Washington continued to examine ways to contain the effects of a default by Bear. As part of these discussions, we began to design a new facility that would build on other liquidity initiatives taken by the Federal Reserve System, and provide a more powerful form of liquidity to major financial institutions. (US Congress 2008c, 117)

The program meant to "put foam on the runway" in the event of a Bear Stearns' bankruptcy was called the Primary Dealer Credit Facility (PDCF). To initiate it the Federal Reserve Bank again had to invoke the emergency clause, section 13(3) of the Federal Reserve Act, citing "unusual and exigent circumstances" as the reason for the program (Federal Reserve Bank 2016b). In general terms, the program was designed to increase financial market stability. As the Fed has put it: "PDCF was established to improve the ability of primary dealers to provide financing to participants in securities markets, and to promote the orderly functioning of financial markets more generally" (Federal Reserve Bank 2016b).

The Federal Reserve Bank had already launched a similar program, the Terms Securities Lending Facility (TSLF), on March 11, 2008. TSLF was launched before the troubles at Bear Stearns became known, so the money from the program was not available to financial institutions before March 27 (Federal Reserve Bank 2008f). As Fed Chairman Ben Bernanke testified before Congress, the events surrounding Bear forced the Federal Reserve Bank to revise its decision and roll out PDCF, a new program that could provide money to financial institutions immediately: "It was precisely the set of conditions that we saw during the week and that led to the Bear Stearns' situation that caused us to reconsider our previously held position ... We made the decision to do so on Sunday" (US Congress 2008c, 23). The establishment of the PDCF was announced by the Board of Governors of the Federal Reserve Bank on March 16, 2008 (Federal Reserve Bank of New York 2008; Geithner 2014, 156; Bernanke 2015, 220).

Ben Bernanke explained the program before Congress in the following way:

> At the time we did it, we did not know whether the Bear Stearns' deal would be consummated or not and we wanted to be prepared, in case it was not consummated, that we would need to have this facility in order to protect what we imagined would be pressure on the other dealers subsequently to that. (US Congress 2008c, 23)

Timothy Geithner has described PDCF as a "credit facility intended to provide liquidity to the investment banks and the broader markets *in case Bear collapsed*" (Geithner 2014, 156; our emphasis).

What is important to understand from a Pragmatist perspective is that the PDCF was intended as a backup instrument in case the negotiations between J.P. Morgan and Bear Stearns failed and Bear Stearns went bankrupt. Fueled by the humility and skepticism we associate with fallibilism (Bernstein 2005), Pragmatist crisis management anticipates negative consequences where other forms of crisis management are confident that the worst is over. While this is a matter of degree, the fact that PDCF was established just after the deal between Bear Stearns and J.P. Morgan was announced provides evidence of anticipation of possible failure. The Fed's implementation of the PDCF program therefore qualifies as fallibilist decision making since it still expected the failure of Bear Stearns and J.P. Morgan when the negotiations were (almost) finished. This provides more evidence for Pragmatist decision making in the Bear Stearns case.

THE ANTI-DUALISM AND EXPERIMENTALISM OF THE BEAR STEARNS RESCUE

Specifications of Pragmatist political crisis management: *Actively searching for third options, ways to transcend dilemmas; avoiding self-imposed commitments; decisions as hypotheses and trials; constant feedback monitoring*

The initial decision to provide Bear Stearns with an indirect loan on March 14, 2008 was not only fallibilist. We also find evidence for anti-dualist and experimentalist crisis management. This analysis will especially focus on the role of Timothy Geithner and Henry Paulson, as they were the main architects of the Bear Stearns' bailout.

The initial loan to Bear Stearns can be regarded as anti-dualist crisis management since the loan was able to overcome the dualist dilemma of either immediate bankruptcy or finding a buyer. Instead the initial short-term loan offered an important middle ground: ensure the financial survival of Bear Stearns until the markets closed for the weekend and then find a buyer. But the decision can also be analysed as experimentalist crisis management. The idea of an indirect loan was a novel and experimentalist idea that was selected because time pressure did not allow for any other solution. The indirect loan served as an initial trial that helped to gather feedback from the financial markets, feedback indicating that confidence in Bear Stearns had not been restored. This feedback led government officials to the conclusion that Bear Stearns needed to find a buyer over the weekend.

The Anti-Dualism of the Indirect Loan

From a Pragmatist perspective, the decision to get Bear Stearns to the weekend with an indirect loan qualifies as anti-dualist crisis management. Faced with the dilemma of either letting Bear Stearns go bankrupt or immediately finding a private buyer, Timothy Geithner's team actively searched for third options to transcend this dilemma and thereby proposed the idea of an indirect loan (Blinder 2013, 106; Geithner 2014, 151; Bernanke 2015, 214).

Under these circumstances of high time pressure, the Federal Reserve Bank could not rely on its "standard preference in dealing with a troubled institution" (Sidel et al. 2008) which was to bring together an industry consortium or interested buyers who could then take over the troubled institution (Kelly 2009, 67). As this option had to be excluded, the primary goal became more humble. As Fed Chairman Ben Bernanke put it: "We need to get to the weekend" (Kelly 2009, 65; also see Paulson 2010, 101; Geithner 2014, 152). The indirect loan via J.P. Morgan was devised as a way to buy time and ensure that Bear Stearns would not go bankrupt until the markets closed for the weekend on Friday evening. As Timothy Geithner has explained in his testimony before Congress:

> This action was designed to allow us to get to the weekend, and to enable us to pursue work along two tracks: first, for Bear to continue to explore options with other financial institutions that might enable it to avoid bankruptcy; and second, for policymakers to continue the work begun on Thursday night to try to contain the risk to financial markets in the event no private-sector solution proved possible. (US Congress 2008c, 116)

The initial loan can be regarded as an example of Pragmatist anti-dualism, employing three strategies to overcome dualisms (Ansell 2011, 10): highlighting the ongoing and continuous relationship between two poles, introducing a third dimension to break out of a two-dimensional space and by linking meaning to action. First, the decision highlighted the continuous relationship between the two possible solutions: Bear Stearns' bankruptcy and finding buyers for Bear Stearns. The indirect loan via J.P. Morgan to Bear Stearns found a middle ground and supported a continuous relationship between these two poles. It enabled a private-sector solution over the weekend without the need to find a buyer right away.

Second, with this idea of an indirect loan, the Federal Reserve introduced a third option that transcended the stark contrast between the two-dimensional decision space. Instead of the options "no bailout" and "unconditional support" the initial loan introduced a third option, much as the blockade during the Cuban Missile Crisis offered an alternative to the dualist decision space of "destroy the missiles" or "do nothing" (Allison 1971).

Third, the one-day loan to Bear Stearns on Friday linked meaning to action by giving the Bush Administration an opportunity to further explore the situation and to discover its meaning "through action" (Ansell 2011, 11). More precisely, the indirect loan can be regarded as a trial that by being enacted—much like the active intervention in an experiment—revealed more information about the financial markets and their exact state (see Ansell and Bartenberger 2016b). This points to the experimentalist aspect of the decision, which will be analysed in more detail in the next section.

Additional evidence for anti-dualist decision making can be found in the flexible 28-day period of the indirect loan that qualifies as an example of "avoiding self-imposed commitments." Under the agreed conditions of the indirect loan it was stated that the loan would be available for "*up to* 28 days." Bear Stearns' CEO Alan Schwartz expected that this would give him the full 28 days to save the investment bank (US Congress 2008c, 24). But the flexible "up to" clause of the indirect loan agreement was deliberatively chosen to adapt to changing circumstances (US Congress 2008c, 78). Despite the indirect loan, the rating agencies downgraded Bear Stearns and the price of its stock continued to fall over the course of March 14 (see next section). Therefore, Geithner and Paulson decided that the indirect loan would not be able to save Bear Stearns over a longer period of time (Kelly 2009, 100). As Timothy Geithner explained before Congress:

> So we took that extraordinary step to buy time to get to the weekend, and … what happened over the course of that day, you can see a little bit about the scale of the loss of confidence, because the dynamics ... accelerated over the course of the day. And the number of customers and counterparties that sought to withdraw funds, the actions by rating agencies on some Bear paper, accelerated that dynamic, despite the access to liquidity and despite the hope that that might buy some time. (US Congress 2008c, 24)

Paulson and Geithner decided that the loan would not be extended after the weekend and that Bear Stearns needed to find a buyer before Monday, March 17 (Sidel et al. 2008; Kelly 2009, 99). They informed Bear Stearns' CEO Schwartz about this decision Friday evening (Paulson 2010, 105; Financial Crisis Inquiry Commission 2011, 289). From an anti-dualist perspective, this "up to 28 days" formulation was an important way to avoid a strict self-imposed commitment and allowed Geithner and Paulson to shorten the time period of the indirect loan on March 14, after the situation of Bear Stearns did not stabilize. For Bear Stearns, this was a surprising move, because a 28-day time period had been used by the Federal Reserve Bank in two of its earlier lending programs—the Term Auction Facility (TAF) and the Term Securities Lending Facility (TSLF), the latter being launched just a few days earlier (Financial Crisis Inquiry Commission 2011, 286; Federal Reserve Bank 2016a). Shortening the loan by relying on the more flexible "up to" clause was therefore a novel decision and avoided a strict self-imposed commitment (Burrough 2008). It allowed Paulson and Geithner to flexibly adapt the conditions of the loan and change its time span from anywhere between 1 to 28 days. The self-imposed commitment of an early deadline was therefore avoided until more evidence was gathered through its character as an experimentalist trial.

The Indirect Loan Decision as an Experimentalist Trial

From a Pragmatist perspective two important dimensions of experimentalist decision making can be identified. First, the decision that the Federal Reserve Bank would indirectly lend to Bear Stearns was a novel solution that was designed as a trial. The reaction from the markets on Friday, however, revealed that confidence in Bear Stearns had not been restored (Financial Crisis Inquiry Commission 2011, 289). A report from the Fed summarizes these findings:

> In light of the further erosion of confidence in Bear Stearns over the weekend by its chief short-term liquidity providers and capital markets transaction counterparties, Bear Stearns likely would have been unable to avoid bankruptcy on Monday, March 17, without either very large injections of liquidity from the Federal Reserve or an acquisition of Bear Stearns by a stronger firm. (Federal Reserve Bank 2008h, 3)

In other words, the trial of the indirect loan from Friday, March 14 raised doubts that the "liquidity we provided would have been sufficient" after the weekend, as Timothy Geithner put it when asked by Congress members (US Congress 2008c, 24). Based on this judgment, Paulson and Geithner decided that Bear Stearns needed to find a buyer over the weekend.

A second dimension of experimentalism in this case is the use of constant feedback monitoring. The reaction of the markets and the direct feedback received by Paulson from banking executives provided crucial information for assessing the "trial" of the indirect loan.

The decision that the Federal Reserve Bank would lend to the investment bank Bear Stearns through J.P. Morgan was an almost unprecedented decision (Landon 2008b). To carry it out, the Fed had to invoke its emergency clause, a clause that had only been used once since the Great Depression (which was actually in the previous week when the Fed opened its TSLF for primary dealers; see Bernanke 2015, 208). We have already seen that the idea for an indirect loan was born out of necessity since the standard solution (finding a buyer or an industry consortium) was thwarted by time pressure. In this context, the idea of an indirect loan was a novel solution and a "creative way ... to buy time" (Paulson 2010, 101). It was a solution that had not been tested before and at the same time can be regarded as a trial that helped to find out more about the situation.

When making the decision for the indirect loan, Paulson and Geithner had expected that the loan would calm the financial markets down and stabilize Bear Stearns (US Congress 2008c, 24). But after the news about the indirect loan for Bear Stearns had been published on March 14, the situation developed in the opposite direction: "Standard & Poor's lowered Bear's rating three levels to BBB. Moody's and Fitch also downgraded the company. By the end of the day, Bear was out of cash. Its stock plummeted 47%, closing below $30" (Financial Crisis Inquiry Commission 2011, 289).

Based on the loan agreement, Bear Stearns' CEO Alan Schwartz expected that the loan would be available for 28 days (US Congress 2008c, 76). As Schwartz testified before Congress:

> I think we interpreted it ... that the initial period would be 28 days, unless we could stabilize the situation in a shorter period of time. As it turns out, and maybe exacerbated by the situation with the run that continued on Friday, and since this was not stabilizing the situation, we were informed that their view of the language was no, it could be up to 28 days but could be removed. (US Congress 2008c, 78–9)

When Bear Stearns received the indirect loan, Paulson had already made clear to Bear Stearns that the government would now take control of the process, telling Bear Stearns' CEO Schwartz: "You're in the government's hands now" (Paulson 2010, 103). When Paulson and Geithner changed their assessment and limited the duration of the loan this change of course caught Bear Stearns by surprise (Kelly 2009, 112; Paulson 2010, 105).

What is especially relevant from a Pragmatist perspective is that this change of course was based on the feedback from the financial markets. As we have seen, the financial markets sent the unanimous message that, in spite of the indirect loan, confidence in Bear Stearns had not been restored. On the contrary, rating agencies had downgraded the investment bank and Bear Stearns' stock value fell drastically (Kelly 2009, 113; Financial Crisis Inquiry Commission 2011, 289). Paulson's and Geithner's changed assessment was also based on direct feedback from bankers, who warned Paulson that Bear Stearns would not survive after the weekend (Sidel et al. 2008).

Henry Paulson's Anti-Dualist Balancing of Moral Hazard and Financial Stability

Specification of Pragmatist political crisis management: Actively searching *for third options and ways to transcend dilemmas*

During the weekend of March 15–16, 2008, Bear Stearns and J.P. Morgan negotiated a possible takeover of Bear Stearns by J.P. Morgan. The government played an important role in these negotiations: "Geithner would keep in touch with both Bear and J.P. Morgan throughout the day, and Paulson would help canvass possible acquirers. In between, the government officials would connect to give each other updates, looping in Bernanke and others as necessary" (Kelly 2009, 127).

Paulson's role is especially noteworthy from an anti-dualist perspective on political crisis management. By influencing the price J.P. Morgan paid for Bear Stearns, Paulson tried to find middle ground between two different objectives: reducing moral hazard while at the same time increasing the stability of the financial system. Paulson's actions were unusual because they can be regarded as governmental intervention in a negotiation between two private companies. This section will describe Paulson's intervention and analyse how it can be regarded as an example of Pragmatist political crisis management.

On Sunday morning, J.P. Morgan's CEO Jamie Dimon informed both Geithner and Paulson that J.P. Morgan would only be interested in taking over Bear Stearns if the Fed would provide financial support (Paulson 2010, 109; Financial Crisis Inquiry Commission 2011, 290). Paulson had been warned by Lloyd Blankfein, his successor as Goldman Sachs' CEO, that "the market expected a Bear rescue" (Paulson 2010, 106; also see Morgenson and Van Natta 2009). He agreed with Geithner and Bernanke that the Federal Reserve Bank should enable a deal between Bear Stearns and J.P. Morgan (Sidel et al. 2008; Kelly 2009, 197; Paulson 2010, 110; Geithner 2014, 155; Bernanke 2015, 218). With the help of BlackRock, an external consulting firm, the Federal Reserve Bank and the Treasury analysed Bear Stearns' assets and decided that the Federal Reserve Bank would take assets worth $30 billion from Bear Stearns and put them in a newly founded entity (US Congress 2008c, 119; Financial Crisis Inquiry Commission 2011, 290). Under the agreement reached between the New York Federal Reserve Bank and J.P. Morgan on March 16, J.P. Morgan would cover the first $1.15 billion of any eventual losses and the Fed the other $28.82 billion (Andrews 2008a; Federal Reserve Bank 2008e; Financial Crisis Inquiry Commission 2011, 290).

What is interesting from a Pragmatist perspective on political crisis management is what happened next. In the decision-making process for the first indirect loan, President Bush and Treasury Secretary Paulson had shifted from a principle-guided position that emphasized moral hazard to a more Pragmatist one that focused on the stability of the financial system. Henry Paulson now faced another dilemma of deciding between moral hazard and financial stability. When it came to the $30 billion loan, he decided to try to balance the two poles in an anti-dualist manner. On the one hand, Paulson supported the decision of the Federal Reserve Bank to acquire $30 billion of Bear Stearns' assets in order to enable a deal between Bear Stearns and J.P. Morgan and prevent Bear Stearns' bankruptcy. This was a decision that catered to the financial stability pole (Axilrod 2009, 154). On the other hand, Paulson also kept the second dimension in mind and tried to minimize the danger of moral hazard. The chief mechanism of doing this was to keep the price J.P. Morgan paid for Bear Stearns low, sending a signal to Bear Stearns and other investment banks that the financial support by the government came with a price (US Congress 2008c, 30; Axilrod 2009, 154).

On Sunday afternoon, Paulson learned from Geithner that J.P. Morgan planned to pay between $4 and $5 per share (Kelly 2009, 202; Paulson 2010, 111; Geithner 2014, 155). From the Treasury Secretary's perspective, this price was too high, so he called J.P. Morgan's CEO Jamie Dimon and suggested a price between $1 and $2 per share (Paulson 2010, 111; Financial Crisis Inquiry Commission 2011, 290; Geithner 2014, 155). On Sunday evening, J.P. Morgan announced that it would buy Bear Stearns for $2 per share (Financial Crisis Inquiry Commission 2011, 290).[5]

In the hearings before Congress the representatives of the Federal Reserve Bank and the Treasury emphasized that they did not set the exact price of the deal but conceded that they influenced it (US Congress 2008c, 22, 34, 58). As Bob Steele from the Treasury stated: "It was our perspective, as I said, that moral hazard wanted to be protected as much as possible. And so therefore a lower price was more appropriate" (US Congress 2008c, 22). It was Treasury Secretary Paulson who pushed for a lower price (US Congress 2008c, 80; Kelly 2009, 204; Paulson 2010, 111; Geithner 2014, 155). This account has

---

[5]   Kelly (2009, 210) has noted how low this price was, highlighting that this valued Bear Stearns at $236 million, "less than a quarter of what its building alone was worth." Later the deal was renegotiated between Bear Stearns and J.P. Morgan and the price increased to $10 per share (Financial Crisis Inquiry Commission 2011, 290).

also been confirmed by J.P. Morgan's CEO Jamie Dimon who testified that Paulson "made it very clear that that [the exact price] was the decision of J.P. Morgan Chase but did express the point of view, which was held by a lot of people including on the J.P. Morgan Chase side that the higher the price, the more the so-called moral hazard" (US Congress 2008c, 80).

From a Pragmatist perspective, we find evidence of the anti-dualist decision-making specification "actively search for third options and ways to transcend dilemmas" in Paulson's pressing for a lower price. As we have seen, by suggesting that J.P. Morgan pay a lower price for Bear Stearns, Paulson tried to achieve two different goals at the same time and to find a middle ground between them: providing financial stability by preventing the bankruptcy of Bear Stearns while also minimizing the danger of moral hazard by keeping the price that the Bear Stearns' shareholders received low. Timothy Geithner has summarized the two poles of this dilemma in his testimony before Congress:

> Two objectives, very important for us. One was there be an agreement reached that would avert the risk of default because of the consequences for the economy as a whole. The second was that the outcome, to the extent possible, not add to the inherent moral hazard risk in this kind of intervention. From my perspective, the outcome reached that evening and the subsequent agreement reached a week later, are fully consistent with those two objectives. (US Congress 2008c, 21)

And the US Treasury's Bob Steele has emphasized the attempt to *balance* the two poles of this dilemma: "This twin responsibility of wanting to be sensitive to the state of the markets and what the situation could cause balanced with also wanting to not encourage a sense of moral hazard" (US Congress 2008c, 58).

This anti-dualist approach to the dilemma was also publicly communicated. As Treasury Secretary Paulson emphasized in a March 16 television interview with George Stephanopolous: "We're very aware of moral hazard ... But our primary concern right now—my primary concern—is the stability of our financial system, the orderliness of the markets" (Landon 2008a).

THE ROLE OF DELIBERATION IN DECISION MAKING DURING THE BEAR STEARNS RESCUE

Specification of Pragmatist political crisis management: *Decisions based on internal deliberation; encouragement of skeptical positions*

In *Human Nature and Conduct*, John Dewey argued that new impulses often disrupt and challenge our existing habits. According to Dewey, we have to rely on the method of "intelligence" to solve such a situation (Dewey 1922).

For Dewey "intelligence" is enacted via deliberation or collective inquiry. As Anderson explains:

> When habit is blocked, people are forced to stop their activity and reflect on the problems posed by their situation. They must deliberate. The aim of deliberation is to find a satisfactory means to resumption of activity by solving the problem posed by one's situation. (Anderson 2014)

Pragmatist deliberation is closely connected to other Pragmatist elements such as fallibilism, experimentalism and its emphasis on consequences. It is characterized by an openness to all feasible options, an emphasis on practical consequences and a quasi-experimentalist attitude. In other words, Pragmatist deliberation can be understood as "an imaginative rehearsal of alternative means" and a "thought experiment designed to arrive at a practical judgment, action upon which is anticipated to resolve one's predicament" (Anderson 2014).

There is also another aspect to Pragmatist deliberation that speaks to the importance of the diversity of opinions in the deliberative process. For Pragmatists, such diversity and the inclusion of dissenting voices is necessary to "maintain the state of doubt" (Dewey 1910, 13) and remain open to other options. This aspect is covered by the specification "encouragement of skeptics" which analyses whether dissenting voices and different opinions have been actively encouraged and included (see George and Stern 2002).

The actors at the center of our discussion of deliberation include President Bush, Treasury Secretary Paulson, New York Federal Reserve President Geithner and Federal Reserve Chairman Bernanke (Ip 2008). They all played an important role in the decision-making process. The Securities and Exchange Commission (SEC) also took part in the discussions around the Bear Stearns decision and was represented by SEC Chairman Chris Cox and his aides, Erik Sirri and Bob Colby (Kelly 2009, 65; Paulson 2010, 100).

Internal Deliberation

Deliberation was an important aspect of decision making throughout the Bear Stearns case. The first and most striking example can be found in the way the decision to provide an indirect loan to Bear Stearns was made on March 13, 2008. Early in the morning, Paulson, Bernanke, Geithner and their aides convened a conference call that also included representatives from the SEC (US Congress 2008c, 115; Kelly 2009, 65; Paulson 2010, 1002; Bernanke 2015, 214). The call lasted for over two hours, during which a possible Bear Stearns rescue or bankruptcy was discussed (Geithner 2014, 152). Jamie Dimon, CEO of J.P. Morgan, joined the call for a few minutes to explain Bear Stearns' situation from his perspective, which was that a bankruptcy of Bear Stearns would have severe consequences (US Congress 2008c, 72; Paulson 2010, 101).

Bernanke led the discussion and inquired about the current situation while Geithner and Kevin Warsh from the New York Fed laid out their assessment that a bankruptcy would have dire consequences, an assessment that was based on their analysis from the night before (Kelly 2009, 63; Bernanke 2015, 214). After examining different options, Geithner introduced the idea of an indirect loan for Bear Stearns via J.P. Morgan, an idea that had been proposed by the New York Fed's general counsel Tom Baxter only hours before the conference call (Geithner 2014, 151; Bernanke 2015, 214). Bernanke agreed that Bear Stearns needed to be rescued and Paulson concurred (Kelly 2009, 66; Paulson 2010, 101; Bernanke 2014, 2015).

After Paulson obtained approval from President Bush, Geithner pointed out that a decision needed to be made soon since the markets were about to open (Wessel 2009, 158; Geithner 2014, 152). At 7 a.m. Bernanke made the final decision to extend the indirect loan to Bear Stearns. Since the indirect loan was issued by the Federal Reserve Bank by invoking the emergency section of the Federal Reserve Act, Fed Chairman Bernanke officially made the decision (Wessel 2009, 156).[6]

Although Bernanke had the final say, the decision was based on extended discussion and on the consensus of all involved government actors. As Kelly has described it: "Mr. Bernanke did a head count. All the top officials agreed a loan was the best option. 'Let's do it,' Mr. Bernanke said" (Kelly 2009, 67; also see Bernanke 2015, 217). In other words, the decision was not made in a top-down manner and dictated by Bernanke or Bush (as would be the case in principle-guided political crisis management) but instead was based on a two-hour long discussion involving the main government actors (Bernanke, Geithner, Paulson and SEC staff).

Three different scenarios and options were discussed and their potential practical consequences assessed: letting Bear Stearns file for bankruptcy; finding another financial institution that could support or take over Bear Stearns; or lending public money to Bear Stearns (Sidel et al. 2008; Kelly 2009, 64). After going through the scenario of a Bear Stearns' bankruptcy, the group reached the conclusion that its potential consequences could destabilize the whole economy and excluded this option. The second option was excluded because the perceived time pressure did not allow for finding a potential buyer

---

[6]   More precisely, it was a decision that had to be approved by the Federal Reserve Board which was chaired by Bernanke. After the conference call ended, Bernanke convened the three available governors and they unanimously supported the decision (Wessel 2009, 162; Blinder 2013, 105; Bernanke 2015, 217).

on Friday. This left the third option as the most feasible way to proceed. This collective inquiry and the weighting of different options via thought experiments qualifies as an aspect of Pragmatist deliberation.

Internal deliberation continued over the course of the weekend. Treasury Secretary Paulson and New York Fed President Geithner stayed in close contact while Bear Stearns and J.P. Morgan negotiated a possible merger, sharing information and discussing next steps (Ip 2008; Kelly 2009, 203; Paulson 2010, 103–10; Geithner 2014, 154). The decision on Sunday, March 15 to support the deal between Bear Stearns and J.P. Morgan with $30 billion from the Federal Reserve Bank was also based on broad internal deliberation. After J.P. Morgan's CEO Jamie Dimon had contacted Geithner on Sunday morning announcing that J.P. Morgan would not be able to take over Bear Stearns without financial support, Geithner called Paulson and Bernanke (Kelly 2009, 203; Paulson 2010, 110; Geithner 2014, 154).

The first idea discussed on this call was that the Treasury should provide the money. But since this required an Act of Congress, the option was deemed impractical under the circumstances of high time pressure (Wessel 2009, 167; Geithner 2014, 155). Geithner suggested that the New York Federal Reserve could cover Bear Stearns' assets and discussed this idea with Bernanke, Paulson and Donald Kohn, the Vice Chairman of the Federal Reserve Board (Paulson 2010, 110; Geithner 2014, 155). After they had agreed on this plan, Bernanke informed his colleagues at international central banks and Paulson talked to President Bush and got his support for the decision (Bush 2008c, 453; Paulson 2010, 113; Bernanke 2015, 220). The Federal Reserve Board approved the $30 billion loan on March 15, 2008 at 3:45 p.m. (Federal Reserve Bank 2008e, 2; Bernanke 2015, 220).

While we find ample evidence of deliberation in this case, we do not find evidence for a second aspect of Pragmatist deliberation—"encouragement of skeptics." We find no indication that attempts were made to include skeptical or dissenting voices in this decision-making process.

External Deliberation

While the decision making during the Bear Stearns weekend was characterized by a high degree of internal deliberation, it also made use of external knowledge. External actors, especially from financial institutions, were consulted and external advisors provided their expertise.

The main role of obtaining this external input was undertaken by the New York Federal Reserve Bank and its president, Timothy Geithner, who Ben

Bernanke called "the Fed's eyes and ears on Wall Street" (Bernanke 2015, 217). Before the crisis, Geithner had

> initiated a series of dinners at the New York Fed's executive dining room, in which five or six executives from a major Wall Street firm would meet his own top people. When the credit crisis deepened, he began calling chief executives nearly every week, asking: What's changed? What's better? What's worse? What worries you? (Ip 2008)

This close contact with Wall Street bankers intensified during the Bear Stearns weekend and was further supported by Treasury Secretary Henry Paulson.

During the negotiations between Bear Stearns and J.P. Morgan, Paulson and Geithner stayed in close contact with the two firms, with Paulson and Geithner acting as "third partner" (Sidel et al. 2008; also see Kelly 2009; NPR 2009). Paulson's aide Neel Kashkari played a key role in this, "shuttling between J.P. Morgan's and Bear's offices" and updating Paulson on recent developments (Wessel 2009, 166; Paulson 2010, 108). Jamie Dimon, the CEO of J.P. Morgan, briefly joined the conference call between Paulson, Geithner, Bernanke and the SEC that resulted in the decision for the indirect loan on March 13. Dimon offered his perspective, explaining that a failure of Bear Stearns would have drastic consequences (Paulson 2010, 101). After the decision for the indirect loan to Bear Stearns was made, Paulson and Geithner held a conference call with executives of the other major banks, explaining the decision on the indirect loan to them (Sidel et al. 2008; Kelly 2009, 77; Paulson 2010, 104). However, the main intent of the call was not collective deliberation, but rather to allow Paulson to ask the other investment banks "to act in a responsible manner" and to continue to lend to Bear Stearns (Kelly 2009, 77; Paulson 2010, 104).

After the call, Geithner met with Paul Volcker, a former chairman of the Federal Reserve, to explain the decision and seek his advice. Geithner explained that the New York Fed tried to bring Bear Stearns to the weekend and hoped to soon find a buyer for the investment bank, an idea that Volcker supported (Kelly 2009, 128; Geithner 2014, 153). The next day, Secretary Paulson received additional external input. In the morning of March 15, 2008, he got a call from Lloyd Blankfein, his successor as Goldman Sachs' CEO. Blankfein warned Paulson that the consequences of a Bear Stearns' bankruptcy would be dramatic and would affect the world economy as well (Morgenson and Van Natta 2009; Paulson 2010, 106).

These examples show that Paulson and Geithner stayed in close contact with external stakeholders, especially executives of the major Wall Street banks, throughout the weekend. The character of these contacts was twofold: some of them were primarily intended to inform external actors about decisions (the conference call with bank executives on March 13). Others gathered information and different perspectives (Paulson's call with Blankfein, Geithner's meeting with Volcker). From a Pragmatist perspective, this does not qualify as deliberation though since it cannot be characterized as collective inquiry. Instead, it was a process of *consultation* that did not include external stakeholders in the decision-making process (Fung 2006). In some cases, these contacts provided additional expertise, as was the case with the hiring of the company BlackRock to help assess the assets that would be used to secure the $30 billion loan as discussed below. Yet, from a Pragmatist perspective this does not qualify as external deliberation either, since this expertise was utilized in very targeted ways. For example, BlackRock's special expertise was used to assess the value of Bear Stearns' assets.

Summary

This section has examined the level of deliberation that took place in the decision-making process of the Bear Stearns decision along two dimensions. It has shown that the level of internal deliberation was high, with the involved government actors (Paulson, Geithner, Bernanke) in constant discussion about the next steps. Both the decisions on the indirect loan for Bear Stearns on March 13 and on the $30 billion loan to support the deal between Bear Stearns and J.P. Morgan on March 15 were based on a process of collective inquiry. We therefore find evidence for the first specification of deliberative decision making, "Decisions based on internal deliberation." However, we do not find any evidence for the other two specifications. External stakeholders were not fully included in the decision making (their role is better described as consultation and as providing expertise) nor were skeptical and dissenting voices encouraged.

MEANING MAKING

The Pragmatist philosopher Richard Bernstein has described President Bush's meaning making after 9/11 as a typical example of anti-pragmatist dualism that framed the events by heavily employing black-and-white dichotomies and as communicating absolute moral certainty (Bernstein 2005). Patterson (2010) has evaluated the economic policies of the Bush government before the financial crisis and found a strong influence of economic ideology (i.e., supply-side economics) and principles. Only a few weeks before the Bear Stearns weekend, Bush framed his economic policies in a similar way, referring to eternal free-market principles. In the following sections, we analyse the meaning-making process of the Bear Stearns case, looking for evidence of

Pragmatist meaning making and examining how the meaning-making dimension of political crisis management compares to decision making.

Explaining Fallibilism with Anti-Dualism: Framing the Decision as Balance

Specifications for Pragmatist political crisis management: Nuanced depiction of events; no dichotomies

In terms of political crisis management, the prior discussion has shown that the Bear Stearns case led to economic decisions that departed from a "clear and consistent philosophy" and from "timeless" (Bush 2008d) economic principles. Instead, Bush and his Treasury Secretary Henry Paulson acted in a fallibilist fashion and left these strict principles behind when they decided to rescue Bear Stearns. The main question here is: How did the Bush Administration publicly frame and explain the decisions to rescue Bear Stearns? This section will examine the strategy that was chosen to frame the decision. The main finding is that Bush, Paulson and the other involved actors explained the fallibilistic decision to save Bear Stearns in a fashion consistent with the Pragmatist idea of anti-dualism.

The Anti-Dualist Balance Between Moral Hazard and Financial Stability

On March 14, only hours after the Federal Reserve Bank had supported Bear Stearns with a \$12.9 indirect loan, President Bush gave a television interview on CNBC. One of the first questions by interviewer Larry Kudlow pointed out Bush's fallibilism: "You have said time and again that you oppose government bailouts, that you oppose the use of taxpayer money to bail out. I want to ask you if that opposition applies to these large banks." To which Bush responded:

> Well, these are unusual times. These are times that—where there's a confluence of housing market risks and financial risks that require unusual action. And it's very important for the American people to know that the Fed and the Treasury *carefully weigh the—necessary to bring some order and stability versus moral hazard. And I think they've struck the right balance in this case*, particularly when people look at the details of the transaction. (Kudlow 2008; our emphasis)

Bush is referring here to the necessity to balance financial stability and moral hazard. From a Pragmatist perspective, the *balancing* of these two opposing poles has been described as anti-dualist decision making and this motif is also expressed in public meaning making. By depicting the events in a nuanced way and avoiding strict dichotomies, this form of meaning making qualifies as anti-dualist.

This anti-dualist framing of the necessity to *balance* financial stability and moral hazard can be identified in other examples of meaning making as well. On March 16, 2008, the Treasury Secretary explained the government's action to ABC's George Stephanopolous in similar terms: "We're very aware of moral hazard ... But our primary concern right now—my primary concern—is the stability of our financial system, the orderliness of the markets. And that's where our focus is" (Landon 2008a; Paulson 2010, 109). In an interview with CNN's Wolf Blitzer, Paulson reiterated his message later the same day:

> I'm as aware as anyone is of moral hazard. I'm also aware of the importance of keeping our economy strong, of orderly capital markets, of the stability of the financial system doing things that promote that orderliness and minimize the disruption ... To me, this was not difficult because the priority, at a time like this, has got to be the stability of our financial system and minimizing the likelihood that this disruption spills over into the real economy. (CNN 2008)

In a nutshell, the message delivered was that financial stability had an equally important place next to the moral hazard principles. As Treasury's Bob Steele testified before Congress on April 3, 2008: "This was an unusual time, as all my colleagues have said, and a specific decision was made with regard to market protection and to the effect on the potential real economy. That was the nature of the decision" (US Congress 2008c, 28). What constitutes the genuine anti-dualist character of this way of meaning making is how it was framed as a *balance* between financial stability and moral hazard. As Fed Chairman Bernanke explained:

> The Federal Reserve *has to strike a very careful balance between actions* to contain risk to the broader economy and actions that might amplify the risk of future financial crises by insulating investors from the consequences of imprudence. (US Congress 2008c, 17; our emphasis)

Framing the decision as a *balance* was done primarily by pointing to the fact that the Bear Stearns rescue was not a bailout, and that the negative effects of moral hazard had been mitigated and minimized. As White House press secretary Perino explained to journalists:

> [T]his isn't about bailing anyone out ... And investors in Bear Stearns are taking large and significant losses in this transaction. And that's not what happens in a bail-out. They bought into a company, they took a financial risk—and it had paid off quite well for them a while ago, but today they're looking at a stock that's only worth $2. (White House 2008a)

This message was also echoed by Ben Bernanke and Timothy Geithner at a Congressional hearing, when confronted with the argument that the bailout of Bear Stearns would create moral hazard. As Bernanke stated:

> I would like to make a comment on the idea that we bailed out Bear Stearns. As President Geithner pointed out, Bear Stearns did not fare very well in this operation. The shareholders took very severe losses. The company lost its independence. Many employees obviously are concerned about their jobs. I do not think it is a situation that any firm would willingly choose to endure. (US Congress 2008c, 30)

As Bernanke further highlighted, if there was a bailout it was a bailout of the market in general and not of Bear Stearns specifically: "So we were—if you want to say we bailed out the market in general, I guess that is true" (US Congress 2008c, 35).

More specifically, the *balancing* of financial stability and moral hazard was highlighted by referring to the low price Bear Stearns received from J.P. Morgan for its shares. The Congressional hearing on April 3, 2008 inquired about the role of the government in setting the price that J.P. Morgan would pay and received mixed answers. The Fed Chairman rejected the idea that the Federal Reserve had anything to do with the price J.P. Morgan paid for Bear Stearns' shares: "We had no interest or no concern about the stock price that was evaluated. That was a secondary issue, as far as we were concerned" (US Congress 2008c, 21). And to Senator Dodd's follow-up question: "So there was no interjection on the part of the Fed at all in this area?" Bernanke responded: "Not to my knowledge" (US Congress 2008c, 21). But Bob Steele, who was representing the Treasury at the hearing, added an important qualifier to Bernanke's answer:

> I think the perspective of Treasury was really twofold. One, was the idea that Chairman Bernanke suggested, that a combination into safe hands would be constructive for the overall marketplace. And No. 2, since there were Federal funds or the Government's money involved, that that be taken into account, and Secretary Paulson offered perspective on that. There was a view that the price should not be very high or should be toward the low end and that it should be, given the Government's involvement, that was the perspective. (US Congress 2008c, 21)

Timothy Geithner was asked next and he sided with Steele's version, explicitly emphasizing that two objectives, the stability of the financial system and the need to keep moral hazard low had to be considered in the decision (US Congress 2008c, 21). Bob Steele further emphasized this point, stating: "As I said, there was a perspective, as President Geithner suggested, that the outcome, with all the different terms and conditions, would be consistent with communicating and making clear moral hazard to the least degree possible" (US Congress 2008c, 22). Treasury Secretary Paulson told reporters on March

17 that "those worried about the government rescue creating a 'moral hazard' should keep in mind that Bear Stearns shareholders face considerable losses with the sale of the investment firm to J.P. Morgan Chase for $2 a share" (Reuters 2008). The $2 price was further emphasized by White House press secretary Dana Perino when asked by a reporter how the Bear Stearns decision squared with the "conservative economic principles of limited government." Perino replied: "Bear Stearns basically went from a company that was doing quite well to failure, and at $2 a share, I should think that those investors are seeing—feeling today the consequences of that risk in a marketplace" (White House 2008a). In explaining and framing their decision, Bush, Paulson and Geithner stressed that moral hazard had been taken care of too.

Comparing this to the strongly dualist framing after 9/11, the Bush Administration offered an interpretation after the Bear Stearns rescue that emphasized the balance it had tried to reach between two opposing poles, avoiding strong black-and-white dichotomies. As the next section will show, meaning making after the Bear Stearns rescue also included a high degree of uncertainty that was openly communicated.

Fallibilist Communication of Uncertainty and Possible Failures

Specification of Pragmatist political crisis management: *communication of uncertainty and possible failures*

Specification of principle-guided political crisis management: *communication of certainty*

We have defined the communication of uncertainty and possible failure as the chief specification of fallibilist meaning making in our model. The manner in which the Bush government has defended its decision and depicted the possible alternative scenarios reveals no evidence for this specification. Instead, we find a high level of communicated certainty that the decision to rescue Bear Stearns was correct and that the alternatives would have been dramatic. We do, however, find examples for communicated uncertainty in the way the Bush Administration framed the Bear Stearns rescue as a decision with an uncertain *outcome*. We also find evidence in the reluctance of government actors to exclude the possibility of further bailouts, referring to the high level of uncertainty that remained.

Communicating Certainty: The *Necessity* of the Decision and Its Alternatives

When it came to defending the decision of the Bear Stearns rescue, the government actors suggested a high level of certainty. This stands in stark contrast to a Pragmatist approach to political crisis management that highlights uncertainty instead. During a press briefing on March 17, the White House Press Secretary stated that:

> a major market disruption would have very damaging consequences and be very painful for everybody, from the small business owner to the homeowner, for everybody all the way up and down the economic food chain. And the goal here is to prevent a major disruption in financial markets. (White House 2008a)

In his testimony before Congress, New York Fed President Timothy Geithner similarly stated that if Bear Stearns would have failed, the "certainty of very substantial losses" (US Congress 2008c, 65) across the financial markets combined with "an abrupt and disorderly unwinding of Bear Stearns would have posed systemic risks to the financial system and magnified the downside risk to economic growth in the United States" (US Congress 2008c, 17). Fed Chairman Ben Bernanke put it in similar terms:

> To prevent a disorderly failure of Bear Stearns and the unpredictable but likely severe consequences for market functioning and the broader economy, the Federal Reserve, in close consultation with the Treasury Department, agreed to provide funding to Bear Stearns through JPMorgan Chase. (US Congress 2008c, 12)

The Treasury's Deputy Secretary Bob Steele supported the position of the Federal Reserve Bank: "We believe the agreements reached were necessary and appropriate to maintain stability in our financial system during this critical time" (US Congress 2008c, 16). Only SEC Chairman Chris Cox raised some doubt concerning the certainty that the decision to rescue Bear Stearns was the right one:

> The question has been asked what might have happened if, notwithstanding the Fed's action, the transaction with J.P. Morgan had not been agreed to before Monday, March 17? Unfortunately, unlike a laboratory in which conditions can be held constant and variables changed while the experiment is repeated, in the social science of the market the selection of one course of action forever forecloses all other approaches that might have been taken. (US Congress 2008c, 14)

But Cox also made clear that despite these doubts he agreed with the decision, noting that "a chaotic unwinding of its [Bear Stearns'] positions not only could have cast doubt on the stability of thousands of the firm's counterparties, but also created additional pressures well beyond the financial system through the real economy" (US Congress 2008c, 14).

The statements of government actors as a whole show that when it came to the *necessity* of the decision to rescue Bear Stearns, the level of communicated uncertainty was low. Instead, the decision was framed as unambiguous and unavoidable. But when it comes to how the *outcome* of the decision and the possible *next step*s were framed, the picture is a very different one.

Communicating Uncertainty: The *Outcome* of the Decision

In his speech at the Economic Club on March 14, 2008, a couple of hours after the Federal Reserve Bank had announced that it would lend $12.9 billion to Bear Stearns via J.P. Morgan, President Bush said that "these are uncertain times" (Bush 2008a).[7] Keeping the Bear Stearns decision in mind, Bush reminded his audience that government actions often had unintended consequences: "And so we got to be careful and mindful that any time the government intervenes in the market, it must do so with clear purpose and great care. Government actions are—have far-reaching and unintended consequences" (Bush 2008a).

Government officials stuck to this frame after the second loan had been issued and Bear Stearns had been taken over by J.P. Morgan.[8] When White House Press Secretary Dana Perino was asked by a reporter on March 17: "[D]oes the President feel we've seen the worst of it?" she responded: "I don't think we know. Obviously in a market economy, economies cycle and they go up and down, and the question is whether or not they are mild disruptions or sharp disruptions" (White House 2008a). On the same day, the *New York Times* reported that Treasury Secretary Paulson "has been cautious about predicting the future of the markets and the possible necessity of further action to stabilize them ... Associates say he has taken a pragmatic approach to the problem and an attitude that the administration would do what it had to do to stabilize the broader markets" (Myers 2008).[9]

---

[7]   It was the same speech in which Bush originally intended to promise that there would be no bailouts, but was advised by Paulson to leave this part out due to the high level of uncertainty (Kelly 2009, 68; Paulson 2010, 92).

[8]   Treasury Secretary Paulson has indicated that the decision to frame the Bear Stearns' loan in this cautious way was made by President Bush, recalling Bush saying that they can't promise that the Federal Reserve Bank would get its money back (Paulson 2010, 113). But we find no further evidence in the sources for this attribution.

[9]   It is important to note that the "pragmatic approach" that is mentioned in this quote refers to the everyday meaning of the term pragmatism and not to the systematic model used in this study (see Posner 2003, ch. 1).

In the Congressional hearing on April 3, Geithner and Bernanke framed the decision in a similar way, highlighting the risks and the uncertainty it entailed. The first aspect concerned the uncertainty if the Federal Reserve Bank, and ultimately the taxpayers, would face any losses from the $30 billion loan. The way the Federal Reserve Bank framed this aspect of the decision was by openly admitting that the $30 billion loan might result in losses but that the alternatives would have been worse. As Timothy Geithner put it in his statement: "[A]s we have been clear, there is risk in this transaction. There is no doubt about it" (US Congress 2008c, 65). Fed Chairman Bernanke further explained that while steps had been taken to reduce the risks—such as hiring of external experts from BlackRock—these risks nevertheless remained:

> We do not know for sure what will transpire, but we have engaged an independent investment advisory firm, who gives us reasonable comfort that if we can sell these assets over a period of time, we will recover principal and interest for the American taxpayer. And certainly under no circumstances are the risks to the taxpayer remotely close to $30 billion. There may be some risk, but it is nothing close to the full amount. We do have collateral, and I would say a good bit of it is very highly rated. (US Congress 2008c, 35)

But as both Geithner and Bernanke made clear, the loan still included a level of risk since it was difficult to value the assets that collateralized the loan. As Geithner explained: "That uncertainty exists today, of course, because these are very complicated markets. It is very unclear over time what the value of those things were likely to be" (US Congress 2008c, 65).

Taken together, the government actors' framing of the outcome of the decision to save Bear Stearns provides evidence for a Pragmatist approach to political crisis meaning making and conforms to our fallibilist specification "communication of uncertainty and possible failure." Additional evidence for this approach can also be found in the way the possibility of further bailouts was communicated.

Communicating Uncertainty: The Possibility of Further Bailouts

On March 14, after the decision on an indirect loan for Bear Stearns, a press release issued by the Federal Reserve Bank made it clear that similar measures might still be necessary: "The Federal Reserve is monitoring market developments closely and will continue to provide liquidity as necessary to promote the orderly functioning of the financial system" (Federal Reserve Bank 2008a). President Bush mirrored the Fed's language in his speech in New York, noting that "events are fast-moving, but the Chairman of the Federal Reserve and the Secretary of the Treasury are on top of them, and will take the appropriate steps to promote stability in our markets" (Bush 2008a). By framing the situation in these open and ambiguous terms the Federal Reserve and President Bush emphasized the uncertainty of possible further steps, a decision that proved wise after the Fed had to support the Bear Stearns purchase by J.P. Morgan with a second loan (Financial Crisis Inquiry Commission 2011, 290).

After Bear Stearns was purchased by J.P. Morgan on March 16, government officials remained reluctant to exclude any further bailouts or similar steps. Treasury Secretary Paulson was cautious about the "possible necessity of further action to stabilize" the financial markets (Myers 2008). When Paulson's deputy Bob Steele was asked by Senator Richard Shelby in a Congressional hearing: "You are not telling us that you have supreme confidence that there is not going to be another problem? You cannot say that, can you?" Steele replied: "No, sir, I cannot" (US Congress 2008c, 28). And Federal Reserve Bank Chairman Ben Bernanke left the possibility open that the Fed might have to react in a similar way: "We do not expect to have to do this, but we are obviously going to be watching and monitoring the markets very carefully, and institutions" (US Congress 2008c, 30).

PRINCIPLE-GUIDED FRAMING OF AN EXPERIMENTALIST DECISION

Specifications of principle-guided political crisis management: Sticking to frames

When it comes to experimentalism in how meaning was made in the Bear Stearns decision, we find no evidence for the specifications that have been defined for experimentalist meaning making. The decision making was neither framed as experimentalist crisis management nor could we identify the trying out of frames or significant frame revision. Instead, the decision to rescue Bear Stearns was framed along the lines of principle-guided political crisis management, with the decision framed as unambiguous and "business as usual" (Donato 2009).

The business-as-usual characterization of the decision can be found in different public statements. In his speech on March 14, President Bush "starkly suggested that much of what was happening was part of the natural cycles of market economies" (Myers 2008) and highlighted that for the government's strategy "it's important to be steady" (Bush 2008a). Despite the fact that the Federal Reserve Bank had for the first time since the Great Depression[10]

---

[10]　While section 13(3) had also been invoked in creating the Term Securities Lending Facility (TSLF) on March 11, 2008, this program did not start until March 27 (Bernanke 2015, 217).

invoked its emergency clause section 13(3) to extend the two loans to Bear Stearns, this particular detail was not mentioned in the press releases issued by the Fed (Federal Reserve Bank 2008a, 2008c). This fact, which would have highlighted the unusual character of the decision, was not subsequently taken up by media reports (Andrews 2008a; Sidel et al. 2008).

In the hearing before Congress on April 3, Fed Chairman Bernanke framed the actions as the usual business of the Federal Reserve Bank: "[Y]ou should recognize that we loan money against collateral all the time. We do not do it usually in quite these unusual circumstances, but we do have the authority to do it" (US Congress 2008c, 59). Later, in a public speech before the Economic Club of New York on June 9, Timothy Geithner highlighted the same point: "Our actions were guided by the same general principles that have governed Fed action in crises over the years" (Geithner 2008). As Geithner elaborated: "The Federal Reserve Act gives us very broad authority to lend in crises. We used that authority in new and consequential ways, but in the classic tradition of central banks and lenders of last resort" (Geithner 2008).

Geithner did hint at the experimentalist character of the decision at the Congressional hearing, noting:

> So Friday morning, we took the exceptional step with extreme reluctance, with the support of the Board of Governors and the Treasury, to structure a way to get them to the weekend so that we could buy some time to explore whether there was a possible solution ... (US Congress 2008c, 24)

This remark summarizes the experimentalist approach of the decision by pointing to the step-by-step approach that started by lending to Bear Stearns indirectly on Friday in order to observe the market feedback to this intervention. After the markets had indicated that this indirect loan had not been able to reestablish confidence in Bear Stearns, Geithner and Paulson changed course and facilitated a purchase of Bear Stearns over the weekend. Geithner's remark, however, is the only instance we find in the sources that hints at the experimentalist character of the decision. Contrasted with the statements that framed the decision as conventional and "business as usual," this sole remark does not qualify as experimentalist meaning making.

We also do not find any instances in which government actors tried out different frames during and after the Bear Stearns decision or engaged in frame revision (revising frames or replacing one frame to another). Instead, the message that was delivered on the Bear Stearns decision, highlighting the anti-dualist character that led to the overruling of moral hazard principles, was consistent over time and voiced by all government actors.

No Evidence for Deliberative Meaning Making

Specifications for Pragmatist political crisis management: Openness to public debate and inquiry

In the decision-making process for the Bear Stearns decision we identified a high level of internal deliberation but found no evidence for external deliberation and the encouragement of skeptics. Analysing the meaning-making process from this perspective, we find no evidence for the specification of deliberative meaning making, "Openness to public debate and inquiry."[11]

While we find no deliberative meaning making in this strict sense, there is an additional aspect that is interesting from a deliberative perspective on meaning making: the fact that the government actors strongly emphasized the deliberative character of the decision-making process publicly, especially in the hearing before Congress. In this context, Geithner has described a conference call on March 14 as deliberative and collaborative decision making:

> After careful deliberation, together we decided on a course of action that would at least buy some time to explore options to mitigate the foreseeable damage to the financial system. With the support of the Secretary of the Treasury, Chairman Bernanke and the Board of Governors agreed that the New York Fed would extend an overnight non-recourse loan through the discount window to J.P. Morgan Chase, so that J.P. Morgan Chase could then "on-lend" that money to Bear Stearns. (US Congress 2008c, 116)

Treasury Deputy Secretary Bob Steele has supported this notion, framing the information gathering and decision-making process as a deliberative and collaborative endeavor as well: "During this period, regulators were continually communicating with one another, working collaboratively, and keeping each

---

[11]   The only remark that comes close to deliberative meaning making was issued by Timothy Geithner during a Congressional hearing. He began his testimony by openly inviting inquiry by Congress: "These are exceptional times. We have taken some very consequential actions. They deserve and require very careful analysis and reflection and oversight. And you are right to begin that process now" (US Congress 2008c, 17). Given that this was the only remark we found that hinted at an openness towards public debate and that it was directed at the Senate's Committee on Banking, Housing and Urban Affairs, which is authorized and obliged by Rule XXV of the Standing Rules of the Senate to inquire on such topics anyway, our judgment is that it does not qualify as an exceptional openness to public debate and inquiry (United States Senate 2014, 27).

other apprised of the changing circumstances" (US Congress 2008c, 116). Steele has further emphasized the importance of deliberation in more detail:

[T]hroughout this process, I can report to all of you that there was good collaboration, and I view that as a good thing, that people were helping each other, trying to think about various issues, and the 96 hours was fairly fraught. And the Secretary was in constant communication and trying to be helpful to Chairman Bernanke and President Geithner as they came to work through this and offered his perspective. (US Congress 2008c, 59)

Fed Chairman Ben Bernanke has also underlined the role of deliberation and collaboration and emphasized its role before Congress:

[T]here was excellent collaboration, and we very much valued not only the Treasury's support as a Department but the market knowledge and insight of Secretary Paulson and Under Secretary Steele. So that was a very useful collaboration, much of it taking place at the wee hours of the morning. (US Congress 2008c, 59)

While these remarks show a pattern that openly communicates and promotes the deliberative aspect of the decision-making process and frames the decision as a deliberative and collaborative one, this does not qualify as deliberative meaning making in a strict sense. Instead, it merely highlights the deliberative character of decision making without extending deliberation to the dimension of meaning making by inviting public debate and inquiry.

SUMMARY: THE BEAR STEARNS RESCUE FROM A PRAGMATIST PERSPECTIVE

This chapter has analysed the rescue of the investment bank Bear Stearns along the lines of the models of political crisis management introduced in Chapter 4. Based on a systematic review of a broad set of sources (internal reports, memoirs, journalistic and scientific accounts, Congressional hearings, press articles, press releases, official statements, press conferences, speeches) it has tried to find evidence for Pragmatist decision making and meaning making. Tables 6.1, 6.2 and 6.3 summarize the results of this analysis.

As the tables show, evidence for Pragmatist decision making has been found for all four of the Pragmatist building blocks: anti-dualism, fallibilism, experimentalism and deliberation. In contrast to this, the results are mixed when it comes to Pragmatist meaning making. Here, we only found evidence for anti-dualism and fallibilism and no examples for experimentalist or deliberative meaning making were identified. This result hints at a possible hypothesis that Pragmatism is more prevalent in decision making than in meaning making, a point that will be further discussed in Chapter 7.

When it comes to the relation of decision making and meaning making, an especially interesting finding from the analysis is the usage of anti-dualist meaning making to frame fallibilist decision making. Confronted with the challenge to explain the decision to rescue Bear Stearns despite their prior beliefs and positions, President Bush and Treasury Secretary Paulson invoked the anti-dualist idea of balancing different objectives. The rescue of Bear Stearns was framed as a middle ground between the objectives of ensuring financial stability and preventing the dangers of moral hazard.

Table 6.1   *Pragmatist decision making in the Bear Stearns case*

SPECIFICATIONS OF PRAGMATIST *DECISION MAKING*	
	Identified
Anti-Dualism	
Actively searching for third options, ways to transcend dilemmas	X
Avoiding self-imposed commitments	X
Fallibilism	
Readiness to change existing beliefs and decisions	X
Avoidance of unrevisable decisions	X
Acceptance of possible failure and unexpected consequences	X
Experimentalism	
Recombination of existing tools	
Decisions as hypotheses and trials	X
Constant feedback monitoring	X
Deliberation	
Decisions based on internal deliberation	X
Deliberation with external stakeholders	
Encouragement of skeptics	

Table 6.2 *Pragmatist meaning making in the Bear Stearns case*

SPECIFICATIONS OF PRAGMATIST *MEANING MAKING*	
	Identified
Anti-Dualism	
Nuanced depiction of events, no dichotomies	X
Fallibilism	
Communication of uncertainty, possible failures	X
Experimentalism	
Framed as experimentalist crisis management	
Trying out of frames, frame reversal	
Deliberation	
Openness to public debate and inquiry	

Table 6.3 *Principle-guided meaning making in the Bear Stearns case*

SPECIFICATIONS OF PRINCIPLE-GUIDED *MEANING MAKING*	
	Identified
Infallibilism	
Communication of certainty	X
"One best way"	
Sticking to frames	X

7. The collapse of Lehman Brothers and the rescue of AIG

The second decision point analysed in this study is the collapse of the investment bank Lehman Brothers in September 2008. At first glance the case looks very similar to the Bear Stearns case. Yet, while Bear Stearns was rescued with financial support from the Federal Reserve Bank, Lehman did not receive such support and had to file for bankruptcy on September 15, 2008. The question of why Lehman Brothers was not saved in the same way as Bear Stearns has received much attention and has been analysed from different political, journalistic and scientific angles (see, e.g., US Congress 2008b, 2008c; Sorkin 2009; Stewart 2009; Swagel 2009; Financial Crisis Inquiry Commission 2011, ch. 18; Blinder 2013, ch. 5; Ball 2016).

We investigate the Lehman Brothers case for evidence of Pragmatist and principle-guided political crisis management. Briefly put, this analysis reveals that government actors engaged in the Lehman case adopted a more principle-guided form of political crisis management than they did in the Bear Stearns case. This is especially true when it comes to the two Pragmatist dimensions of anti-dualism and fallibilism which are largely absent in the Lehman example. While focusing on the Lehman case, we also contrast it with two other important decisions made only days later: the rescue of the insurance company AIG and the rescue of the money market mutual funds. These two decisions again illustrate a more Pragmatist form of political crisis management.

DUALIST DECISION MAKING

Specification of principle-guided political crisis management: *Decisions are framed in either-or terms (dilemmas)*

The US Treasury and the Federal Reserve Bank approached the Lehman case with a strategy that was built on two premises: first, that a buyer for Lehman was needed; second, that no public money would be provided this time. We argue that this perspective qualifies as principle-guided crisis management because it employs the anti-Pragmatist concept of dualism. Framing the decision in the dichotomous contrast of *buyer or bankruptcy* the Federal Reserve Bank and the Treasury limited the scope of their possible responses.

From the perspective of this study, this decision therefore qualifies as dualist crisis management since it framed the decision as an either-or dilemma—that is, "*either* we find a buyer for Lehman Brothers *or* we will let the company fail." As Ben Bernanke recalls Timothy Geithner saying: "Our whole strategy was based on finding a buyer" (Bernanke 2015, 268). The second horn of the dilemma excluded the possibility of public financial support—that is, "*either* we find a solution that does not require public money *or* we will let Lehman Brothers fail."

In highlighting these two dilemmas it is important to note that the decision to let Lehman fail was not the first choice of the Bush Administration. But by framing the decisions in the form of two dilemmas (buyer or bankruptcy; solution without public money or bankruptcy) the bankruptcy of Lehman was the only remaining outcome after no buyer was found and the commitment to not use public money was made. The previous chapter showed how the Bear Stearns decision transcended such a dualism: first, by providing a limited indirect loan on March 14, 2008 that was intended to allow Bear Stearns to get to the weekend and allow further exploration of options; second, by balancing the two poles of moral hazard and systemic stability by pushing for a low price for Bear Stearns' shares. For the Lehman decision, however, we find no substantial examples of anti-dualist decision making.

The Insistence on Finding a Buyer as Dualist Crisis Management

The premise that a buyer for Lehman was necessary was developed at the Federal Reserve Bank. In an internal mail from July 12, 2008, the New York Fed's James McAndrews suggested that from the Fed's perspective—similar to the Bear Stearns scenario—a buyer was necessary in order to save Lehman: "If we think it [Lehman Brothers] can be sold, then proceed as in BS [Bear Stearns]. If not, discuss with the Treasury its appetite for a permanent addition to the government's balance sheet by lending to the distressed firm" (Financial Crisis Inquiry Commission 2010, 69). If the Treasury did not show an "appetite" to help out, Andrews suggested that Lehman would have to file for bankruptcy.

The view that a buyer was needed for Lehman showed up in another internal email of the Federal Reserve Bank from July 20, 2008 with the subject "Our Options in the Event of a Run on LB [Lehman Brothers]." Written by Patrick Parkinson, Director of the Division of Banking Supervision and Regulation of the Federal Reserve Board, it summarized the Fed's position: "But even if we are willing to extend as much as $200 billion of financing to LB [Lehman Brothers], absent an acquirer our action would not ensure LB's survival"

(Financial Crisis Inquiry Commission 2008e, 4). An internal Fed analysis from September 10, 2008 reached the same conclusion and found a dilemma that included only two basic options: finding a buyer for Lehman or the failure of the company (Financial Crisis Inquiry Commission 2011, 331). As New York Fed director Geithner summarized the position of the Federal Reserve Bank: "We had no alternative to a merger" (Geithner 2014, 185).

The view at the Treasury was in line with the Fed's assessment stating that a buyer for Lehman was necessary. For political and legal reasons, Treasury Secretary Paulson insisted that the Treasury was not willing to help Lehman Brothers (as discussed in the next section) so he facilitated the negotiations between Lehman and its two potential buyers (Sorkin 2009, 131; Paulson 2010, 178). After these negotiations failed, the Treasury's Phillip Swagel emphasized how the absence of a buyer was the chief reason why Lehman could not be rescued: "In the end there was no one prepared to buy Lehman with any realistic amount of government assistance as had been the case with Bear Stearns" (Swagel 2009, 40). This was also how Treasury Secretary Paulson explained the decision to President Bush: "There was just no way to save Lehman. We couldn't find a buyer even with the other private firms' help" (Paulson 2010, 216; also see Sorkin 2009, 226; Bush 2010, 457).

The meeting with leading Wall Street bankers on September 12, 2008 was also structured according to this dilemma. Geithner and Paulson had convened the executives of major financial institutions at the New York Federal Reserve Bank to explore ways in which these financial institutions could help to facilitate the sale of Lehman to one of the two potential buyers: the Bank of America or Barclays (Sorkin 2009, ch. 13; Stewart 2009; Financial Crisis Inquiry Commission 2011, 334). Geithner divided the bankers into three working groups along the two lines of the dilemma (Mollenkamp 2008). The first two groups prepared a sale of Lehman while the third group prepared for the alternative, a Lehman bankruptcy (Stewart 2009; Wessel 2009, 17; Paulson 2010, 193).

Excluding the Possibility of Financial Support as Dualist Crisis Management

This sense of only two possible options was further increased by Paulson's stance on the question of whether public money would be used to rescue Lehman Brothers. While the Federal Reserve Bank, with support from President Bush and the Treasury, had supported the sale of Bear Stearns in

March 2008 with $30 billion, Treasury Secretary Paulson excluded a similar solution for Lehman:

> In a conference call with Bernanke and Geithner, Paulson stated unequivocally that he would not publicly support spending taxpayer's money—the Fed's included—to save Lehman. "I'm being called Mr. Bailout," he said. "I can't do it again." (Wessel 2009, 14; also see Sorkin 2009, 141)

Without support from Paulson, Bernanke was reluctant to spend the Fed's money on a Lehman deal (Wessel 2009, 14).

The moral hazard-infused stance that no public money would be spent on Lehman Brothers was repeated in internal discussions and public statements. In meetings with Wall Street bankers on the evening of September 12, 2008 both Paulson and Geithner stressed that "the government would not bail out Lehman and that it was up to Wall Street to solve its problems" (Sorkin 2008; also see Bajaj 2008). The reluctance to rescue Lehman Brothers is also noted in the internal agenda that the Treasury and Fed prepared for the meeting, which lists one of the key elements of Paulson's introductory remarks: "Paulson conveys willingness of the official sector to let Lehman fail" (Financial Crisis Inquiry Commission 2008d, 2). Early on, Paulson and Geithner also let the two potential buyers of Lehman Brothers know that there would be no public money (Stewart 2009; Paulson 2010, 184). Additionally, Paulson believed "that we should emphasize publicly that there could be no government money for a Lehman deal" (Paulson 2010, 181).

President Bush stayed out of sight during the Lehman weekend and "left most of the details about the crisis to ... Paulson" (Labaton 2008; also see Stolberg 2008; Mann 2015, 132). As Wessel (2009, 11) puts it: "Bush and his team had delegated almost unconditional responsibility for managing the Great Panic to the Treasury and the Fed." When Paulson informed Bush on September 14, 2008 that Lehman would have to file for bankruptcy, Bush expressed relief that his government would no longer be associated with government bailouts, telling Paulson

> that he was unhappy about the bankruptcy, but that allowing Lehman Brothers to fail would send a strong signal to the market that his administration wasn't in the business of bailing out Wall Street firms any longer. (Sorkin 2008, 226)

Internally, Timothy Geithner was opposed to Paulson's position of excluding the possibility of any public support. Wessel has described Geithner as "the one most ready to intervene to stop something bad from happening" and the "most 'forward leaning'" compared to Paulson and Bernanke (Wessel 2009, 20). Geithner himself recalls how the days of the Lehman decision were one of the few instances where there were substantial opinion differences between himself, Paulson and Bernanke (Geithner 2014, 180). Geithner sensed that Paulson and Bernanke were influenced by political pressure and especially did not agree with Paulson's strategy to *publicly* state that there would be no financial support for Lehman (Stewart 2009; Paulson 2010, 187; Geithner 2014, 179).

Paulson later claimed that his position was part of a negotiation tactic that was meant to prevent Lehman, its potential buyers and other Wall Street banks from expecting that the government would step in again (Wessel 2009, 14; Paulson 2010, 187). There is evidence for this explanation (Financial Crisis Inquiry Commission 2008d, 2011, 332; Valukas 2010, 618) but as the next section will show, Paulson's reluctance can also be traced back to increased political pressure against the bailout of another investment bank.

Whatever the exact reasons for Paulson's position, the internal and public exclusion of the possibility of any financial support for the rescue of Lehman Brothers can be qualified as dualist decision making since it included a dualist account of possible options. Although Geithner did not want to exclude the possibility of public financial support, he has pointed out this led to a situation where the Treasury and Federal Reserve Bank were not able to preserve their options: "I didn't want us to commit to inaction and box ourselves in" (Geithner 2014, 179). Publicly reinforcing the "no-bailout" position further led to a self-imposed commitment that made it difficult to change course. From the perspective of Pragmatist political crisis management, such self-imposed commitments should be avoided. The Bear Stearns case has provided an important example of how such commitments are avoided, with Treasury Secretary Paulson advising President Bush not to promise that there would be no further bailouts. This action preserved optionality and enabled the Federal Reserve Bank to financially support the deal between Bear Stearns and J.P. Morgan two days later.

For the Lehman case, we find an example of dualist decision making—that is, that *decisions are framed in either-or terms (dilemmas)*. The concluding section examines the question of why the Bush Administration engaged in this principle-guided form of political crisis management, in contrast to its earlier Pragmatist approach in the Bear Stearns case.

The Infallibilist Lehman Decision and the Fallibilist AIG Shift

Specifications of Pragmatist political crisis management: *Readiness to change existing beliefs and decisions (AIG); avoidance of unrevisable decisions (AIG)*

Specifications of principle-guided political crisis management: *Sticking to existing beliefs and decisions (Lehman)*

From a Pragmatist perspective, the Lehman decision is notable because it departed from the fallibilist stance of the Bear Stearns decision and shifted back to a position of infallibilism. A key specification that has been identified for infallibilist political crisis management in the model (see Chapter 4) is *Sticking to existing beliefs and decisions*. This section finds evidence for this behavior in the Lehman decision. But with the decision to rescue the insurance company AIG two days after Lehman filed for bankruptcy, government officials reversed course again and engaged in fallibilist decision making by leaving free-market and moral hazard principles behind. The two specifications that can be identified for the fallibilism of the AIG decision are *Readiness to change existing beliefs and decisions* and *avoidance of unrevisable decisions*. They will be discussed below in the section entitled "The Fallibilism of the AIG Decision: Changing Existing Beliefs and Avoiding Unrevisable Decisions."

The Infallibilism of the Lehman Decision: Sticking to Existing Beliefs

In the discussion of the Bear Stearns case we have seen how government officials in the Bush Administration initially departed from the principles of free-market economics and the doctrine of moral hazard. Confronted with the financial troubles of Bear Stearns and their importance for the systemic stability of financial markets ("too interconnected to fail"), Paulson and Geithner decided to leave these existing beliefs behind and rescued Bear Stearns. For the Lehman decision, however, this was not the case. Instead, by giving in to increasing political pressure and assuming that the financial markets were prepared for the failure of Lehman, the established beliefs in free-market economics and the doctrine of moral hazard prevailed.[1]

The resistance against a bailout of Lehman was especially strong inside the Federal Reserve Bank and carried by "a group of hawkish regional Fed presidents" (Geithner 2014, 130). On September 16, 2008, one day after Lehman Brothers had to file for bankruptcy, this resistance became obvious during a meeting of the Federal Reserve Bank's Open Market Committee (FOMC). This committee consists of the members of the Federal Reserve Board and five of the Fed's presidents. Thomas Koenig, President of the Federal Reserve Bank in Kansas City, highlighted that the bailouts by the Federal Reserve Bank had "raised some real moral hazard issues" and concluded: "I think what we

---

[1]   From a meta-perspective this shift from fallibilism (Bear Stearns) to an infallibilist emphasis on existing principles (Lehman) to a fallibilist stance on these principles (AIG) might be described as Pragmatist adaptation. Here we stick to the micro-analysis of these decisions and discuss this aspect in the following chapter.

did with Lehman was the right thing because we did have a market beginning to play the Treasury and us, and that has some pretty negative consequences as well" (Federal Reserve Bank 2008d, 50–1). Jeffrey Lacker, President of the Federal Reserve Bank of Richmond, supported this notion and highlighted the importance of moral hazard too: "What we did with Lehman I obviously think is good. It has had an effect on market participants' assessment of the likelihood of other firms getting support" (Federal Reserve Bank 2008d, 48). A concern about moral hazards had also become more central at the Treasury, with Treasury Secretary Paulson explaining on September 15 that he "never once considered that it was appropriate putting taxpayer money on the line in resolving Lehman Brothers," adding: "Moral hazard is not something I take lightly" (White House 2008b; also see Cohan 2008).

These established beliefs in the functioning of free markets and the doctrine of moral hazard prevailed in the decision to let Lehman fail. We therefore find evidence for the specification of infallibilist decision making *Sticking to existing beliefs and decisions* in the Lehman decision. While the Treasury and the Federal Reserve Bank did depart from the Bear Stearns decision, they did so to return to their initial principles of free-market economics and moral hazard.

THE FALLIBILISM OF THE AIG DECISION: CHANGING EXISTING BELIEFS AND AVOIDING UNREVISABLE DECISIONS

With the decision to save the insurance company AIG, the infallibilist course of the Lehman decision was reversed and fallibilist decision making was again apparent. More specifically, we can identify two specifications of fallibilist decision making in the AIG case: *Readiness to change existing beliefs and decisions* and *avoidance of unrevisable decisions.*

Contradicting the assumption that the markets were prepared, the Lehman bankruptcy on September 15, 2008 had severe effects on the financial markets and caused the Dow Jones to fall by more than 500 points, the "biggest one-day point drop since Sept. 17, 2001, the first trading day after the Sept. 11 terrorist attacks" (Berenson 2008). On the same day, AIG was downgraded by the major rating agencies and media reports emerged that the Federal Reserve was considering support for the insurance company with a $75 billion credit line (Walsh and Merced 2008). Initially the Treasury and the Federal Reserve Bank had hoped that a private-sector solution for AIG would emerge, but after AIG had ended its negotiations with private investor Christopher Flowers and an industry consortium led by the investment banks J.P. Morgan and Goldman Sachs could not agree on a solution, this scenario became increasingly unlikely (Congressional Oversight Panel 2010, 50; Financial Crisis Inquiry Commission 2011, 348). Yet, government officials were reluctant to consider a public bailout of AIG. In a hearing of the Congressional Oversight Panel, New York Fed President Timothy Geithner later stated that in the night that Lehman filed for bankruptcy "it still seemed inconceivable that the Federal Reserve could or should play any role in preventing AIG's collapse" (Congressional Oversight Panel 2010, 52). At a press conference at the White House the day after Lehman's bankruptcy, Treasury Secretary Paulson also rejected the idea that the government would help AIG: "Let me say, what is going on right now in New York has got nothing to do with any bridge loan from the government. What's going on in New York is a private sector effort" (White House 2008b).

Inside the Fed, an assessment of AIG's situation had already started over the weekend (Financial Crisis Inquiry Commission 2011, 348). In a meeting with New York Fed officials on September 12, AIG executives had asked if they could obtain a loan from the Federal Reserve under its emergency section (Financial Crisis Inquiry Commission 2008a). As in the Lehman case, there were concerns at the Fed about moral hazard. In an internal memo, Adam Ashcraft from the New York Fed noted that AIG's request for an emergency loan was an attempt to "avoid making otherwise hard but viable options" (Financial Crisis Inquiry Commission 2008c, 2). In another analysis, entitled "Pros and cons of lending to AIG" the dangers of moral hazard featured prominently: a bailout of AIG, the analysis concluded "[c]ould diminish incentive to pursue private sector solutions ... Increases moral hazard as other insurance companies seek protection ... [and] could reward poor risk management practices" (Financial Crisis Inquiry Commission 2008f, 2). But the analysis also found reasons to support a public bailout, chiefly that a "[c]ollapse would be extremely complex to resolve given global nature of the firm" (Financial Crisis Inquiry Commission 2008f, 1). Or as another internal memo, which was sent to Timothy Geithner, noted on the topic of directly contrasting the AIG case to the Lehman decision: "In important ways, AIG's failure ... is more systemic in nature due to size, franchise, and the wholesale and retail dimensions of its business" (Financial Crisis Inquiry Commission 2008g, 1).

Similar to the Bear Stearns case, the concerns about systemic stability prevailed over moral hazard worries in the end. Internally it was Timothy Geithner who pushed for a public rescue of AIG (Sorkin 2009, 245; Geithner 2014, 194; Bernanke 2015, 278). Together with Bernanke, Geithner got the support of Paulson (Sorkin 2008, 247; Wessel 2009, 194).

On September 16, 2008, the Federal Reserve Bank announced that it would loan $85 billion to AIG, invoking its emergency section 13(3) (Federal Reserve Bank of New York 2012). In exchange, the Fed took 79.9 percent of AIG's ownership and replaced its CEO (Sorkin 2009, 253; Geithner 2014, 196). President Bush resisted the bailout at first, but was convinced by Bernanke's assurances that the $85 billion loan would be secured by good collateral and the goal to preserve systemic stability (Sorkin 2009, 252). As Bush remembered:

> There was nothing appealing about the deal. It was basically a nationalization of America's largest insurance company. Less than forty-eight hours after Lehman filed for bankruptcy, saving AIG would look like a glaring contradiction. But that was a hell of a lot better than a financial collapse. (Bush 2010, 458)

In summary, this behavior qualifies as fallibilist decision making since we find evidence for the specification *Readiness to change existing beliefs and decisions* here. President Bush and Treasury Secretary Paulson, who had pushed for a hard course in the Lehman case, had to overcome their moral hazard principles and give in to the importance of systemic stability. Similar to the Bear Stearns case this change of mind was triggered by the internal analysis from the Federal Reserve Bank, which emphasized the severe consequences an AIG failure would likely have due to its size and interconnectedness.

Besides its size and global interconnectedness, the other main reasons for a bailout of AIG concerned the problem of contagion. The hypothesis of the Fed's internal analysis was that if a company as big and well known as AIG filed for bankruptcy, neither market participants nor the general public would know which company would be next, thereby further decreasing the level of confidence and trust in the financial system (Financial Crisis Inquiry Commission 2008g, 1). This fear of the severe and *unrevisable* consequences of an AIG failure played a significant role in the decision-making process. An internal Fed analysis noted the "[l]arger surprise factor than Lehman" and found that a failure of AIG would happen "on the back of Lehman bankruptcy" which had unsettled the financial system already (Financial Crisis Inquiry Commission 2008g, 2). Another memo warned about possible "spillover effects on other firms involved in similar activities" including major companies such as General Electric (Financial Crisis Inquiry Commission 2008f, 1). In this effort to avoid the uncertain and unrevisable consequences of an AIG bankruptcy, we therefore find evidence for fallibilist decision making, and more specifically an *avoidance of unrevisable decisions*. This attempt to avoid an unrevisable decision can be traced to the consequentialist approach of governmental actors towards AIG. While the Lehman decision was strongly influenced by general principles of moral hazard, governmental actors put the practical (and potentially unrevisable) consequences of an AIG bankruptcy at the center of their decision. We therefore argue that such an approach qualifies as Pragmatist political crisis management.

"One Best Way" and the Experimentalist Shift with the Money Market Funds

Specifications of Pragmatist political crisis management: Recombination of existing tools (money market funds)

Specifications of principle-guided political crisis management: Decisions derived from "objective" evidence (legally impossible to lend to Lehman, not perceived as judgment call)

We find no evidence for Pragmatist experimentalism in the case of the Lehman decision. Instead a specification of principle-guided decision making can be identified for the Lehman case, *decisions derived from "objective" evidence*. Similar to fallibilism, however, we can also identify a shift away from this principled "one best way" approach to a more Pragmatist one after Lehman had to file for bankruptcy. By experimentally using the Exchange Stabilization Fund to rescue the money market funds after the Lehman failure, the US Treasury engaged in the creative *recombination of existing tools*, a specification of experimentalist decision making identified in our model. What is interesting from this study's perspective is how the role of legal considerations changed between the Lehman decision and the money market funds rescue. In the anti-experimentalist atmosphere of the Lehman decision, strict and narrowly interpreted legal rules predetermined the possible options and dictated one way to react to the crisis: the bankruptcy of Lehman Brothers. In terms of the experimentalist decision to save the money market funds, legal considerations were interpreted more flexibly and did not predetermine possible solutions.

Legal Principles Defining "One Best Way" for the Lehman Decision

Strictly speaking, the decision of whether the Federal Reserve Bank should rescue Lehman Brothers or not depended on the interpretation of its "emergency clause," section 13(3) of the Federal Reserve Act. This clause states that:

> "*under unusual and exigent circumstances*, the Board of Governors of the Federal Reserve System, by the affirmative vote of not less than five members, may authorize any Federal reserve bank" to lend to any institutions if these loans "are indorsed or otherwise secured *to the satisfaction of the Federal Reserve bank*". (Federal Reserve Bank 2013; our emphasis)

We highlight the two passages of this section that show how the decision to invoke section 13(3) is not a clear-cut one but always a matter of interpretation. First, the Fed's Board of Governors must decide if the concrete situation qualifies as "unusual and exigent circumstance". Second, if this is the case, the governors must decide if the loan they plan to extend is "secured to the satisfaction of the Federal Reserve Bank." Given the general formulation of these two conditions the governors' decision remains a judgment call that leaves room for interpretation (Financial Crisis Inquiry Commission 2011, 340–1).

In the case of Bear Stearns, the Fed's Board of Governors had decided that both of these conditions were met and invoked section 13(3) to lend $30 billion to Bear Stearns. For Lehman, however, this was not the case. Instead, building on a narrow interpretation of the legal clauses, the main government actors argued that the Lehman situation could not meet the second condition and that a loan to Lehman could not be covered "to the satisfaction of the Federal Reserve Bank." After the two potential buyers, Bank of America and Barclays, had dropped out, the decision for Bernanke was stark: "Without a buyer, and with no authority to inject fresh capital or guarantee Lehman's assets, we had no means of saving the firm" (Bernanke 2015, 268). As Wessel indicates, "neither Bernanke nor Geithner was prepared to nationalize Lehman without Paulson's backing" (Wessel 2009, 21). But Paulson insisted that the "Fed could not legally lend to fill a hole in Lehman's capital" and that the Treasury had no authority either (Paulson 2010, 209). This was also the way in which Paulson explained the decision to President Bush, insisting that it was impossible to rescue the investment bank (Bush 2010, 457; Paulson 2010, 216).

This assessment was based on the assumption that without a buyer, Lehman would not only be illiquid but insolvent, and that the Fed alone could not stop the run on the bank (Blinder 2013, 127). When Bernanke asked Geithner about the possibility to rescue Lehman without a buyer Geithner rejected the possibility, replying: "We would only be lending into an unstoppable run" (Geithner 2014, 267). A similar story was told to journalist James Stewart by a Treasury official:

> So there were really two issues: legal and practical. Paulson insists that we didn't have the legal authority, and I won't question that. But, even if we did have the authority, it wasn't practical. All the Fed money in the world wasn't going to stop a run on Lehman. (Stewart 2009)

Internally, the Fed assumed that the capital hole of Lehman was around $12 billion (Financial Crisis Inquiry Commission 2008b), with Bernanke insisting that the necessary authority to lend to Lehman was first created at a later stage with the Troubled Asset Relief Program (Wessel 2009, 25; Financial Crisis Inquiry Commission 2011, 340). When Bernanke testified before Congress, he indicated that this was the main direction in which the Fed had pushed:

> On Sunday night of that weekend, what was told to me—and I have every reason to believe—was that there was a run proceeding on Lehman …; that Lehman did not

have enough collateral to allow the Fed to lend it enough to meet that run. (Financial Crisis Inquiry Commission 2011, 340)

This argument has played an important role in how the decision to let Lehman fail was publicly framed. Here it is crucial to note that this strict reference to legal principles and the insistence that, without a buyer, bankruptcy was the best and only option for Lehman qualifies as principle-guided political crisis management. More precisely, we find evidence for the specification *Decisions derived from "objective" evidence*, with section 13(3) of the Federal Reserve Act serving as quasi-objective evidence in this case. As we have seen, the provision of section 13(3) is "very broad" (Financial Crisis Inquiry Commission 2011, 340), providing the Federal Reserve Bank with a substantial amount of latitude when deciding on specific cases. Or as legal scholar Peter Conti-Brown has put it: "The point is that 'satisfaction,' in the midst of a financial crisis, is an entirely discretionary concept" (Conti-Brown 2015b). Yet, during the Lehman decision this latitude was largely denied and the decision framed as inevitable. As Blinder has shown, Bernanke, Paulson and Geithner insisted that section 13(3) unambiguously did not apply to the Lehman case, arguing that "*saving Lehman with a loan from the Fed was illegal*" (Blinder 2013, 127, emphasis in the original; also see Ball 2016).

Even the general counsel of the Federal Reserve Bank, Scott Alvarez, has found the strict interpretation in the Lehman case to be too narrow, highlighting that requiring 13(3) loans to be fully secured would "undermine the very purpose of section 13(3), which was to make credit available in unusual and exigent circumstances" (Financial Crisis Inquiry Commission 2011, 341). The *New York Times* revealed later that there was a group inside the New York Fed that believed that Lehman could be legally bailed out but Paulson, Bernanke and Geithner claimed that they never learned about these findings (Stewart and Eavis 2014).

The decision to rescue AIG only a few days later, even if there was no buyer for the insurance company, showed that the argument that prevented a loan for Lehman could not "objectively" be found in the provisions of section 13(3). Instead, from the perspective of this study, the Lehman decision was an attempt to implement a more principle-guided form of political crisis management that referred to allegedly "objective" legal principles to defend its decision. With AIG, a more fallibilist approach returned to the decision-making process, with Bernanke deciding that the Fed "couldn't risk another sudden collapse of a systemic institution at a moment of such intense turbulence" (Geithner 2014, 194). After the AIG rescue, Pragmatist experimentalism also reemerged. More precisely, as the next section will show, experimentalism can be identified in the Treasury's decision to rescue the money market funds.

Creative Experimentalism to Rescue the Money Market Funds

Before Congress passed the Troubled Asset Relief Program (TARP) in October 2008, Treasury Secretary Paulson insisted that the Treasury had no funds that could be used for public bailouts (Wessel 2009, 169; Paulson 2010, 114–15; Geithner 2014, 156). This was the reason why the Federal Reserve Bank had to provide the financial resources for the bailout of Bear Stearns and AIG (Blinder 2013, 126). But after Lehman had to file for bankruptcy the troubles of the financial markets could no longer be unilaterally tamed by the Federal Reserve Bank, especially when it came to money market funds.

Money market funds have a similar function for big companies as bank accounts have for individuals, including similar expectations regarding their reliability. In the words of Ben Bernanke:

> investors who put their money into a money market fund expect that they can take their money out at any time, dollar for dollar … The money market funds in turn have to invest in something, and they tend to invest in short-term assets such as commercial papers. (Bernanke 2013, 79)

These commercial papers were widely regarded as safe investments. But after Lehman failed and its own commercial papers became virtually worthless, many money market funds were not able to pay back investors the full share of their accounts (Financial Crisis Inquiry Commission 2011, 356–60). This triggered a classic bank run: investors pulled out more money from the money market funds ($350 billion in one week), making it even harder for the funds to pay out all their depositors (Blinder 2013, 144). To regain liquidity, the money market funds had to sell an equal amount of commercial papers, which led to a "broad-based run on commercial paper markets," as Geithner explained before Congress (Financial Crisis Inquiry Commission 2011, 145). Since commercial papers were used by major companies like General Electric or IBM to fund many of their short-term transactions, concerns within the Fed and the Treasury increased that these companies might not be able to continue their business (Cheney 2011, 505; Financial Crisis Inquiry Commission 2011, 358; Blinder 2013, 145).

To solve this problem the Federal Reserve Bank and the Treasury decided to use a twofold strategy: the Treasury provided guarantees for money market funds through its Exchange Stabilization Fund (ESF) and the Fed provided additional liquidity through its Asset-Backed Commercial Paper Money Market Fund Liquidity Facility (AMLF). For Ben Bernanke there was nothing unusual about this solution: "This was an absolutely classic bank run and a classic response: providing liquidity to help the institution being run provide cash to its investors, and providing guarantees. That successfully ended the run" (Bernanke 2013, 83). But if we look more closely at this supposedly "classic response," we see that it was a quite unusual and creative decision, especially the Treasury's guarantee that employed the ESF.

The ESF, which originated in the Gold Reserve Act of 1934, had a very "specific purpose: to stabilize the international value of the dollar when necessary by buying or selling foreign currency" (Blinder 2013, 146; also see US Congress 1934; Richardson et al. 2013). The ESF was controlled by the US Treasury and its usage did not require Congressional authorization, a feature that brought it to the center of public debate when the Clinton Administration used it in 1995 to loan $20 billion to Mexico to prevent a default of the country (Schwartz 1996; Geithner 2014, 49–52).

So while there was a precedent for the unusual usage of the ESF, the decision to use the ESF to guarantee the deposits of the money market funds was "nevertheless quite unprecedented. Never before had the fund been used to issue guarantees of any kind" (Wallach 2015b, 75). From a Pragmatist perspective, it is especially interesting to see how legal concerns were negotiated in this decision. In March 2008, Timothy Geithner had asked Henry Paulson if the Treasury could use the ESF to rescue Bear Stearns, but the Treasury's lawyers argued that this was not possible (Geithner 2014, 155). With the troubles in the money market funds, this assessment changed. Treasury Secretary Paulson tried to establish a link between the money market funds and the original intention of the ESF to stabilize the dollar:

> Now money market funds were being hit by massive redemptions, some of them from skittish overseas investors. A collapse of the money fund industry could easily lead to a run on the dollar. (Paulson 2010, 253)

Blinder has called this reasoning "quite a stretch" (Blinder 2013, 252) and Wallach has described how this "farcically thin legal justification was developed during exchanges between the Treasury and the White House on the evening of Thursday, September 18, when legal fastidiousness was clearly not a primary concern" (Wallach 2015b, 76). Even Robert Hoyt, the Treasury's general counsel, admitted that the decision "was a bit of a legal stretch to say how that [use of the ESF to guarantee money market funds] related to the exchange rates, but we said, well, if you knew what would have happened if we hadn't done this, you would understand" (Wallach 2015b, 76). In other words, the decision-making process shifted away from strict legal considerations (which were dominant in the Lehman decision) to a *consequentialist* perspective. Such a perspective looks at consequences of an action and not at its principles.

Internally, the idea to use the ESF as a guarantee for the money funds was brought up by the Treasury's Steve Shafran and Paulson supported the idea immediately (Paulson 2010, 252; Wallach 2015b, 74). For Paulson the usage of the ESF was an "inspired idea" (Paulson 2010, 252) and an "extraordinary improvisation" (Paulson 2010, 263) that allowed the Treasury to do what Paulson thought was necessary: guaranteeing the deposits in money funds to prevent a run on them that would affect not only the financial sector but the whole economy (Financial Crisis Inquiry Commission 2011, 358).

Looking back at the financial crisis, Paulson later noted how the government was often forced "to use the inadequate tools" at hand in a novel and creative way to target an unprecedented crisis (Paulson 2010, 438). The ESF example qualifies as such a *recombination of existing tools* and therefore as an example of experimentalist political crisis management. The two existing tools that were recombined in this example were the idea of governmental guarantees and the ESF. The power of governmental guarantees was a concept well known in the prevention of bank runs, with the Federal Deposit Insurance Corporation (FDIC) insuring all bank accounts up to $100,000 (Geithner 2014, 203). The ESF, which was originally intended and used for a very different purpose, was identified as the tool that could provide the necessary financial resources to guarantee the deposits of money market funds and stop the run on them (Blinder 2013, 145).

THE ROLE OF DELIBERATION IN DECISION MAKING DURING THE LEHMAN CASE

Specification of Pragmatist political crisis management: *Decisions based on internal deliberation*

Specification of principle-guided political crisis management: *Exclusion of skeptics*

When it comes to the role of deliberation in the decision-making process around the Lehman decision, the findings are similar to the ones from the Bear Stearns case. Internally, the level of deliberation was high. The main governmental actors were in constant discussion about Lehman and AIG. This deliberation provides evidence for a Pragmatist approach to political crisis management. An (ideal-typical) principle-guided approach to political crisis management would refrain from (internal and external) deliberation. Instead, in the principle-guided mode of "dictation," decisions would be made by a single leader, similar to what Carl Schmitt imagined for his (commissary and sovereign) dictator.

Contrary to the Bear Stearns case, we can also identify tensions in internal discussions around the Lehman case. When it comes to external deliberation, however, we can only identify the inclusion of external stakeholders in a process of consultation and find no evidence of any direct influence in decision making.

Internal Deliberation

Similar to the Bear Stearns case, the level of internal deliberation for the Lehman decision was high. Starting on September 9, Paulson, Bernanke and Geithner were in daily contact either through direct meetings or via conference calls (for a list of these meetings and calls, see Financial Crisis Inquiry Commission 2010, 6). To facilitate the internal discussion, Treasury Secretary Paulson and his team flew to New York on September 12 and worked alongside Timothy Geithner and his team for the rest of the weekend (Paulson 2010, 190; Geithner 2014, 182).

Internal discussions were dominated by the question of whether public money should be used in order to save Lehman or not. Geithner later noted that the Lehman weekend:

> was one of the few times during the crisis when there was any distance between Hank [Paulson] and me. There was even some distance between Ben [Bernanke] and me. I sensed their advisers pulling them toward expedience, trying to distance them from the unpalatable moves we had made and the even less palatable moves I thought we'd have to make soon. (Geithner 2014, 180)

Paulson also stated that Geithner "expressed concern about my public stand on government aid" (Paulson 2010, 187), with Wessel reporting that "Geithner lost his customary cool" (Wessel 2009, 16) when it came to the question of whether public money should be used for a Lehman rescue. Bernanke took a middle ground position: on the one hand, he felt political pressure similar to that experienced by Paulson and wanted to reduce moral hazard (Geithner 2014, 180), but on the other hand, through his knowledge of the policy responses during the Great Depression, he also sided with Geithner's more interventionist approach (Wessel 2009, 21).

In the end these internal discussions were rendered obsolete after Lehman's last potential buyer, the British bank Barclays, did not get approval for the deal from its regulator in the UK. Until then, for Geithner, a "last-minute Fed assistance still seemed possible" (Geithner 2014, 185) but when Lehman could not find a buyer he supported Paulson's position that bankruptcy was the only option left (Wessel 2009, 21; Geithner 2014, 187).

We therefore find evidence for the specification *decisions based on internal deliberation* in the Lehman case. In contrast to the Bear Stearns case we also find evidence for internal tension, especially between Geithner and Paulson when it came to a possible public bailout of Lehman. President Bush played only a minor role in these discussions. He was informed by Paulson about the latest events and supported the course that was decided upon by Paulson, Bernanke and Geithner (Labaton 2008; Wessel 2009, 11; Bush 2010, 456).

We could not identify another specification of deliberative decision making—*encouragement of skeptics*. Timothy Geithner was skeptical about Paulson's strict no-bailout course but he was not actively encouraged to influence decision making. Instead, he was part of the core decision-making team by virtue of his position. His inclusion therefore does not account as an example for the Pragmatist specification of encouraging skeptics.

One skeptic, Chairman of the US FDIC Sheila Bair, was excluded from the decision-making process. Her skepticism came from the exact opposite direction as Geithner's. Bair argued that the Bush Administration should have let Bear Stearns fail and that debt holders of AIG should have taken some losses (Nocera 2011). Geithner therefore considered Bair a proponent of "moral hazard fundamentalism" (Geithner 2014, 217) and the *New York Times* noted that Bair "favored 'market discipline'" and abhorred bailouts (Nocera 2011).

Bair described how her dissent led to her systematic exclusion from the decision-making process:

> we [FDIC] were rarely consulted. They [Treasury and Federal Reserve Bank] would bring me in after they'd made their decision on what needed to be done, and without giving me any information they would say, "You have to do this or the system will go down." If I heard that once, I heard it a thousand times. "Citi is systemic, you have to do this." No analysis, no meaningful discussion. It was very frustrating. (Nocera 2011)

In her memoirs, Bair speculates that she was excluded because of her gender from "the all-boys network" in the Treasury and Federal Reserve but also because her moral hazard principles conflicted with the decisions taken in the Bear Stearns and AIG cases (Bair 2012, 98).

In any case, this exclusion of Bair and the FDIC led to a situation where the FDIC had to actively intervene to correct a mistake that was made in the guarantees for the money market funds. Drafting the guarantees under high time pressure the Treasury decided that it would use the ESF to guarantee *all* amounts in money market funds (Blinder 2013, 146–7). For normal bank accounts, however, the insurance provided by the FDIC only covered $100,000. Therefore, the new Treasury program created incentives for investors to withdraw their money from their bank accounts and move it into money market funds. As Bair remarked: "Unfortunately, they [Paulson and his team] did not consult with us and did not even consider that the unlimited coverage would create liquidity issues for banks" (Bair 2012, 108). After calling Paulson and explaining the problem, Paulson agreed to change the program so that it would only cover deposits that were already in money market funds when the guarantee program started (Paulson 2010, 262; Blinder 2013, 147).

From the perspective of this study, Bair's exclusion from the decision-making process provides evidence for a specification of principle-guided decision making, *exclusion of skeptics*. What is interesting about Bair is that her skepticism was based on moral hazard principles. So while her exclusion points at principle-guided political crisis management it might have enabled the Pragmatism of the Bear Stearns and AIG decision.

External Deliberation

For external deliberation we find a pattern very similar to the Bear Stearns case. External stakeholders were only included in consultation processes and when their help and expertise in implementing specific measures was needed. Chief among these external stakeholders were Wall Street bankers and finance lawyers. Officials from the Federal Reserve Bank and the Treasury were in contact with many Wall Street bankers in the weeks before the Lehman bankruptcy to get external opinions and assessments (for an overview, see Financial Crisis Inquiry Commission 2010). On September 11, for instance, Goldman Sachs' executive Susan McCabe sent an email to William Dudley, who also had worked at Goldman Sachs before he joined the New York Fed, warning him that a failure of Lehman could be worse than Bear Stearns: "They [Lehman] have much bigger counter-party risk than Bear did, especially in Derivates market, so [t]he market is getting very spooked, nervous" (Financial Crisis Inquiry Commission 2011, 332). Hayley Boesky, another member of Timothy Geithner's team at the New York Fed, received the same message from hedge fund managers (Financial Crisis Inquiry Commission 2011, 333). Geithner also called investor Warren Buffet to get his opinion on AIG (Geithner 2014, 193).

The most systematic inclusion of Wall Street bankers took place in the New York Fed building from September 12–14 where leading bank executives were convened in order to form an industry consortium that would help rescue Lehman (Mollenkamp 2008; Stewart 2009; Wessel 2009, 17; Paulson 2010, 193). During these negotiations, private investor Christopher Flowers also provided Treasury Secretary Paulson with details about AIG's situation and advised him to replace AIG's management (Paulson 2010, 200).

Where special expertise was needed, finance lawyers were also included (Frankel 2015). In the case of the AIG rescue, "Marshall Huebner, the co-head of insolvency and restructuring at the law firm Davis Polk & Wardwell, who was already working on AIG for J.P. Morgan" was brought on board to advise the Federal Reserve Bank (Sorkin 2009, 249). Congress, on the other hand, was only marginally included, with Barney Frank, Chairman of the House

Financial Services Committee, later noting: "I would say with regard to Bear Stearns or Lehman or AIG, Congress was never consulted. We were never asked our opinion. We were informed that this was happening" (PBS 2009).

Summary

To summarize, we find evidence for specifications of internal deliberation for the Lehman case but no evidence for external deliberation that goes beyond the level of consultation. For internal deliberation we find a higher degree of internal tension compared to the Bear Stearns case, with Paulson and Geithner having advocated different positions on the possibility of public financial support for Lehman Brothers. The dispute ended when no buyer for Lehman could be found and Geithner agreed that Lehman's bankruptcy was the only option left. For external deliberation we find a strong inclusion of Wall Street bankers and finance lawyers. Similar to the Bear Stearns case, however, this inclusion took place on the level of information gathering and consultation but not decision making.

MEANING MAKING

After having analysed decision making in the Lehman case, the following sections will concentrate on the meaning-making process. By looking for specifications of Pragmatist and principle-guided meaning making in the Lehman case, we will compare the meaning-making dimension of political crisis management to decision making.

From Dualist "No More Bailouts" to Nuanced Case-by-Case Frames

Specifications of Pragmatist political crisis management: Nuanced depiction of events, no dichotomies

Specifications of principle-guided political crisis management: Usage of black-and-white dualisms

In the days before the Lehman decision was made, Treasury Secretary Paulson had widely communicated his position that there would be no public support for Lehman Brothers (Paulson 2010, 181). His press secretary intentionally leaked this position to reporters (Wessel 2009, 15; Paulson 2010, 186) leading to media reports that Paulson was "drawing a line in the sand" and excluding the possibility of another Bear Stearns solution (Zumbrun 2008; Wessel 2009, 15). As the *New York Times* reported on September 12:

> Treasury officials let it be known that, this time, they would not be putting any taxpayer money on the line. People with knowledge of the thinking of the Treasury Secretary, Henry M. Paulson Jr., said Friday that he was opposed to providing tax-payer money to push through a deal that could save Lehman. (Anderson et al. 2008)

After Lehman had to file for bankruptcy, Paulson was pushed by Jim Wilkinson, his chief of staff, to defend this position, with Wilkinson advising Paulson to emphasize that the Bush Administration "is not in the business of bailouts" (Sorkin 2009, 234). During a press conference at the White House on September 15, Paulson reinforced his position, stating: "… I never once considered that it was appropriate to put taxpayer money on the line in resolving Lehman Brothers" (White House 2008b).

When AIG was rescued with public money on the next day, the government faced the problem of perceived inconsistency. As economist Alan Blinder has highlighted: "The Lehman decision abruptly and surprisingly tore the perceived rulebook into pieces and tossed it out the window. Market participants were thus cut adrift, no longer knowing what game they were playing" (Blinder 2013, 128).

The way this perceived inconsistency was framed at first was by pointing to the differences between the Bear Stearns, Lehman Brothers and AIG cases. Bernanke has called the varying decisions "a different response to different circumstances" (Bernanke 2015, 292) and Paulson has framed the decision-making process as a sequence of case-by-case decisions that took into account the diverse characteristics of each case: "[W]e have worked together on a case-by-case basis addressing problems at Fannie Mae and Freddie Mac, working with market participants to prepare for the failure of Lehman Brothers and lending to AIG so it can sell some of its assets in an orderly manner" (US Congress 2008a, 27, also see 2008c, 37). And at the White House press conference Paulson remarked: "The situation in March and the situation and the facts around Bear Stearns were very, very different to the situation we are looking at here in September" (White House 2008b).

The main difference between Bear Stearns and Lehman that was publicly identified by Bernanke and Paulson was that the markets were prepared for a Lehman failure (Financial Crisis Inquiry Commission 2011, 340). In his testimony before Congress shortly after Lehman failed, Bernanke explained:

> In the case of Lehman Brothers, a major investment bank, the Federal Reserve and the Treasury declined to commit public funds to support the institution. The failure of Lehman posed risks, but the troubles at Lehman had been well known for some time and investors clearly recognized as evidenced for example by the high cost of

insuring Lehman's debt in the market for credit default swaps that the failure of the firm was a significant possibility. Thus, we judge that investors and counterparties had time to take precautionary measures. (US Congress 2008b, 30)

Similar to the Bear Stearns case, Bernanke and Paulson also stressed the anti-dualist balance of two main concerns in their decisions: the systemic stability of the financial markets and the problem of moral hazard. Especially for the AIG rescue, as Bernanke put it, "it is a very tough deal that we struck. We did that because we wanted to protect the taxpayer. At the same time, we were concerned about the implications for the markets of the failure of this large company" (US Congress 2008b, 44). Treasury Secretary Paulson stressed the same point:

> Let me just say that, with regard to Freddie and Fannie and AIG, in case you or your constituents do not know, in those cases CEOs were replaced, the Government got warrants for 79.9 percent of the equity, golden parachutes were eliminated, strong action was taken. (US Congress 2008b, 26, also see 2008a, 30)

From the perspective of our model of political crisis management, the findings are mixed for the (anti-)dualist dimension. On the one hand, Paulson's absolute rejection in public of any financial support for Lehman Brothers qualifies as dualist meaning making by evoking a strict black-and-white dualism, with Paulson communicating that he was "adamant that there will not be government money used in the resolution of the situation" (Lawder 2008). On the other hand, by emphasizing the case-by-case character of the decisions and its nuanced differences government officials also engaged in anti-dualist meaning making. At first, this anti-dualist emphasis on nuances and gray tones was also the key strategy to target the problem of perceived inconsistency. But as the next section will show, this framing strategy was later revised and replaced by a more principle-guided approach.

Experimentally Changing the Frame to Principled Legalism

Specifications of Pragmatist political crisis management: Trying out of frames, frame revision

Specifications of principle-guided political crisis management: Framed as unambiguous and "evidence-based"

The biggest challenge for the Bush Administration when framing the Lehman and AIG decisions was to explain the perceived inconsistency. Governmental actors reacted to this challenge by experimentally reversing their frame from the nuanced depiction of differences to principled legalism.

As economist Paul Krugman has highlighted, the problem of the perceived inconsistency is closely connected to the public's *trust* in government's actions:

> Some are saying that we should simply trust Mr. Paulson, because he's a smart guy who knows what he's doing. But that's only half true: he is a smart guy, but what, exactly, in the experience of the past year and a half—a period during which Mr. Paulson repeatedly declared the financial crisis "contained," and then offered a series of unsuccessful fixes—justifies the belief that he knows what he's doing? He's making it up as he goes along, just like the rest of us. (Krugman 2008)

In assessing the actions of the US Treasury during the financial crisis, Acharya et al. have arrived at a similar conclusion:

> It is relatively more difficult to see a coherent logic behind the US Treasury's actions and the design of bailout packages. Clearly, given the magnitude of the problems and the urgent need for some solutions, a certain improvisatory quality entered into the Treasury's actions as well. Increasingly however, these actions have taken the form of a discretionary approach (that is, ad-hoc or institution by institution) rather than a principles-based one. (Acharya et al. 2009, 126)

From the perspective of this study it is interesting to see how Acharya et al. criticize the provisional and "ad-hoc" character of the Treasury's decisions and argue for a "principle-based" approach. Paulson rejected such a strict principle-based approach, arguing that "if you get too dug in on a position, the facts change, and you don't change to adapt to the facts, you will never be successful" (Landler and Dash 2008). He noted on the AIG decision: "If we had to reverse ourselves over the weekend, so be it" (Paulson 2010, 187). But government officials worried how to explain the perceived inconsistency of the different decisions. Geithner, for instance, highlighted the "why-AIG-but-not-Lehman? public relations challenge" and noted: "I don't have the burden of explaining to the public the zig and the zag" (Geithner 2014, 194).

As the last section has shown, the immediate explanation Paulson and Bernanke offered publicly for the allegedly contradicting decisions was to highlight the nuanced differences of the cases, especially noting their assumption that the markets were better prepared for a Lehman failure. Over time, this framing strategy shifted and instead employed a more legalistic explanation, pointing to the fact that under section 13(3) of the Federal Reserve Act any emergency loan must be "secured to the satisfaction of the Federal Reserve bank" (Federal Reserve Bank 2013). Based on the narrow reading of this phrase, Bernanke, Paulson and Geithner increasingly argued that Lehman was not bailed out because it was *legally impossible*. As Bernanke later told the Financial Crisis Inquiry Commission: "We are not allowed to lend without a reasonable expectation of repayment. The loan has to be secured to the satisfaction of the Reserve Bank" (Financial Crisis Inquiry Commission 2011, 340). This version was supported by Paulson (2010, 209) and Geithner, who stated: "[W]e didn't think we could legally do the rescue ourselves" (Geithner 2014, 187).

David Wessel has shown how the shift towards this legalistic explanation took place in the months after the Lehman decision and summarized: "By the end of 2008, Bernanke, Paulson, and Geithner had coalesced around the explanation that—without a buyer—neither the Treasury nor the Fed had the authority to spend what it would have taken to save Lehman" (Wessel 2009, 24).

From a Pragmatist perspective on political crisis management, this shift away from an anti-dualist explanation that highlighted the nuanced differences of the Lehman case to an unambiguous legal interpretation qualifies as *frame revision* and therefore as experimentalist meaning making. After trying out the frame that highlighted the nuanced details of the Lehman decision (assumption that markets were prepared, hope for a private-sector solution) Paulson, Bernanke and Geithner switched to a more principle-based frame: that it was legally impossible to rescue Lehman Brothers because a loan would not have been secured "to the satisfaction" of the Federal Reserve Bank. Paulson, Bernanke and Geithner later stated that the reason why they did not use the legalistic frame earlier was that they did not want to publicly admit that both the Treasury and the Federal Reserve had been powerless in the Lehman case. As Bernanke stated:

> But we [Paulson and Bernanke] had agreed in advance to be vague because we were intensely concerned that acknowledging our inability to save Lehman would hurt market confidence and increase pressure on other firms. (Bernanke 2015, 289; also see Wessel 2009, 24; Geithner 2014, 190)

Legal scholar Peter Conti-Brown and economist Laurence Ball found this shift to a principle-based and legalistic framing of the Lehman decision was not a mere tactical and legal one but also a political decision that reacted to the negative feedback from the previous explanation (Donato 2009, 55; Ball 2016): "[T]he Fed reached for legal cover when the Lehman bankruptcy turned out very differently than they had hoped. It was a political decision, not a legal one" (Conti-Brown 2015a).

Through the legalistic framing of the Lehman decision in the later phase we also find evidence for principle-guided meaning making, more precisely in the form of the specification *Framed as unambiguous and "evidence-based."* By employing a narrow legalistic interpretation of section 13(3) and by stating that a rescue of Lehman was legally impossible the decision was framed as unambiguous and based on the "objective" evidence of legal rules (Wallach 2015a). By evoking these legal principles as unequivocal, the Lehman decision was explained as the only possible choice. As Paulson later put it: "the central bank could not legally make a loan" (Paulson 2010, 230).

(In)Fallibilism: Communication of Both Certainty and Uncertainty

Specifications of Pragmatist political crisis management: *Communication of uncertainty, possible failure*

Specifications of principle-guided political crisis management: *Communication of certainty*

When it comes to the roles of fallibilism and infallibilism in meaning making we find that government officials employed a mix of both approaches, communicating uncertainty and possible failures while also stressing the certainty of the outcomes of their decisions on other occasions.

Communicating Uncertainty

In a press conference the day after Lehman's failure, Treasury Secretary Paulson was confronted with questions regarding the government's next steps, especially if the Lehman decision marked the definitive end of public bailouts. At first Paulson tried to avoid answering this question: "… I think it's important that regulators remain very vigilant. We're very vigilant, but we do not take, and I don't take, lightly ever putting the taxpayer on the line to support an institution" (White House 2008b). But when reporters followed up with the question if this statement should be read as "no more bailouts," Paulson replied: "Don't read it as no more; read it as that it's important, I think, for us to maintain the stability and orderliness of our financial system" (White House 2008b).

This communication of uncertainty and publicly leaving all possible options open can be found in other instances of Paulson's answers during this press conference as well. When asked if the worst of the financial crisis was over, Paulson again avoided public commitments:

I think we've got to go back to the housing correction and where are we in the housing correction. And I believe that there is a reasonable chance that the biggest part of that housing correction can be behind us in a number of months. I'm not saying two or three months, but in months as opposed to years. I think we're going to have housing issues in this country for—and mortgage issues for years, but in terms of getting by the biggest part of this correction, if we can make this Fannie

Mae-Freddie Mac effort work the way I would like to see it work, I think we'll make real progress here. (White House 2008b)

It is especially interesting how Paulson did not promise that the government efforts to tame the crisis would work. Instead, he highlighted that a possibility for ending the crisis was that the government's solution "work[s] the way I would like to see it work," though at the same time indicating that this would not necessarily be the case. A similar argument can be found in another statement by Paulson, framing the government's strategy in modest terms and pointing to the non-linearity of future developments: "As I've said, we're not going to move through this in a straight line. There are going to be some real rough spots along the road, but I believe we're making progress" (White House 2008b).

In a speech on September 19, 2008, President Bush also highlighted the risk of the government's strategy while at the same time pointing out that the risks would otherwise be even higher:

These measures will require us to put a significant amount of taxpayer dollars on the line. This action does entail risk. But we expect that this money will eventually be paid back. The vast majority of assets the government is planning to purchase have good value over time, because the vast majority of homeowners continue to pay their mortgages. And the risk of not acting would be far higher. (Bush 2008b)

Paulson brought forward a similar argument in a Congressional hearing on September 23, admitting risks for taxpayers but also emphasizing that the risk of failed governmental action would be more dramatic:

The taxpayer is already on the hook. The taxpayer is going to suffer the consequences if things do not work the way they should work. And so the best protection for the taxpayer and the first protection for the taxpayer is to have this work. (US Congress 2008b, 27)

Compared to Paulson and Bush, Fed Chairman Bernanke's public meaning making put a stronger emphasis on the aspect of certainty. But when advocating for the necessity of the Troubled Asset Relief Program, even Bernanke admitted that the situation had not been resolved by the government's intervention and remained precarious:

Despite the efforts of the Federal Reserve, the Treasury, and other agencies, global financial markets remain under extraordinary stress. Action by Congress is urgently required to stabilize the situation and avert what otherwise could be very serious consequences for our financial markets and for our economy. (US Congress 2008c, 93)

From a Pragmatist perspective, these are examples of fallibilist meaning making that highlight the uncertainty of decisions and acknowledge the possibility of failures. For the Lehman case, however, we also find frames used by Bush and Paulson that lean more towards principle-guided political crisis management, highlighting the certainty of decisions and future developments, as the next section will show.

Communicating Certainty

In a press statement released immediately after the decision to let Lehman fail, Paulson tried to bolster public confidence and highlighted that the Treasury together with the Federal Reserve Bank, the SEC and major investment banks had taken all steps necessary to prepare the market for a Lehman fail (US Department of Treasury 2008a). The press release published by the Federal Reserve Bank took a similar position (Federal Reserve Bank 2008b).

In the press conference at the White House the next day, Paulson communicated certainty, starting off by remarking "that the American people can remain confident in the soundness and the resilience of our financial system" (White House 2008b). When asked about the soundness of the commercial bank system Paulson reiterated this position:

> Well, I've got to say our banking system is a safe and a sound one. And since the days when we've had federal deposit insurance in place, we haven't had a depositor who's got less than $100,000 in an account lose a penny. So the American people can be very, very confident about their accounts in our banking system. (White House 2008b)

President Bush framed the situation in a similar way. Speaking about the general situation of the financial system, Bush emphasized the need for painful adjustments while at the same time remarking: "In the long run, I'm confident that our capital markets are flexible and resilient, and can deal with these adjustments" (Labaton 2008). Bush especially tried to spread confidence and emphasize certainty when it came to the security of finances:

> In this difficult time, I know many Americans are wondering about the security of their finances. Every American should know that the federal government continues to enforce laws and regulations protecting your money. Through the FDIC, every savings account, checking account, and certificate of deposit is insured by the federal government for up to $100,000. The FDIC has been in existence for 75 years, and no one has ever lost a penny on an insured deposit—and this will not change. (Bush 2008b)

Bush repeated this argument when it came to the insurance the Treasury provided for money market funds: "For every dollar invested in an insured fund,
you will be able to take a dollar out" (Bush 2008b).

It is interesting to note that certainty was communicated when it came to the
general stability of the financial system and the soundness of public guarantees
(as provided by the FDIC and others). For the proposed solutions, however,
we find a larger degree of communicated uncertainty, with Paulson and Bush
emphasizing the risks of the government's decisions.

No Evidence for Deliberative Meaning Making

Identified specifications: None

For the Lehman and AIG cases, we find no evidence for deliberative meaning
making. Similar to the Bear Stearns case, the only instance that even hints in
this direction is a remark by Henry Paulson during a Congressional hearing on
September 24, 2008:

> I appreciate that we are here to discuss an unprecedented program, but these are
> unprecedented times for the American people and for our economy. I also appreciate
> that the Congress and the Administration are working closely together and we have
> been for a number of days now so that we can help the American people by quickly
> enacting a program to stabilize our financial system. (US Congress 2008a, 26)

Just as in the Bear Stearns case, we would characterize this statement not as
an example of deliberative meaning making but as a courtesy remark towards
a Congressional committee that was legally authorized to inquire in to these
topics. If anything, we find evidence in the direction of non-deliberative
meaning making in the sense of preventing public debate and inquiry. As
Treasury Secretary Paulson remarked during the same hearing, public debate
and inquiry were not the first priority: "Many of you here also have strong
views. And we must have that critical debate, but we must get through this
period first" (US Congress 2008a, 28).

We have also seen how Paulson and Bernanke claimed that they did not
reveal the "real" reasons for Lehman's failure (that they had no legal authority
to do so) during the Congressional hearing, thereby preventing public debate
on the decision. In a similar sense, the bailout of the government-sponsored
enterprises Fannie Mae and Freddie Mac in early September 2008 was planned
and implemented in a highly secretive way that Fed Chairman Bernanke has
described as "like planning a surprise attack in hostile territory" (Bernanke
2015, 244; also see Paulson 2010, 163). But since these examples are too
blurry, and in the case of Fannie Mae and Freddie Mac not within the timeframe

of this study, we also find no sufficient evidence for non-deliberative meaning making. Instead, from the perspective of the model, meaning making in the Lehman case was somewhere between the two ideal types of Pragmatist and principle-guided political crisis management when it comes to deliberation.

Summary

In short, the analysis of the Lehman case has yielded the following results. For *decision making* we have found that both the Treasury and the Federal Reserve Bank took a dualist stance towards Lehman, insisting on a buyer for the firm and excluding the possibility of financial support. The Lehman decision has also been described as an infallibilist shift back to ideological principles. This infallibilist stance, however, was reversed with the decision to save the insurance company AIG shortly after Lehman's failure. Similar mixed results were found for the role of experimentalism, where the Lehman decision was characterized by a strong principle-guided approach that invoked a narrow reading of legal rules. Yet, a more experimentalist approach was used to rescue the money market funds, creatively using the ESF to provide insurance for the money market funds. For deliberation we have found that the degree of internal deliberation was high, but external deliberation remained on the level of consultation and did not influence decision making.

Meaning making in the Lehman and AIG cases was set in motion by Treasury Secretary Paulson's strong dualist stance against any further bailouts, which led to a situation in which the Bush Administration's actions were perceived as inconsistent after the AIG rescue. The way Bernanke and Paulson tried to frame this situation at first was through anti-dualism, highlighting the nuanced differences of both cases and communicating their assumption that the markets were prepared for Lehman's failure. Later they shifted the frame and brought forward a more principle-based explanation, highlighting the legal impossibility of saving Lehman. This frame revision, from Pragmatist anti-dualism to principle-based legalism, is in itself an example for the experimentalist adaption of frames. With respect to fallibilism, we have found evidence for both fallibilist and non-fallibilist meaning making. However, no convincing evidence could be identified for (non-) deliberation.

Taken together we find mixed results for the Lehman case that include both elements from Pragmatist and principle-guided political crisis management. These results are summarized in Tables 7.1 to 7.4.

Table 7.1   Decision making in Pragmatist crisis management

SPECIFICATIONS OF PRAGMATIST *DECISION MAKING*	
	Identified
Anti-Dualism	
Actively searching for third options, ways to transcend dilemmas	
Avoiding self-imposed commitments	
Fallibilism	
Readiness to change existing beliefs and decisions	X
Avoidance of unrevisable decisions	X
Acceptance of possible failure and unexpected consequences	
Experimentalism	
Recombination of existing tools	X
Decisions as hypotheses and trials	
Constant feedback monitoring	
Deliberation	
Decisions based on internal deliberation	X
Deliberation with external stakeholders	
Encouragement of skeptics	

Table 7.2   Meaning making in Pragmatist crisis management

SPECIFICATIONS OF PRAGMATIST *MEANING MAKING*	
	Identified
Anti-Dualism	
Nuanced depiction of events, no dichotomies	X
Fallibilism	
Communication of uncertainty, possible failures	X
Experimentalism	
Framed as experimentalist crisis management	
Trying out of frames, frame reversal	X
Deliberation	
Openness to public debate and inquiry	

Table 7.3   *Decision making in principle-guided political crisis management*

SPECIFICATIONS OF PRINCIPLE-GUIDED *DECISION MAKING*

	Identified
Dualism	
Decisions are framed in either-or terms (dilemmas)	X
Infallibilism	
Sticking to existing beliefs and decisions	X
No expectance of failure, no backup plans	
"One best way"	
Decisions derived from "objective" evidence	X
Decisions from existing cases applied unaltered	
Dictation	
Decisions based on a priori principles without deliberation	
Exclusion of skeptics	X

Table 7.4   *Meaning making in principle-guided political crisis management*

SPECIFICATIONS OF PRINCIPLE-GUIDED *MEANING MAKING*

	Identified
Dualism	
Usage of black-and-white dualisms	X
Infallibilism	
Communication of certainty	X
"One best way"	
Framed as unambiguous and "evidence-based"	X
Sticking to frames	
Dictation	
Prevention of public debate and inquiry	

8.   Comparative reflections and new hypotheses

The previous chapters have analysed two decision points from the US financial crisis according to our perspectives on political crisis management—the decision to rescue the investment bank Bear Stearns in March 2008 and the decision to let the investment bank Lehman Brothers fail in September 2008. Many of the specifications for Pragmatist political crisis management were identified in the Bear Stearns case. The results for the Lehman case are mixed, including evidence for both Pragmatist and principle-guided political crisis management. The Lehman decision can therefore be analysed as a shift towards a more principle-guided form of political crisis management that was reversed again with the bailout of AIG and the money market funds.

As explained in the Introduction, the main research objective of this study has been to build a model of Pragmatist crisis management and to demonstrate how this model can be used in empirical research. Contrasting this Pragmatist model with a principle-guided crisis management model, we specified both models and used them to analyse two decision points during the US financial crisis. This analysis has found evidence for both models and identified shifts between them as well as hybrid forms that combined them both. Since part of the research objective is to demonstrate how this model can be used in empirical research, this chapter will pave the way for future empirical research by briefly introducing and discussing two questions:

1. What were the *causes* of the shift from a Pragmatist approach in the Bear Stearns case to a more principle-guided approach in the Lehman case followed by the shift back to Pragmatism in the AIG decision? This chapter will discuss several potential reasons and formulate hypotheses that offer answers to this question.
2. How were elements of both Pragmatist and principle-guided political crisis management *combined* in the Lehman case? By analysing this question, we will reconsider the general relation between Pragmatism and strict principles and briefly examine the role of hybrid forms of Pragmatist and principle-guided political crisis management.

It is important to note that given that this study is primarily a plausibility probe for identifying a Pragmatist model, no definite answers can be provided for these questions. However, addressing them can help us articulate hypotheses that may serve as starting points for future research projects. After all, hypothesis generation is one of the core strengths of case study research (see George and Bennett 2005, 20; Blatter 2008, 68).

EXPLAINING SHIFTS BETWEEN PRAGMATIST AND PRINCIPLE-GUIDED CRISIS MANAGEMENT

The last chapter left us with the following puzzle: Why did the Bush Administration—while believing in free-market principles—bail out the private investment bank Bear Stearns in March 2008? And why did the same governmental actors let Lehman Brothers fail in September 2008 while rescuing the insurance company AIG only two days later? Tables 8.1 and 8.2 summarize the identified specifications of our models for both cases.

Some have perceived this shift as mere political inconsistency (Krugman 2008; Acharya et al. 2009, 126; Blinder 2013, ch. 5), but the conceptual framework developed for this study offers a novel perspective on this shift. The perceived inconsistency between the decision regarding Bear Stearns, AIG and the money funds, on the one hand, and the Lehman decision, on the other, can be understood as a shift between Pragmatist and principle-guided political crisis management. From this perspective, the decision to let Lehman fail represented an attempt to implement a more principle-guided form of political crisis management, an attempt abandoned with the decisions to save AIG and the money funds only a few days later.

So far we have not systematically dealt with the possible *reasons* for this shift. In other words, if we understand the differences of the three decisions (Bear Stearns and AIG, on the one hand, and Lehman, on the other) as differences between Pragmatist and principle-guided political crisis management, we should take a step back and ask what caused these shifts. We offer some preliminary thoughts here on how to explain what Geithner called the "zig and the zag" of their decision making (2014, 194).

One hypothesis offered by many commentators to explain these shifts is that political pressure and public opinion drove Bush Administration decisions. While this hypothesis appears highly plausible for explaining the shift to the principle-guided approach of the Lehman decision, we argue it is less likely to explain the Pragmatism of the Bear Stearns and AIG decision. In other words, this explanation accounts for the shift from *Pragmatist* to *principle-guided political crisis management* in our cases. But what explains the shift in the other direction, from a *principle-guided* to a *Pragmatist* approach?

We offer four hypotheses for this shift that might be considered in future research. Before introducing them, it is useful to offer a few remarks on how we formulated them. These hypotheses are abductive inferences derived from

Table 8.1   *Overview of decision making in the Bear Stearns and Lehman cases*

Pragmatist Political Crisis Management			Principle-Guided Political Crisis Management	
DECISION MAKING			DECISION MAKING	
Anti-Dualism			*Dualism*	
Actively searching for third options and ways	B	L	Decisions are framed in either-or terms	
to transcend dilemmas	B		(dilemmas)	
Avoiding self-imposed commitments				
Fallibilism			*Infallibalism*	
Readiness to change existing beliefs and	B, L	L	Sticking to existing beliefs and decisions	
decisions	B, L		No expectance of failure, no backup plans	
Avoidance of unrevisable decisions	B			
Acceptance of possible failure and unexpected				
consequences				
Experimentalism			*"One best way"*	
Recombination of existing tools	L	L	Decisions derived from "objective	
Decisions as hypotheses and trials	B		evidence	
Constant feedback monitoring	B		Decisions from existing cases applied	
			unaltered	
Deliberation			*Dictation*	
Decisions based on internal deliberation	B, L		Decisions based on a priori principles	
Deliberation with external stakeholders			without deliberation	
Encouragement of skeptics		L	Exclusion of skeptics	

Note: B = Bear Stearns, L = Lehman Brothers.

inductive insights drawn from the cases themselves. In developing them, we follow Karl Popper's advice to formulate "bold hypotheses" (Popper 2002). As such, these hypotheses make bold generalized claims that can serve as starting points for future research projects that may falsify and modify them. This is especially true for hypotheses 1, 2 and 3. We do not see any a priori reason why political pressure should always push towards principles, while bureaucratic or technocratic decision making necessarily pushes towards Pragmatism. Yet, these cases point towards that inference. The claims of the hypotheses find additional support in the literature on crisis management.

Hypothesis to explain the shift from Pragmatism to principle-guided management:

H1: A high level of political pressure (e.g., election season) leads to principle-guided political crisis management.

Table 8.2   *Overview of meaning making in the Bear Stearns and Lehman cases*

Pragmatist Political Crisis Management			Principle-Guided Political Crisis Management	
MEANING MAKING			MEANING MAKING	
Anti-Dualism			*Dualism*	
Nuanced depiction of events; no dichotomies	**B, L**	**L**	Usage of black-and-white dualisms	
Fallibilism			*Infallibalism*	
Communication of uncertainty, possible failures	**B, L**	**B, L**	Communication of certainty	
Experimentalism			*"One best way"*	
Framed as experimentalist crisis management		**L**	Framed as unambiguous and	
Trying out frames, frame reversal	**L**	**B**	"evidence-based" Sticking to frames	
Deliberation			*Dictation*	
Openness to public debate and inquiry			Prevention of public debate and inquiry	

Notes: B = Bear Stearns, L = Lehman Brothers.

Hypotheses to explain the shift from principle-guided to Pragmatist management:

H2: A low level of political pressure (e.g., "lame duck") leads to Pragmatist political crisis management.
H3: Administrative actors push for Pragmatist political crisis management.
H4: A higher level of uncertainty leads to Pragmatist political crisis management.
H5: Time pressure leads to Pragmatist political crisis management.

Hypothesis 1: A high level of political pressure leads to principle-guided political crisis management.

Hypothesis 1 is a prevalent hypothesis in the literature on the Lehman decision (see Sorkin 2009, 339; Stewart 2009; Wessel 2009, 14; Blinder 2013, 123; Ball 2016) and it has been taken up in the empirical chapters already. In the context of our case studies, the hypothesis postulates that the decision to let Lehman fail was caused by increasing political pressure and the negative public opinion towards public bailouts. In this scenario, increasing political pressure disabled the Pragmatism of the earlier Bear Stearns decision and facilitated a principle-guided approach. If we look at the empirical evidence for this hypothesis—as the following paragraphs will do—we find that the hypothesis can very well account for the Lehman decision but falls short when it comes to explaining the AIG decision.

Political pressure opposing governmental "bailouts" increased after Bear Stearns was rescued in March and was reinforced only a week before the Lehman decision when the government placed Fannie Mae and Freddie Mac under conservatorship. Treasury Secretary Paulson was heavily criticized, particularly by Conservatives (Stewart 2009; Wessel 2009, 14). Republican Kentucky Senator Jim Bunning stated that Paulson "is acting like the minister of finance in China" (Benjamin 2008) and the conservative Heritage Foundation spoke of "signs of creeping socialism in today's America" (Istook 2008). Both presidential candidates, Senators Obama and McCain, spoke out against any further rescues (Geithner 2014, 175) and Republican candidates John McCain and Sarah Palin promised in a commentary for the *Wall Street Journal* that they would "protect taxpayer from more bailouts" (McCain and Palin 2008). When Henry Paulson met with leading members of Congress on September 11, 2008, they too made it clear that they opposed a bailout of Lehman Brothers (Paulson 2010, 183). As Ben Bernanke noted, "popular, political, and media views were hardening against the idea of the Fed and the Treasury taking extraordinary measures to prevent the firm's failure" (Bernanke 2015, 260).

Wessel points out that Paulson and Bernanke reacted to this political pressure by becoming increasingly reluctant to support a Lehman purchase with public money (Wessel 2009, 20–1). Andrew Ross Sorkin has found that "it seems undeniable that the fear of a public outcry over another Wall Street rescue was at least a factor in how he [Paulson] approached Lehman's dilemma" (Sorkin 2009, 339). This account is supported by Timothy Geithner who, when Paulson began to repeat his strong opposition to another bailout,

> began to worry that he actually meant it … I could hear the influence of his political advisers, who had been trying to steer Hank [Paulson] away from supporting any Fed role, urging him not to let me talk him into another Bear. (Geithner 2014, 179)

Geithner also noted a similar development for Bernanke (Geithner 2014, 180). Inside the Treasury, on September 9, Jim Wilkinson, Paulson's chief of staff, worried in an internal email to Michele Davis, the Assistant Secretary for Public Affairs: "I just can't stomach us bailing out Lehman … Will be horrible in the press don't u think?" (Financial Crisis Inquiry Commission 2011, 330). And the *Wall Street Journal* quoted a person involved in the internal discussions with the remark: "We've re-established 'moral hazard'" (Solomon et al. 2008).

After Lehman had to file for bankruptcy the decision to let Lehman fail was politically and publicly supported. Bush told Paulson he was pleased that this would send a strong signal that his administration did not support any further bailouts (Sorkin 2008, 226) and both presidential candidates, Barack Obama and John McCain, "supported the government's refusal to step in with a rescue deal" (Timiraos and Holmes 2008). The *Washington Post* issued an editorial, finding that "the U.S. government was right to let Lehman tank" (Washington Post 2008). Vincent Reinhart, from the conservative American Enterprise Institute, found that "this was the right time for the government to draw the line" (Reinhart 2008) and economics professor Jeremy Siegel predicted in the *Wall Street Journal* that "there is good evidence that the worst is over" (Siegel 2008).

The hypothesis that Lehman was cut loose because of political pressure also finds support in poll data. In the case of Bear Stearns, after examining the situation closely and under Timothy Geithner's influence, the Bush Administration decided to rescue the investment bank. Bush's approval rate fell by four points (Figure 8.1), but according to a survey conducted by Rasmussen Reports two-thirds of the American voters approved the bailout, with 30 percent thinking that the Federal Reserve Bank did an "excellent job" in handling the Bear Stearns situation while 37 percent said that it did a "fair job." Only 17 percent said that the Fed had handled the situation "poorly" (Rasmussen Reports 2008a). Yet, over time, skepticism grew and when Gallup polled Americans at the end of March 2008, 61 percent opposed governmental support for Wall Street investment companies (Gallup 2008) and over the course of the following months public and political opposition against further bailouts grew. Paulson (2010, 183), Bernanke (2015, 260) and Geithner (2014, 175) have noted that they felt this increasing political pressure after the rescue of Bear Stearns and Fannie Mae and Freddie Mac, especially from the conservative wing of the Republican Party (Sorkin 2009, 339; Stewart 2009; Wessel 2009, 14).

If we look at President Bush's approval rating over the course of 2008 (Figure 8.1) we notice not only the drop by four points after the decision to bail out Bear Stearns in March 2008. Bush's approval rate also fell by two points after the decision to bail out Fannie Mae and Freddie Mac announced on September 7. Parsing President Bush's approval rating along party lines reveals that the drop after the Bear Stearns decision can be attributed, in particular, to decreasing support among Republicans, which fell by five points. The drop after the Fannie Mae and Freddie Mac rescue was due to an eight-point drop among independents, while approval among Republicans remained constant.

For the Lehman decision, it is difficult to derive any insights from the approval ratings. We can observe a drop of four points between September 8–11 to

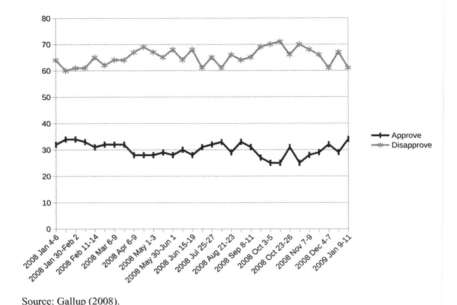

Source: Gallup (2008).

Figure 8.1   Approval rating of President Bush in 2008

September 26–27,[1] but it is difficult to determine what caused this drop since this timeframe covers the Lehman decision, the AIG decision and the beginnings of Congressional debates about the Troubled Asset Relief Program (TARP).[2] However, in a survey conducted briefly after Lehman's failure, 65 percent of Americans approved of the government's decision, stating that if "a large financial institution like Lehman Brothers is in financial trouble" it should file for bankruptcy; only 7 percent favored the usage of taxpayer funds (Rasmussen Reports 2008b). This indicates that a broad public majority probably supported the Bush Administration's decision to let Lehman fail.

This finding is further supported by surveys conducted in the second half of September that took into account the bailout of AIG and the plans for a com-

---

[1]   The polls for each observation point were conducted over several days.
[2]   This problem is even more pronounced in the presidential approval ratings compiled by Rasmussen, ABC/Washington Post, CNN, Fox News and NBC/Wall Street Journal, which are conducted on a monthly basis only. The Gallup poll used here is the most fine-grained survey, but even it does not permit a conclusion.

prehensive Congressional bailout package (TARP). In a poll from September 19–22, "the vast majority of Americans say the government is doing only a fair (44%) or poor (33%) job handling the problems on Wall Street" (Pew Research Center 2008). And a poll by Gallup from September 26–27 found that 68 percent of Americans disapproved of Bush's response to the financial crisis with only 28 percent approving the response (Jones 2008).

Taken together, these findings indicate that a majority of the general public (especially Republicans) was highly skeptical about governmental bailouts.[3] While the approval for Bush increased modestly among Democrats in September (from three to five points), it significantly decreased among Republicans, from 71 percent on September 8–11 to 55 percent on October 3–5 (Lehman declared bankruptcy on September 15; the Fed loaned AIG $85 billion on September 16; authority for TARP was passed October 3). This opposition among Republicans towards public bailouts (as exemplified by AIG and TARP) was also present in the political pressure that was predominantly exerted by (conservative) Republican members of Congress (Sorkin 2009, 339; Stewart 2009).

The hypothesis therefore offers a relevant explanation for the principled shift of the Lehman decision. By pointing out how political pressure against another bailout grew, it finds evidence in survey data, the Financial Crisis Inquiry Report (Financial Crisis Inquiry Commission 2011, ch. 19) and the personal accounts of the involved actors (Paulson 2010, 183; Geithner 2014, 175; Bernanke 2015, 260). The political stakes were further accentuated by the upcoming presidential and Congressional elections.

But it is hard to see how this hypothesis can account for the shift that took place in the other direction, from a principle-guided approach to a Pragmatist one. This is true for the initial decision to bail out Bear Stearns despite strong free-market sentiments among the decision makers. But it is also true for the shift back to a Pragmatist form of political crisis management with the AIG decision. As has been discussed above, the direction of political and public pressure did not change during this time. The Lehman decision was met by broad approval and the majority of the general public (as well as both presidential candidates) was still critical about any further bailouts (Benjamin 2008; McCain and Palin 2008; Wessel 2009, 14; Geithner 2014, 175). To summarize, while the hypothesis can account for the shift to a principle-guided political crisis management with the Lehman decision, it does little to explain the Pragmatist approach to the Bear Stearns and AIG decision. The following hypotheses try to explain this lacuna by drawing on the findings of the two

---

[3] For a long-term perspective on public opinion and government interventions, see Kenworthy and Owens (2011).

case studies and by suggesting alternative explanations that might be explored in future research.

Future research

Hypothesis 1 offers an explanation for the shift from Pragmatist to principle-guided political crisis management. By pointing to the fact that political and public pressure can make Pragmatist political crisis management difficult to pursue, this hypothesis offers an idea that is worth examining in future research. The hypothesis has been explored already for Pragmatist experimentalism, departing from Campbell's early insight about the "political vulnerability" of experimentalism (Campbell 1969, 409). Recent studies have supported Campbell's claim and have highlighted the political challenges to Pragmatist experimentalism (Ansell and Bartenberger 2016b; Bartenberger and Sześciło 2016).

Hypothesis 2: A low level of political pressure leads to Pragmatist political crisis management.

It is a well-established finding in the literature on the American presidency that the last phase of a presidential term bears a special character. Presidents in this phase are described as "lame ducks"; they lack political power and influence while at the same time they are being freed from the pressure of reelection, thereby increasing their political options (see Hedtke 2002; Shafie 2013; Franklin 2014). In the context of our study, this second aspect is important. As journalist Peter Baker has described the role of President Bush during the financial crisis:

> ... Bush recognized that he was in a better position to confront the catastrophe than his successor would be. He understood by now the levers of government and, moreover, could do what was necessary without worrying about political fallout. (Baker 2013, 609)

In the same key, Norman Ornstein has written: "It is also clear that Bush has agreed to make a few difficult or unpopular decisions on his way out so as not to burden Obama with them ..." (Ornstein 2009).

Many commentators, however, have pointed in the opposite direction, emphasizing Bush's weak position in the final months of his presidency, especially after Republicans in Congress had voted against his TARP bill (Walsh 2008). Morgan described how the "lame-duck status limited Bush's influence as party leader" (Morgan 2010, 199) and, in October 2008, Mooney noted the "diminished role" President Bush played in the financial crisis (Mooney 2008).

The hypothesis is also countered by the fact that the year 2008 was shaped by the presidential race between Barack Obama and John McCain. While there was no electoral pressure on President Bush personally, his decisions still affected the Republican Party and its candidates. As media analyses have shown, media coverage of the presidential race became increasingly shaped by the financial crisis in September 2008 (Jurkowitz 2008), leading to a more negative tone towards the McCain campaign in the media (Holcomb 2013). For the Bush Administration, political pressure was therefore not completely disabled but had shifted to the candidates for the presidential and Congressional elections.

Hypothesis 2 can be regarded as the logical complement of hypothesis 1. Whereas hypothesis 1 argues that political pressure will lead to principle-guided political crisis management, hypothesis 2 claims that the absence of political pressure will lead to Pragmatist political crisis management. Taken together, the two hypotheses allow us to analyse the relation of political pressure and Pragmatist/principle-guided political crisis management from both directions.

Future research
Hypothesis 2 has been chiefly developed in the context of the Congressional bailout bill and the bailout of the automobile industry (see Cassidy 2012). It remains unclear if it applies to the AIG decision as well. As the preceding section has shown, political pressure did not change in the time between the Lehman and AIG decision. We find no evidence that the internal perception of political pressure inside the Bush Administration changed in this time period. Perhaps future research can help to clarify these issues.

Even if the finding is that a higher level of political pressure will lead to principle-guided political crisis management and a lower level will lead to Pragmatism, future research should remain open to exploring this connection further. While the literature on political crisis management has found that established principles and values might be reinforced during crises (Boin and 't Hart 2003, 549), we see no strict a priori reason why political pressure should always push towards principles and away from Pragmatism. But as mentioned in the introduction to this section, this hypothesis (as well as the others) should be understood as "bold hypotheses"—in the sense advanced by Karl Popper—that might be qualified or falsified by future research.

Hypothesis 3: Administrative actors push for Pragmatist political crisis management.

"The field of administration is a field of business. It is removed from the hurry and strife of politics ..." (Wilson 1887, 209). In his article "The study of administration," from which this quote is taken, Woodrow Wilson established what later became known as the *politics-administration dichotomy*. This dichotomy suggests that bureaucracy deals with the organization of the state's business and focuses more on "technical" questions, which are isolated from political considerations and partisan politics (see DeLeon 2005; Kane and Patapan 2009). Hypothesis 3 picks up on this idea and suggests that the main agents behind Pragmatist political crisis management are *administrative* rather than political actors, that is, decision makers and leaders in public agencies. Hypothesis 3 thereby offers a possible refinement to hypothesis 1, which asserts that political pressure is one of the main influences driving the approach to political crisis management.

In the context of the cases, hypothesis 3 states that political pressure was reduced because the center of Bush Administration decision making throughout the financial crisis was not the White House but the US Treasury and the Federal Reserve Bank. We have already discussed how the main actors who shaped the government's response were Treasury Secretary Henry Paulson and Ben Bernanke and Timothy Geithner from the Federal Reserve Bank. In an interview in December 2008, Paulson emphasized that President Bush never overruled one of his decisions and that Bush understood "that when you're dealing with something as unprecedented and fast-moving as this we need to have a different operating style" (Becker et al. 2008). This "different operating style" included Bush's guarantee to Paulson "that Treasury, not the White House, would have the dominant role in shaping economic policy" (Becker et al. 2008). Republican strategist Rich Galen has suggested that Bush put Paulson in charge to depoliticize the crisis response, noting: "It takes the politics essentially out of it" (Raum 2008).

The empirical analysis of the Bear Stearns, Lehman Brothers and AIG decisions has shown how Paulson kept President Bush in the decision-making loop while demonstrating that Bush supported the strategy previously agreed upon by Paulson, Bernanke and Geithner. These decisions were strongly influenced by reports and analyses conducted by the bureaucracies of the Treasury and the Federal Reserve Bank that outlined scenarios and examined potential consequences on the financial markets (see Chapters 5 and 6).

The hypothesis states that the analyses that were drafted by the bureaucracies of the Treasury and the Federal Reserve Bank were close to Pragmatism's emphasis on practical consequences and problem-solving. However, with its conflicts between moral hazard hawks and interventionists, the Federal Reserve Bank was certainly not an ideology-free zone. As Mitchel Abolafia has noted, the Federal Reserve—while allowing space for an emphasis on consequences—was partly captured by the "dogma of efficient markets" (Abolafia 2012, 111, also see Abolafia 2010). Still, with decision making centered at the Fed and the Treasury, partisan political pressure was somewhat reduced and the logic of practical consequences and problem-solving played a stronger role.

Timothy Geithner was the actor who came closest to this more technocratic logic of efficacy and problem-solving. Geithner himself remarked that he was glad to be removed from the political pressure that Paulson as Treasury Secretary and Bernanke as Fed Chairman had to deal with to a greater degree (Geithner 2014, 194). Paulson and Bernanke had to explain their decisions in Congressional hearings (US Congress 2008a, 2008b, 2008c) while Geithner could work in the background. In the Lehman case, Paulson and Bernanke responded to the increasing political pressure and favored a principle-guided approach while Geithner did not want to exclude a public solution (Wessel 2009, 20–1).

Future research
This hypothesis adds another layer to hypothesis 1 by stating that political pressure is reduced when administrative actors play a greater role compared to political actors (in our cases, a greater role for the more technically oriented US Treasury and the Federal Reserve Bank as opposed to the more partisan White House). A question this hypothesis raises that cannot be discussed at greater length is the question of where Pragmatism is located in government. In other words, why did the Bush Administration act pragmatically in certain situations (Bear Stearns, AIG) but not in others (Lehman)? Was it because different actors were involved in these decisions or did institutional settings play a role as well? Addressing this question might be a fruitful point of departure for future research.

Hypothesis 4: A higher level of uncertainty facilitates Pragmatist political crisis management.

As Chapter 2 discussed, the concept of uncertainty lies at the center of philosophical Pragmatism. In a nutshell, Pragmatism's approach to uncertainty is to shift our focus from strict principles to an inquiry into the *practical consequences* of action. This Pragmatist emphasis on consequences is encapsulated in the Pragmatist elements of anti-dualism, fallibilism, experimentalism and deliberation that have provided the foundations for our empirical analysis.

Hypothesis 4 takes up these Pragmatist insights and argues that what enabled Pragmatist decision making in the cases of Bear Stearns and AIG was the uncertainty of possible consequences, which pushed abstract principles into the background. For the Lehman decision, however, *perceived* uncertainty about potential consequences was lower, with government actors assuming that the markets were already prepared for the bankruptcy of the investment bank. This lower level of uncertainty in the Lehman decision arguably enabled a principle-guided approach to political crisis management.

By contrast, the troubles of Bear Stearns caught the Bush Administration by surprise and while the initial reaction was to let the investment bank fail, a Federal Reserve analysis of the potential consequences led to a change of mind (see Chapter 6). The uncertainty of the size of the threat, in particular, plus the question of whether the threat posed a risk to the systemic stability of financial markets, worried government actors (US Congress 2008c, 14).

A similar scenario played out in the case of AIG. As investment banker Michael Lewitt highlighted in the *New York Times*, AIG

> is a central player in the unregulated, Brobdingnagian credit default swap market that is reported to be at least $60 trillion in size. Nobody knows this market's real size, or who owes what to whom, because there is no central clearinghouse or regulator for it. (Lewitt 2008)

The high level of uncertainty surrounding AIG was further amplified by the global character of the firm and the already fragile condition of financial markets after the Lehman bankruptcy (Financial Crisis Inquiry Commission 2008f, 2008g). As Fox has noted: "The best case for the bailout seems to be that nobody has the faintest idea what the consequences of AIG's failure for financial markets would be, but the fear was that it could lead to total chaos" (Fox 2008). Fox also emphasized that the Federal Reserve Bank could not "afford to stand on principle" (Fox 2008), while Mann summarized the AIG decision as an emphasis on necessity: "The only rationale that could serve to explain the administration's policies was one of necessity: Bush set principles aside and did whatever he had to do to keep the economy afloat" (Mann 2015, 133). After AIG got bailed out, *The Economist* commented: "The prospect of letting such a large and interconnected institution fail was not a gamble the government was willing to take (especially while caught in the riptide of Lehman)" (The Economist 2009).

For the Lehman decision, the situation looked different. Since Lehman had moved to the focus of concern right after the Bear Stearns rescue, governmental actors assumed that the financial markets had had enough time to prepare for a Lehman bankruptcy (Hilsenrath et al. 2008; Labaton 2008; Swagel 2009, 40; Wessel 2009, 11). While Paulson, Bernanke and Geithner anticipated that a Lehman bankruptcy would cause turmoil on the financial markets, it seemed to be a risk that could be calculated and contained. As Lewitt put it: "Regulators knew that if Lehman went down, the world wouldn't end" (Lewitt 2008).

According to hypothesis 4, this different level of uncertainty was decisive when it comes to explaining these different decisions. While the uncertainty of potential consequences was high in the cases of Bear Stearns and AIG, uncertainty was regarded as lower and more controllable in the Lehman case. From the perspective of this hypothesis, a lower level of uncertainty facilitated principle-guided political crisis management while a higher level of uncertainty led to a Pragmatist approach. The reason for this seems to be found in the fact that a higher level of (perceived) uncertainty facilitates Pragmatist fallibilism, that is, the insight "that there is never a metaphysical guarantee to be had that such-and-such a belief will never need revision" (Putnam 1995, 152). Under crisis conditions that accentuate surprise, threat and uncertainty, fixed principles and beliefs are replaced by the fallibilist insight that these principles and beliefs might be flawed after all. Under such conditions, the hypothesis postulates, finding guidance in strict principles will give way to Pragmatist anti-dualism, fallibilism, experimentalism and deliberation.

Future research
Hypothesis 4 offers a fruitful perspective by highlighting the role of uncertainty and how it influences political crisis management. Uncertainty is not only an element of crises according to our definition, but it has also been identified as a key concept in Pragmatist thinking. Exploring the role of uncertainty in greater detail through additional research therefore seems promising. Connections with the work of Karl Weick on sensemaking (Weick 1993, 2006, 2015) and Charles Lindblom on incrementalism (Lindblom 1959, 1979), as well as with the literature on "bounded rationality" (Simon 1957; Kahneman 2003), might be valuable avenues for further exploration.

Hypothesis 5: A high level of time pressure facilitates Pragmatist political crisis management.

The hypothesis that under time pressure established principles are replaced by a Pragmatist approach has been described for financial crises by Henry B. Steagall, Chairman of the House Banking and Currency Committee, in 1932:

> Of course, [fixing the crisis] involves a departure from established policies and ideals, but we cannot stand by when a house is on fire to engage in lengthy debates over the methods to be employed in extinguishing the fire. In such a situation we instinctively seize upon and utilize whatever method is most available and offers assurance of speediest success. (quoted in Shiller 2008, 101)

Hypothesis 5 puts this assumption in a general form and thereby highlights another key element of crisis situations: urgency.[4]

Both cases where we witnessed a Pragmatist approach to political crisis management (Bear Stearns, AIG) included a high level of time pressure. As President Bush noted for the Bear Stearns case: "I was surprised by the sudden crisis ... I assumed any major credit troubles would have been flagged by the regulators or rating agencies" (Bush 2010, 453). Henry Paulson and Timothy Geithner learned about a possible bankruptcy when they were called by Bear Stearns' CEO Alan Schwartz on March 13 (Kelly 2009, 17; Paulson 2010, 93). The decision to temporarily save Bear Stearns was made the next morning and only two days later, on March 16, the final decision to rescue Bear Stearns was made. With Bear Stearns' cash reserves melting away quickly, the opening of the markets on Monday (with the Asian markets opening on Sunday night) was perceived as setting a hard deadline that mandated a quick decision. Figure 8.2 depicts this rapid drain of Bear Stearns' liquidity in a matter of days.

Bear Stearns Liquidity

In the four days before Bear Stearns collapsed, the company's liquidity dropped by $16 billion.

IN BILLIONS OF DOLLARS, DAILY

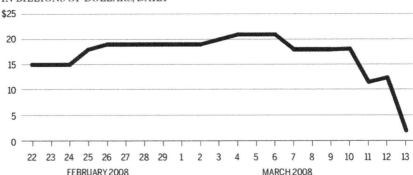

Source: Financial Inquiry Commission (2011, 289).

Figure 8.2   Liquidity level of Bear Stearns in March 2008

---

[4]   Gary Klein's (1998) research has found that firefighters and rapid response teams under time pressure act in a way that resembles Pragmatist behavior.

The situation was similar to the AIG circumstances. Treasury Secretary Paulson only learned about the severe troubles at AIG from private investor Christopher Flowers on Saturday, September 13, three days before the decision to rescue AIG was made (Sorkin 2009, 173; Paulson 2010, 200). When the financial markets opened on Monday, the rating agencies further downgraded AIG and the stock prices of the insurance company fell by 61 percent (Financial Crisis Inquiry Commission 2011, 349). As Figure 8.3 shows, this drop of stock prices—which was accompanied by increased margin calls from AIG's counterparties—happened over a couple of days, leaving governmental actors little time to make a decision. As Fox noted:

> unlike with Lehman—where the possibility of failure was openly discussed for months and to a certain extent planned for—federal officials and market participants don't seem to have really focused on AIG's problems until this week. (Fox 2008)

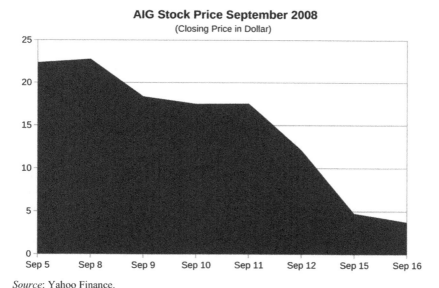

Source: Yahoo Finance.

Figure 8.3   *Stock price of AIG in September 2008*

The principle-guided Lehman decision, on the other hand, was anticipated for a longer period of time, with governmental actors contemplating the scenario of a possible Lehman bankruptcy since July 2008 (Financial Crisis Inquiry

Commission 2008e, 2010, 69). Different options and scenarios were internally discussed and a strategy developed that resembled the Bear Stearns case: in case of troubles find a buyer for Lehman or let Lehman go bankrupt. Although there was time pressure involved in the Lehman decision as well (with negotiations happening over the course of a weekend) government actors could rely on their prepared plans to a greater degree. According to hypothesis 5, this decreased sense of urgency (together with the assumption that the financial markets had enough time to prepare for a failure of Lehman) promoted a principle-guided approach to political crisis management.

Future research

One concern about the Pragmatist emphasis on deliberation might be that it is highly constrained by time, and thus is unlikely to occur in urgent situations. Although we have pointed out that deliberation is not about optimization and may be conducted on the fly, the degree to which urgency constrains Pragmatist deliberation is worth further analysis. For the cases analysed here we have found a high degree of internal deliberation but little evidence for external deliberation that went beyond consultation. Future research could explore hypothesis 5 in greater detail by analysing how (external) deliberation and the other elements of Pragmatism are affected by urgency (on crisis deliberation, see Boin and Nieuwenburg 2013).

INTERSECTIONS AND COMBINATIONS OF PRAGMATIST AND PRINCIPLE-GUIDED POLITICAL CRISIS MANAGEMENT

By describing the shifts between Pragmatist and principle-guided political crisis management during the US financial crisis in 2008, we do not intend to imply that these two approaches to political crisis management are necessarily strictly separated.[5] In designing the model of Pragmatist and principle-guided political crisis management we have noted that they should be understood as ideal-typical in the Weberian sense. As such they mark the two poles of a continuous scale (as illustrated in Figure 4.1). In empirical research, we should also expect to find hybrid forms that combine elements of both models.

This section briefly discusses instances where combinations and intersections of Pragmatist and principle-guided political crisis management were

---

[5]   In this sense the tables that summarize the empirical results should also not be interpreted as depicting dualist on-off dichotomies. They instead try to summarize important findings and provide a rough overview of where evidence can be found for certain model specifications.

found in our empirical analysis. In these instances, the boundaries between the models seem to be unclear or dependent on which perspective we apply. Examining these instances can clarify and refine the relation of Pragmatist and principle-guided political crisis management.

The Shifts Between Pragmatist and Principle-Guided Political Crisis Management: A Case of Meta-Pragmatism?

The empirical analysis in Chapters 6 and 7 has found a shift between Pragmatist and principle-guided political crisis management in the Bush Administration's response to the financial crisis. After the Pragmatist bailout of Bear Stearns, the Bush Administration shifted to a more principle-guided approach with the Lehman decision, before shifting back to Pragmatist political crisis management with the AIG decision a few days later. From a meta-perspective, these shifts might themselves be interpreted as Pragmatist behavior. Did the Bush Administration simply choose whatever form of political crisis management worked under the changing circumstances? After political pressure had increased with the bailouts of Bear Stearns and Fannie Mae and Freddie Mac, was the shift towards principle-guided political crisis management just a Pragmatist adaptation that reacted flexibly and experimentally to external feedback? These are thorny questions but we would argue that while these shifts might be understood as experimentalist, they do not qualify as Pragmatism in the sense that we have described it.

In general, these questions take us back to the initial discussions about the differences of philosophical Pragmatism and "everyday" pragmatism. In setting out to develop a substantiated understanding of Pragmatism, we noted that the term encapsulates two meanings. On the one hand, it is a term that is used in our everyday language to refer to a "practical" approach to problems that is undogmatic, concentrates on "what works"—a meaning that borders on opportunism (see Merriam Webster n.d.). On the other hand, Pragmatism refers to a distinct philosophical tradition that was founded by American philosophers such as Charles Peirce, William James and John Dewey and that refers to the model of practical rationality we set out in Chapter 2. These meanings are not necessarily antithetical, but they differ in important ways.[6]

The everyday meaning of pragmatism refers to a simplified version of philosophical Pragmatism, one that encapsulates some of its ideas but does not include its whole depth and breadth. Emphasizing practical aspects

---

6   From a Hegelian perspective one might speak of an example of "Aufhebung" in this context where the meaning of philosophical Pragmatism is both preserved and at the same time abolished in the everyday meaning of the term.

and "whatever works" while being skeptical about dogmatic principles—as everyday pragmatism does—is one aspect of philosophical Pragmatism, an aspect highlighted by Hilary Putnam and Nicholas Rescher as the "primacy of practice." But Pragmatism, as a philosophical perspective, offers much more than this. With the concepts of anti-dualism, fallibilism, experimentalism and deliberation (not to mention the richer account of practical rationality set out in Chapter 2), philosophical Pragmatism offers ideas that specify what it means to focus on practice and consequences. These elements go beyond a "whatever works" practicality and offer richer accounts of how to explore the question of "what works."

If Pragmatism is understood in terms of "readiness to change existing beliefs and decisions" (fallibilism), the shift to principle-guided decision making in the Lehman case was *not* an example of Pragmatism since the existing beliefs and decisions of the Bush Administration were based on the moral hazard doctrine which stated that troubled private companies should not be bailed out by governments. The Bear Stearns decision partially set aside this doctrine and therefore qualifies as an example of fallibilism. With the Lehman decision, however, the Bush Administration returned to their initial beliefs and did not overrule them again. According to our framework the shift towards principle-guided political crisis management was therefore *not* fallibilist.

Yet the shifts between Pragmatist and principle-guided political crisis management do qualify as Pragmatist experimentalism according to our specification, *decisions as hypotheses and trials*. Reacting to the feedback (i.e., political pressure) after the bailouts of Bear Stearns and Fannie Mae and Freddie Mac, the Bush Administration switched to a principle-guided approach that emphasized a "no more bailouts" position. With the AIG decision, however, this course was again adapted and a shift back to Pragmatist political crisis management followed. The hypotheses in the previous section have discussed possible reasons for this shift.

A similar example for such meta-experimentalism that shifted from Pragmatism to a principle-guided approach has been identified in the framing of the Lehman decision. We have identified a frame revision in this case with government actors shifting from an explanation that emphasized the nuanced differences of the decisions to a strict legalism. This legalist meaning making invoked section 13(3) of the Federal Reserve Act as an unambiguous constraint that strictly excluded the possibility of a Lehman rescue. While this shift was a shift away from Pragmatism towards principle-guided political crisis management, the shift itself might be described as experimentalism according to the specification, *trying out of frames, frame revision*.

From a meta-perspective, the shifts of the Bear Stearns, Lehman and AIG decisions can be understood in a similar way. Analysing decision making and meaning making from a micro-perspective, as Chapter 7 has done, the

Lehman decision qualifies as principle-guided political crisis management. But from a meta-perspective the shift towards this principle-guided political crisis management can be analysed as Pragmatist experimentalism. A similar example of such ambiguity can also be found on the micro level, as the next section will show.

Future research
The importance of the different levels of analysis could be taken up by future research. The question that might guide this future research is the following: How does our characterization of Pragmatist and principle-guided political crisis management change if we change our level of analysis? Do we find further instances where we can speak of principle-guided political crisis management on the micro level but can find elements of Pragmatism on the meta level? Such an analysis would need to include additional theoretical research as well, further refining our understanding of the exact relation between Pragmatism and principles and between everyday pragmatism and philosophical Pragmatism.

Excluding Moral Hazard Skeptics to Enable Pragmatism?

Our analysis has examined the deliberations during the Lehman and AIG decisions and noted that Sheila Bair, Chairman of the US Federal Deposit Insurance Corporation (FDIC), was systematically excluded from decision making because of her insistence on moral hazard principles. Bair opposed the rescue of Bear Stearns and advocated for a stricter policy towards AIG (Bair 2012, 98). From the perspective of our model this exclusion of Bair qualifies as principle-guided political crisis management according to the specification, *exclusion of skeptics*. Yet, excluding moral hazard hawks like Bair from the decision-making processes might have facilitated the Pragmatist decisions to bail out Bear Stearns and AIG, since Bair opposed both decisions and argued against them.

This issue poses a thorny question about the relation between Pragmatist and principle-guided political crisis management: Can we still speak of Pragmatist decision making when the way these decisions were reached included elements contradicting the main pillars of Pragmatist thinking, such as the exclusion of skeptics? In a dispute with Leon Trotsky, John Dewey argued that means and ends are closely connected and that ends "*can be attained only by means that accord with those ends*" (Dewey 1987, 298, original emphasis). This refers to Pragmatism in its ideal-typical form. But as this study has argued, Pragmatist and principle-guided political crisis management should be understood as opposing poles of a continuous scale. The space between the poles is populated by gray areas and hybrid combinations of both ideal types.

We argue that the exclusion of Sheila Bair from the decision-making process is an instance of a hybrid form that combines both Pragmatism and principle-guided political crisis management. More specifically, the exclusion of Bair is an example of Pragmatist behavior being facilitated by principle-guided means, that is, the exclusion of actors that opposed a Pragmatist approach. Focusing on these intersections and combinations of Pragmatist and principle-guided political crisis management, it is important to highlight the fact that it is not an either-or question where crisis responses can be strictly schematized as either Pragmatist or principle-guided. Depending on our level of analysis, we can find instances and cases where Pragmatist and principle-guided elements are closely intertwined. Nevertheless, the models still have value because they make it possible to analytically identify these different elements and analyse how they relate and combine.

Future research
Future research could focus on these combinations of Pragmatist and principle-guided political crisis management, and especially on instances where the borders between the two approaches appear blurry. The means and ends debate that draws on Dewey's arguments could serve as a starting point for this, posing the question: Are Pragmatist ends in political crisis management (i.e., crisis responses and policies) achieved through a *process* of Pragmatist means or can we also find examples where principle-guided means are used for Pragmatist ends and vice versa?

CONCLUSION

This chapter has discussed some of the main findings of the empirical analysis and has suggested some opportunities for future research. We have taken a step back to explore what causes political leaders to adopt either a Pragmatist or principle-guided approach to political crisis management and have examined intersections and combinations of both approaches.

In the first part of this chapter, we introduced several hypotheses to explain the potential causes of shifts between Pragmatist and principle-guided political crisis management. Political pressure has been identified as one hypothesis for explaining the shift towards a principled approach in the Lehman decision. Yet, this hypothesis was found to be insufficient for explaining the shifts towards Pragmatist political crisis management. Hypothesis 2 and 3 added additional perspectives on this hypothesis by stating that political pressure was reduced by the "lame duck" status of the Bush Administration and by the fact that the centers of decision making were not located at the White House but in the Treasury and the Federal Reserve Bank. Hypotheses 4 and 5 emphasized the role that uncertainty and urgency may have played in the shifts between the two approaches to political crisis management.

The second part of this chapter has further examined the relation of Pragmatist and principle-guided political crisis management by discussing two examples. The first example has found that the characterization of Pragmatist and principle-guided political crisis management also depends on the level of analysis. From a meta-perspective, the shift towards principle-guided political crisis management can be understood as Pragmatist experimentalism. The second example has recounted a case where the principle-guided exclusion of skeptics might have facilitated Pragmatist decision making.

Taken together, these findings pose challenges for future research to explore (1) the causes of the two different approaches to political crisis management and (2) how these approaches are combined in practice and how different levels of analysis change our understanding of the two approaches. The concluding chapter of this study will discuss another possible future research objective: identifying empirical indicators for Pragmatist and principle-guided political crisis management.

9. Conclusion: the practical rationality of crisis leadership

The Pragmatist philosopher and psychologist William James was visiting Stanford University in 1906 when the infamous San Francisco earthquake struck. Eight days later, James visited San Francisco and marveled at:

> the rapidity of the improvisation of order out of chaos. It is clear that just as in every thousand human beings there will be statistically so many artists, so many athletes, so many thinkers, and so many potentially good soldiers, so there will be so many potential organizers in times of emergency. In point of fact, not only in the great city, but in the outlying towns, these natural ordermakers, whether amateurs or officials, came to the front immediately. (James 1911, 221–2)

Successful public governance of crises requires leaders who can manage the uncertainty, the urgency and the threat entailed by crisis conditions—to improvise order out of chaos. To do so, James argues, is a skill, a talent. Yet James also notes that this skill lies "latent in human nature" (James 1911, 223). Great crisis leaders may be a special breed, but this book has argued they can learn much from ordinary practical rationality—that is, if they appreciate its hidden resources.

This study began by describing Pragmatism's model of practical rationality and has ended with an empirical analysis of two of the most important decision points in the US financial crisis of 2008. The general aspiration of this journey was to develop a model of Pragmatist political crisis management that builds on the hidden resources revealed by Pragmatism's rich interpretation of practical rationality—resources such as anti-dualism, fallibilism, experimentalism and deliberation. In this concluding chapter we briefly assess the outcomes of this study, reflect on its limitations and discuss elements of a possible future research agenda.

This study has tried to bring together philosophical Pragmatism and studies of political crisis management. This agenda was constructed around the idea that Pragmatism's emphasis on uncertainty might offer insights for a theory of effective crisis management. Towards that end, we have traced the role of uncertainty in Pragmatist thinking and contrasted an account of Pragmatist and principle-guided political crisis management. A key point of this contrast is that Pragmatism firmly rejects relying on strict and fixed principles and opposes a principle-guided "quest for certainty" (Dewey 1990). Pragmatism does not try to overcome or eradicate uncertainty but rather cautions us that uncertainty is a part of the human condition that can never be fully overcome. This is not an insight that leaves Pragmatists in a sense of despair or nihilistic relativism. Instead, Pragmatism offers us tools and approaches that allow us to live and act under such conditions of uncertainty—to create order out of chaos. Pragmatism can be therefore understood as a "meliorist" philosophy asserting that we can always improve our situation, even under critical or tragic circumstances (Hook 2002; Glaude 2004).

In a nutshell, this meliorism and the ability to enable "successful action under conditions of uncertainty" (Joas 2000, 39) constitute the promise that Pragmatism makes to political crisis managers. This study has identified four core elements that specify what a Pragmatist approach to political crisis management might look like: anti-dualism, fallibilism, experimentalism and deliberation. Defining Pragmatism with the help of these four core elements has provided this study with a solid theoretical foundation and a fairly precise understanding of Pragmatism. Yet, this schematic approach to Pragmatism also came at a price. Each of these four elements could easily merit a book-length treatment. Anti-dualism, fallibilism, experimentalism and deliberation are complex concepts and it is almost impossible to do them justice in a single study.

Our broader but more schematic approach does have the advantage of keeping the full panoply of Pragmatist ideas in view. These ideas are not as rich as those set out in our discussion of practical rationality in Chapter 2, but they are more empirically tractable. The empirical chapters have provided first probes of the plausibility of these ideas. By looking at cases of political crisis management through the lenses of Pragmatist and principle-guided political crisis management, we gain a novel and fruitful perspective. The following section briefly assesses the analytical and practical value of the model of Pragmatist political crisis management.

THE ANALYTICAL AND PRACTICAL VALUE OF THE MODEL

We can evaluate the usefulness of the model developed by this study along two dimensions: an analytical and a practical one. The analytical dimension poses the question: Does the model of Pragmatist political crisis management help to understand what leaders did during the financial crisis? The practical dimension focuses on the question: Can a Pragmatist approach towards crisis management be useful for decision makers and crisis managers in practice? We discuss each of these two questions in turn.

Analytical Value

Hopefully, the empirical analysis in Chapters 6 and 7 demonstrated to readers that the Pragmatism model provides a novel and fruitful perspective on the Bush Administration's handling of the financial crisis of 2008. From the perspective advanced by this study, the bailing out of Bear Stearns and the bankruptcy of Lehman Brothers was not mere political inconsistency, as other observers have charged (Krugman 2008; Acharya et al. 2009, 126; Blinder 2013, ch. 5), but can be traced back to two different modes of political crisis management—Pragmatist and principle-guided. In our examples, these two different modes of political crisis management were based on different understandings of the crisis at hand.

For the Bear Stearns case, the Pragmatist model has shown how the Bush Administration overcame its established principles of free-market ideology and moral hazard. Instead, the analysis of the expected consequences of Bear Stearns' bankruptcy drove the decision to rescue the firm. The Bush Administration's response occurred in the context of a high level of uncertainty concerning the importance of Bear Stearns for the stability of the entire financial system. Worrying that Bear Stearns might be too big (and too intertwined) to fail and fearing the negative consequences for the global economy, the Bush Administration decided to rescue the investment firm.

The case was different with Lehman Brothers. When confronted with the troubles at Lehman, the Bush Administration was relatively certain that the financial system was prepared for the bankruptcy of the investment bank. This decreased level of uncertainty allowed for a shift back to a more principle-guided approach that was meant to send a strong message that the Bush Administration had returned to its free-market principles. But with the decisions to save the insurance company AIG and the money market funds immediately after Lehman failed, the Bush Administration returned to a more Pragmatist approach.

The analytical value of our two models is that they reveal how (perceived) uncertainty has led to different forms of political crisis management and they demonstrate that Pragmatist and principle-guided action both shape crisis response. The study has illuminated the different kinds of "rationality" that can guide political crisis management and has set out a broad set of building blocks and specifications that might serve as starting points for additional research.

While this study has helped to gain a deeper understanding of what happened in the Bush Administration during the crisis, it could not fully explore the reasons why Pragmatist political crisis management was favored at certain times and principle-guided political crisis management at others. Chapter 8, however, has offered a set of hypotheses that might guide future research.

Practical Value

It is difficult to evaluate the practical value of Pragmatist political crisis management for decision makers and crisis managers. In the Introduction, we noted that other authors have (implicitly) described Pragmatist modes of crisis management on the operational level—notably, Karl Weick, Gary Klein and high reliability researchers. Operational crisis managers may thus recognize their own behavior in our Pragmatist crisis management model. For them the main value of the model lies in the systematic portrayal of the Pragmatist approach. Our systematic elaboration of the Pragmatist approach might also provide an important counterweight to the prevalent rationalism in the practical literature on crisis management (see Harvard Business School 2004).

But what is the value of this study for *political* crisis managers? While we highlight that practical rationality may illuminate hidden decision-making and meaning-making resources, we also acknowledge that a Pragmatist approach might be difficult for political crisis managers. While handling a crisis, political crisis managers cannot solely concentrate on practical consequences and functional problem-solving. Political crisis managers must keep the symbolic dimension of politics in mind (Edelman 1985; 't Hart 2008) and think about the political dimensions of a crisis and its public perception as well.

For a Pragmatist approach to political crisis management, the difficulties lie especially in the area of meaning making. Publicly admitting possible failures, emphasizing the uncertainty of decisions and inviting public debate and critique can be an extremely challenging task for political leaders. Depending on political culture, Pragmatist meaning making can lead to significant political costs for public leaders.

Despite these difficulties, a Pragmatist approach might be valuable for political crisis managers when confronted with two forms of crisis: crises that involve a high level of uncertainty and crises that strongly challenge established values. As defined in Chapter 1, all crises involve some degree of uncertainty and a threat to established values. But a Pragmatist approach to crises might be particularly valuable to political crisis managers as the level of uncertainty and the threat to established values increases. As Pragmatists would argue, the uncertainty of a crisis often disables the capacity for comprehensive rational analysis. During such crises, the applicability of strict principles and fixed dogmas also becomes more uncertain, leaving a Pragmatist approach as a valuable alternative for responding to the crisis.

Crises that strongly challenge established values might make it impossible for governments to draw on these values and principles in order to respond to the crisis. When the Fukushima catastrophe challenged the established principle that nuclear energy was necessary for a prospering economy in Germany, the crisis made it impossible for the conservative German government to draw on this principle in order to respond to the crisis. Instead, in a surprising and pragmatic move, the German government drafted and passed a bill to ban nuclear energy from Germany in the near future (Wittneben 2012).

In the end, the practical usefulness of the Pragmatist political crisis management model also depends on the personal character of crisis managers. That is, whether you think the Pragmatist crisis management model has practical value depends on your ontological and epistemological position (see Marsh and Furlong 2010). A crisis manager who holds the position that it is possible to identify fixed laws and principles that provide the definitive answers to decisions will reject the value of a Pragmatist approach towards crisis management. On the other hand, a crisis manager who holds the position that answers to decisions can only be found through an open and probing search and that all our beliefs remain fallible will be more open to a Pragmatist approach and willing to employ it in practice.

To sum up, the value of the model of Pragmatist political crisis management needs to be further explored in future research. In the remainder of this Conclusion, we briefly sketch out elements of a research agenda that could build on this study. Chief among them is the identification of specific empirical indicators for Pragmatist and principle-guided political crisis management.

INDICATORS FOR PRAGMATIST AND PRINCIPLE-GUIDED POLITICAL CRISIS MANAGEMENT

Chapter 4 suggested a list of specifications of what we expect to see in Pragmatist and principle-guided political crisis management. These specifications built on the theoretical writings of Pragmatism, but we argued that it is impossible to derive a comprehensive list of specific empirical indicators from the Pragmatist literature. Based on our empirical analysis in Chapters 6 and 7, however, we can suggest other potential indicators that might be useful for future research.

These empirical indicators have been identified in the course of the analysis (Tables 9.1 and 9.2). They do not represent a definitive list of empirical indicators for Pragmatist and principle-guided political crisis management. Rather, it is a list that can be further refined, expanded and corrected in future research projects.

Table 9.1   *Summary of Pragmatist political crisis management*

Pragmatist Political Crisis Management
DECISION MAKING
Anti-Dualism
-Working groups are established to explore additional options
-Decisions and contracts are formulated in flexible terms
Fallibilism
-Stated objectives of the crisis management process are changed
-Established approaches and solutions are not used
-Decisions try to buy time, not to conclusively solve the problem
-Continuous preparation of backup plans throughout the crisis
Experimentalism
-Tools (agencies, programs, resources) are used in a way that is not in line with their intended purpose or area of expertise
-Unprecedented solutions are used to manage the crises
-Mechanisms are implemented that allow the continuous monitoring of feedback
Deliberation
-Regular meetings to discuss decisions
-External stakeholders are involved in decision making
-Skeptics are actively invited and included in decision making (devil's advocate, multiple advocacy, etc.)
MEANING MAKING
Anti-Dualism
-Importance of a "balance" between different aspects is publicly communicated by government actors
Fallibilism
-Public acknowledgement by government actors that the planned solution might not solve the crisis
-Government actors avoid making any promises about the future
Experimentalism
-Decisions are explained differently by government actors in the course of time

INDICATORS FOR PRAGMATIST POLITICAL CRISIS MANAGEMENT

Decision Making

Working groups are established to explore additional options (anti-dualism)

An important feature of Pragmatist anti-dualism is the avoidance of dilemmas and the exploration of additional options. In crisis management, an indicator for such an anti-dualist exploration of additional options is the establishment of

Table 9.2   Summary of principle-guided political crisis management

Principle-Guided Political Crisis Management
DECISION MAKING
Dualism
-Strategy to solve the crisis is based on one option
Infallibilism
-Established standard solutions are used to solve the crisis
"One best way"
-Legal rules are emphasized and narrowly interpreted
Dictation
-Internal critics are cut off from decision making
MEANING MAKING
Dualism
-Dichotomous interpretations are publicly communicated by government actors
"One best way"
-Decisions are publicly framed by referring to strict legal principles
-Decisions are framed in the same way over the course of time

working groups that explore these options. In the case of Bear Stearns rescue, the indirect loan via J.P. Morgan can be regarded as an additional option that avoided the dilemma of finding a buyer or letting Bear Stearns fail. Timothy Geithner created an ad hoc working group with his team at the New York Fed to explore this option. The establishment of this working group provides an example of this indicator of Pragmatist political crisis management.

Decisions and contracts are formulated in flexible terms (anti-dualism)
The avoidance of self-imposed commitments has been identified as an important aspect of anti-dualism in our model of Pragmatist political crisis management. One indicator to identify this specification is the formulation of decisions and contracts in flexible terms. In the case of the indirect loan that the Federal Reserve Bank provided Bear Stearns with, for instance, the loan agreement determined that the loan would be available for "up to 28 days." This flexible formulation allowed Paulson and Geithner to shorten the duration of the loan when they anticipated that Bear Stearns needed to find a buyer immediately. This flexible "*up to*" formulation prevented a self-imposed commitment and allowed Paulson and Geithner to change course as the crisis developed. This flexible formulation of the contract with Bear Stearns therefore is a good indicator of Pragmatist political crisis management.

Stated objectives of the crisis management process are changed (fallibilism)

This indicator tries to identify the adaptability of existing beliefs and decisions. In the case of Bear Stearns, for example, both President Bush and Treasury Secretary Henry Paulson departed from a position that emphasized "moral hazard." At the heart of this position was the belief that the economic policies should secure the functioning of the free market and that companies who run into trouble should fail. But with the Bear Stearns case this objective shifted and was replaced by the importance of "systemic stability." From this perspective, Bear Stearns needed to be saved in order to safeguard the financial and economic system as a whole. Such a change of stated objective indicates the adaptability of existing beliefs and thus the presence of Pragmatist political crisis management.

Established approaches and solutions are not used (fallibilism)

Existing beliefs and decisions are often "codified" in established approaches, processes and solutions that can be used to target a specific type of crisis. If these established routines are left behind in order to solve the crisis, this is an indicator of Pragmatist political crisis management since it leaves behind existing beliefs and decisions in a fallibilist way. For a financial crisis at a major bank the main precedent has been set by the hedge fund Long Term Capital Management (LTCM) in 1998, which was saved by a consortium of banks and financial institutions that were brought together by the Federal Reserve Bank. In the case of Bear Stearns, this established approach of creating a consortium of private buyers was not used due to time constraints; instead, the novel idea of an indirect loan was chosen. The usage of the indirect loan is thus an example for this indicator of Pragmatist political crisis management.

Decisions try to buy time, not to conclusively solve the problem (fallibilism)

The indirect loan intended to rescue Bear Stearns over the weekend was not meant to be a solution that would solve the crisis once and for all, but rather an interim solution meant to buy time. Such decisions to buy time might be used as an indicator of Pragmatist political crisis management since they avoid unrevisable decisions (e.g., the collapse of Bear Stearns). Such time-buying decisions emphasize that a definite solution might not be available at an early stage of a crisis and that a probing step-by-step approach might be more appropriate.

Continuous preparation of backup plans throughout the crisis (fallibilism)

Backup plans are not an exclusive characteristic of Pragmatist political crisis management. Nonetheless, Pragmatist political crisis management might put an especially strong emphasis on backup plans and continue to develop them even as other forms of crisis management might become convinced that the crisis is solved and that backup plans are no longer needed. In this sense, the continuous preparation of backup plans can serve as an indicator of Pragmatist political crisis management. For example, an indicator of Pragmatist crisis management in the case of Bear Stearns might be where the Federal Reserve Bank rolled out the Primary Dealer Credit Facility (PDCF) in order to prepare for a bankruptcy of Bear Stearns. The PDCF was developed at a stage when negotiations between Bear Stearns and J.P. Morgan were already progressing and where it had become increasingly clear that Bear Stearns probably could be saved. Preparing backup plans at such a late stage during a crisis where the solution seems imminent already qualifies as an indicator of Pragmatist fallibilism.

Tools (agencies, programs, resources) are used in a way that is not in line with their intended purpose or area of expertise (experimentalism)

The recombination of existing tools has been identified as one of the specifications of experimentalism in our model of Pragmatist political crisis management. This indicator tries to identify such recombinations by checking if "tools" (agencies, programs, resources, and so on) are used in a way that is not in line with their intended purpose. After Lehman's failure, for instance, money market funds were saved by the Bush Administration with the help of the Exchange Stabilization Fund (ESF). As its name indicates, the ESF was not intended to be used for such a purpose; instead, it was originally designed to be used to stabilize the US dollar in international markets. This creative usage of the ESF indicates an experimentalist approach and qualifies as Pragmatist political crisis management.

Unprecedented solutions are used to manage the crises (experimentalism)

The fact that "established approaches and solutions are not used" has already been identified as an indicator for Pragmatist fallibilism. This indicator complements this insight by looking for examples where unprecedented solutions are used to manage a crisis. Such a usage of novel solutions qualifies as Pragmatist political crisis management. In the case of Bear Stearns, we have seen how the government's standard repertoire was to establish an industry consortium that would rescue the investment bank. This option was not possible in this case due to time constraints. Instead, the novel solution of an indirect loan was devised, an approach that made it necessary to invoke the

Federal Reserve Bank's emergency clause. This outcome provides an indicator of Pragmatist political crisis management.

Mechanisms are implemented that allow the continuous monitoring of feedback (experimentalism)

While feedback monitoring alone is not a sufficient indicator of Pragmatist experimentalism, it is a necessary one since feedback monitoring is an important prerequisite of experimentalism. Through constant feedback monitoring, the outcome of Pragmatist experiments is evaluated and the experimentalist "intervention" can be adapted accordingly. The implementation of continuous feedback monitoring mechanisms therefore qualifies as an indicator (albeit weak) of Pragmatist experimentalism. In our empirical cases we have seen how government actors monitored market developments closely and stayed in constant contact with external experts (banking executives, lawyers) to gather feedback. In the case of the indirect loan for Bear Stearns, this feedback led to a change of course when the duration of the loan was limited to the weekend. This incident thus can be regarded as an example for this indicator of Pragmatist political crisis management.

Regular meetings to discuss decisions (deliberation)

This indicator tries to identify internal deliberation, one of the characteristics of Pragmatist political crisis management. It points to whether internal meetings took place regularly and were used to discuss possible options and make decisions. In our cases we have seen how discussions in internal meetings (especially between Paulson, Bernanke and Geithner) played an important role in the decision-making process. This deliberative approach provides an example for this indicator of Pragmatist political crisis management.

External stakeholders are involved in decision making (deliberation)

This indicator looks for evidence of external deliberation, with external stakeholders being actively involved in decision making. To identify external deliberation, this involvement must go beyond the level of consultation. Instead, external stakeholders must have an active influence on the decisions that are being made in order to qualify as deliberation. In our cases we found little evidence for this indicator, because although external stakeholders were consulted, they had no direct influence on the decision-making process.

Skeptics are actively invited and included in decision making (devil's advocate, multiple advocacy, and so on) (deliberation)

Pragmatist deliberation puts a strong emphasis on the diversity of actors' perspectives. This indicator tries to identify Pragmatist deliberation by looking at whether skeptical and dissenting voices were actively included in the decision-making process. This might be accomplished by the usage of techniques such as devil's advocacy or multiple advocacy that make sure that dissenting voices are heard.

Meaning Making

Importance of a "balance" between different aspects is publicly communicated by government actors (anti-dualism)

This indicator aims at Pragmatist anti-dualism in meaning making. Anti-dualist meaning making depicts events in a nuanced way and avoids dichotomies. One possible indicator to measure anti-dualist meaning making is to examine whether government actors communicate the importance of "balancing" different values and needs. In the case of Bear Stearns, for example, government actors emphasized how their decision to rescue Bear Stearns balanced the aspects of moral hazard and financial stability. In explaining the decision, the Bush Administration indicated that both aspects were important and that the decision tried to encompass both aspects at once. This approach therefore provides an example for this indicator of Pragmatist political crisis management.

Public acknowledgment by government actors that the planned solution might not solve the crisis (fallibilism)

In our model of Pragmatist political crisis management, fallibilist meaning making has been identified as the communication of uncertainty and possible failures. This communication of uncertainty can refer to (1) the planned solution and (2) the possible outcome of the crisis. The two indicators regarding fallibilist meaning making try to measure these two aspects. This indicator targets the first aspect by searching for public acknowledgments by government actors that the planned solution is not strictly necessary and that other solutions might have a chance of working. Admitting this publicly qualifies as fallibilist meaning making since it communicates uncertainty and the government's fallibility. Perhaps unsurprisingly, we found no evidence for this indicator in our cases!

Government actors avoid making any promises about the future (fallibilism)

The second indicator of fallibilist meaning making targets the communication of uncertainty concerning the *outcome* of the crisis. It measures communicated uncertainty by searching for instances where government actors have avoided making promises about the future. When President Bush was about to give a speech briefly before the Bear Stearns rescue, Treasury Secretary Paulson advised him not to make any promises that there would be no bailout. In Congressional hearings after the Bear Stearns' bailout, government officials also left open whether further bailouts might be needed. This behavior provides an example for this indicator of Pragmatist political crisis management.

Decisions are explained differently by government actors over the course of time (experimentalism)

Frame revisions and trying out different frames are key characteristics of experimentalist meaning making according to our model of Pragmatist political crisis management. This indicator tries to measure experimentalist meaning making by looking at how decisions are explained over time and whether these explanations change. In the Lehman Brothers case, for example, the decision to let the investment bank fail was at first explained by government officials by pointing to the fact that the markets were already prepared for a Lehman bankruptcy. After this argument had been proven wrong by the turmoil caused by Lehman's demise, government officials like Paulson and Bernanke shifted to a different framing of the decision that highlighted how it was legally impossible to save Lehman. This shift in meaning making provides an example for this indicator of Pragmatist political crisis management.

INDICATORS FOR PRINCIPLE-GUIDED POLITICAL CRISIS MANAGEMENT

In many ways, the empirical indicators of principle-guided political crisis management can be thought of as the counterparts of the Pragmatist political crisis management indicators. Yet, principle-guided political crisis management cannot be identified through the absence of Pragmatist political crisis management alone (this would just identify *non-Pragmatist* political crisis management). Instead, to advance empirical research on principle-guided political crisis management, a specific set of indicators is needed. The following list may provide a starting point for this endeavor, based on our empirical analysis.

Decision Making

Strategy to solve the crisis is based on one option (dualism)

Our analysis has identified the portrayal of decisions as either-or dilemmas as a key characteristic of principle-guided political crisis management. To identify this principled approach to decision making we can examine the strategy to solve the crisis and check if it was based on one or more options. If the strategy was based on one option, such an approach qualifies as principle-guided political crisis management.

The Lehman decision has provided an example for such a principle-guided approach to political crisis management. In this case the strategy to solve the crisis was based on one option: to find a buyer for Lehman Brothers. When a buyer could not be found, Lehman had to file for bankruptcy. To find support for this indicator it is useful to analyse internal materials (memos, mails, minutes from meetings, and so on) and see if different options were considered or if the crisis-solving strategy was based on one option. In our cases it has also proven useful to examine if working groups were formed to explore different options, as discussed above. For Lehman, this was apparently not the case.

Established standard solutions are used to solve the crisis (infallibilism)

Principle-guided political crisis management sticks to existing beliefs and decisions. An indicator for this infallibilist approach to decision making is that established standard solutions are used to solve a crisis. In the case of Lehman Brothers, we have seen how the Bush Administration followed the established standard solution by trying to find a private buyer for Lehman. The Lehman example therefore has been qualified as an example of principle-guided political crisis management.

Legal rules are emphasized and narrowly interpreted ("one best way")

In principle-guided political crisis management, decisions are based on what is regarded as "objective evidence." The Lehman case has shown that one example of such "objective evidence" is legal rules and regulations. Internally, Paulson and Bernanke argued that a bailout of Lehman Brothers would be illegal, a stance that was based on a narrow interpretation of the Federal Reserve's emergency clause. The emphasis upon and the narrow interpretation of legal rules therefore can serve as an indicator of principle-guided political crisis management.

Internal critics are cut off from decision making (dictation)

Chapter 4 has shown how the exclusion of skeptical and dissenting voices from the decision-making process is a characteristic of principle-guided political crisis management. An indicator to identify this exclusion of skeptics is to examine if people were cut off from the information and decision-making process because of their skeptical stance (even if their formal position would have required their inclusion).

One such internal critic who was cut off during the financial crisis was Sheila Bair, the head of the Federal Deposit Insurance Corporation (FDIC). Bair was highly skeptical about public bailouts and opposed the Pragmatist approach that the Bush Administration took in the Bear Stearns and AIG decision. While her formal position as the head of an important banking-related agency would have made her a prime candidate for the governmental crisis management team, evidence suggests that she was excluded from the information and decision-making process because of her skeptical and dissenting opinions.

Meaning Making

Dichotomous interpretations are publicly communicated by government actors (dualism)
The usage of black-and-white dualisms is an important aspect of principle-guided political crisis management. The framing of 9/11 as a "war against terror" against an "axis of evil" provides an example for such dualist meaning making. In a similar vein, the decision to let Lehman Brothers fail was framed by strongly excluding the possibility of a public rescue and "drawing a line in the sand." We argue that when such univocal and dichotomous interpretations of crises are publicly communicated by government actors, this communication qualifies as an indicator of principle-guided political crisis management.

Decisions are publicly framed by referring to strict legal principles ("one best way")
Just as strict legal principles are important in principle-guided decision making, they might also be used in public meaning making. We argue that framing decisions in an unambiguous way and underlining that "there is no alternative" qualifies as an indicator of principle-guided political crisis management. The Lehman decision has been framed in such a strict legalist way as we have seen in the empirical analysis. By pointing out that it was legally impossible to save Lehman Brothers, Treasury Secretary Paulson and Fed Chairman Bernanke framed the decision as unambiguous and without any alternative. Their framing of the situation in this fashion provides an indicator of principle-guided political crisis management.

Decisions are framed in the same way over time ("one best way")
A final indicator for principle-guided meaning making is the fact that decisions are framed in the same way over time. While Pragmatist meaning making is characterized by the adaptation of frames over time (frame revisions) principle-guided meaning making sticks to the frames it uses. In our empirical cases, the meaning making of the Bear Stearns decision followed such a pattern of frame continuity. The decision to save Bear Stearns was consistently explained by referring to the importance of systemic stability. This consistent framing provides an example for this indicator of principle-guided political crisis management.

ADDITIONAL OBJECTIVES FOR FUTURE RESEARCH

Aside from extending and refining the list of empirical indicators, the following general issues might also be worth considering in future research.

The Locus of Pragmatism

This analysis has focused on the role of the Bush Administration in shaping the response to the financial crisis of 2008. It has shown how the influence of government actors has varied over the course of the crisis and how the government adopted diverse positions. This finding speaks to Graham Allison's classic description of "organizational process" and "governmental politics" models, which outlined how governments in crises are composed of pluralist actors and interests (Allison 1971). In this context, it is interesting to ask where the locus of Pragmatist crisis management is located. In other words, who or what exactly are the drivers of Pragmatist and principle-guided political crisis management? Why for example did the Bush Administration act (at least partly) in a Pragmatist fashion in the financial crisis but not after 9/11 (see Halper and Clarke 2004; Bernstein 2005)? Is it because different people were involved (with Paulson and Geithner pushing for a Pragmatist approach during the financial crisis and the neo-conservatives for a principle-guided approach after 9/11)? Or does it also have to do with the fact that different organizations and departments dealt with these different crises? In other words, is Pragmatism located in persons, routines and/or institutions? Chapter 8 took up this issue and hypothesized that Pragmatist political crisis management is more likely to prevail when and where administrative or technocratic actors have a greater role in decision making. However, this hypothesis is not particularly nuanced, and we suspect that this issue is worthy of more fine-grained investigation.

The Relation of Decision Making and Meaning Making and Beyond

Two dimensions of political crisis management were at the center of this study: decision making and meaning making. Both dimensions were analysed according to a set of specifications and the results were compared and contrasted. One of the findings of our analysis was that meaning making was less Pragmatist than decision making. This poses the question of "political vulnerability" (Campbell 1969). Or to put it more bluntly: Do governments make decisions in a Pragmatist fashion only to present themselves as principled actors to the public?

This is a question that could be further explored along the lines of the four elements of Pragmatism: anti-dualism, fallibilism, experimentalism and deliberation. This question has already been addressed for experimentalism (Campbell 1969; Ansell and Bartenberger 2016b; Bartenberger and Sześciło 2016) but research on the other elements is still missing. Such research could also include other important dimensions of political crisis management that have not been discussed in this study: early recognition of crises, sensemaking during crises and learning and accountability after crises.

Expanding the Analysis to Other Types of Crisis

This study has tried to show the usefulness of the model of Pragmatist and principle-guided political crisis management by analysing two decision points from the financial crisis of 2008. This focus should not imply that the usefulness of the model is only limited to financial crises. Expanding the reach by applying the model to other types of crises—such as natural catastrophes, terrorist attacks or major accidents—could therefore be one of the main objectives of future research.

The analysis of the political response to terrorist attacks might be a field worth considering here, especially when it comes to principle-guided political crisis management. Strong principles ("war against terror," "no negotiations with terrorists") are often at the center of political responses after terrorist attacks, as the examples of 9/11 and the recent attacks in Paris have shown (Bernstein 2005; Sharma 2015). Analysing whether we can also find examples of Pragmatist political crisis management that refrain from evoking strict principles in the aftermath of terror attacks might therefore be a promising endeavor. Possible examples worth examining in greater depth are the response to the 2011 terror attacks in Norway or the adaptive approach the Austrian government took towards terrorism in the 1970s and 1980s (see Riegler 2011).

Economic crises are another field where principle-guided political crisis management might play an important role. As we have seen in our case, economic ideologies often take the form of strict principles and dogmas that can influence the government's response to economic turmoil. At first glance, a prime example for such a principled approach might be the role the German government has played in the eurozone crisis. Many commentators have noted the strong ordo-liberal principles that have guided the response to the eurozone crisis, especially towards Greece (e.g., Habermas 2010; Kollewe 2012; Beck 2013; Van Esch 2014; Van Esch and Swinkels 2015). Examining the role of the German government in the eurozone crisis might provide a valuable starting point to further analyse the role of principle-guided political crisis management.

FINAL WORDS

To summarize, this study has tried to develop a model of Pragmatist political crisis management. "Pragmatism" remains a thorny concept that is hard to grasp in all its diversity. However, by focusing on Pragmatism as a distinctive perspective on practical rationality, by further specifying four elements of this perspective for empirical analysis (anti-dualism, fallibilism, experimentalism and deliberation), and by drawing a distinction between Pragmatist and principle-guided political crisis management, we hope to have provided a more solid conceptual foundation for the future use.

Given the current state of world affairs, political crisis management is unfortunately a topic of heightened importance. This study provides a small step towards advancing our understanding of political crisis management and it can hopefully foster further investigation into different approaches to political crisis management. After all, the successful governance of crises—whether terrorist attacks, natural catastrophes or economic turmoil—is one of the biggest contemporary challenges to modern democracies.

Bibliography

Abolafia, M.Y. (2010), 'Narrative construction as sensemaking: How a central bank thinks', *Organization Studies*, **31** (3), 349–67.

Abolafia, M.Y. (2012), 'Central banking and the triumph of technical rationality', in K. Knorr Cetina and A. Preda (eds), *The Oxford Handbook of the Sociology of Finance*, Oxford: Oxford University Press, pp. 94–112.

Abrams v. United States (1919), http://www.law.cornell.edu/supremecourt/text/250/616#writing-USSC_CR_0250_0616_ZD (accessed June 20, 2019).

Acharya, V., T. Philippon, M. Richardson and N. Roubini (2009), 'The financial crisis of 2007–2009: Causes and remedies', *Financial Markets, Institutions & Instruments*, **18** (2), 89–137.

Agamben, G. (2005), *State of Exception*, Chicago, IL: University of Chicago Press.

Alexander, T.M. (1990), 'Pragmatic imagination', *Transactions of the Charles S. Peirce Society*, **26** (3), 325–48.

Aliseda, A. (2005), 'The logic of abduction in the light of Peirce's Pragmatism', *Semiotica*, **153** (1), 363–74.

Allison, G.T. (1971), *Essence of Decision: Explaining the Cuban Missile Crisis*, Boston, MA: Little, Brown.

Allison, G.T. and P. Zelikow (1999), *Essence of Decision: Explaining the Cuban Missile Crisis*, New York: Longman.

Anderson, E. (2014), 'Dewey's moral philosophy', in E.N. Zalta (ed.), *The Stanford Encyclopedia of Philosophy*. http://plato.stanford.edu/archives/spr2014/entries/dewey-moral/ (accessed March 10, 2014).

Anderson, J., A.R. Sorkin and B. White (2008), 'Shares continue decline as Lehman looks for buyer', *New York Times*. http://www.nytimes.com/2008/09/12/business/12lehman.html (accessed April 7, 2016).

Anderson, P.A. (1983), 'Decision making by objection and the Cuban missile crisis', *Administrative Science Quarterly*, **28** (2), 201–22.

Andrews, E.L. (2008a). 'Fed acts to rescue financial markets', *New York Times*. http://www.nytimes.com/2008/03/17/business/17fed.html (accessed January 27, 2016).

Andrews, E.L. (2008b), 'Fed chief shifts path, inventing policy in crisis', *New York Times*. http://www.nytimes.com/2008/03/16/business/16bernanke.html (accessed February 24, 2016).

Anheier, H.K. and L. Moulton (1999), *When Things Go Wrong: Organizational Failures and Breakdowns*, Thousand Oaks, CA: Sage Publications.

Ansell, C.K. (2001). *Schism and Solidarity in Social Movements: The Politics of Labor in the French Third Republic*, Cambridge: Cambridge University Press.

Ansell, C.K. (2009), 'Mary Parker Follett and pragmatist organization', in P. Adler (ed.), *The Oxford Handbook of Sociology and Organization Studies: Classical Foundations*, Oxford: Oxford University Press, pp. 464–85.

Ansell, C.K. (2011), *Pragmatist Democracy: Evolutionary Learning as Public Philosophy*, Oxford: Oxford University Press.

Ansell, C.K. (2012), 'What is a "democratic experiment"?', *Contemporary Pragmatism*, **9** (2), 159–80.

Ansell, C.K. (2015), 'Pragmatist intepretivism', in M. Bevir and R.A.W. Rhodes (eds), *The Routledge Handbook of Interpretive Political Science*, London: Routledge, pp. 86–98.

Ansell, C.K. (2016), 'Pragmatism', in J. Torfing and C.K. Ansell (eds), *Handbook on Theories of Governance*, Cheltenham, UK and Northampton, MA, USA: Edward Elgar Publishing, pp. 392–401.

Ansell, C.K. and M. Bartenberger (2016a), 'Unruly problems', in C. Ansell, J. Trondal and M. Øgård (eds), *Governance in Turbulent Times*, Oxford: Oxford University Press, pp. 107–36.

Ansell, C.K. and M. Bartenberger (2016b), 'Varieties of Experimentalism', *Ecological Economics*, **130**, 64–73.

Ansell, C. and A. Boin (2017), 'Taming deep uncertainty: The potential of pragmatist principles for understanding and improving strategic crisis management', *Administration & Society*, 0095399717747655.

Ansell, C. and J. Gingrich (2007), 'The United Kingdom's response to the BSE epidemic', in D. Gibbons (ed.), *Communicable Crises: Prevention, Response, and Recovery in the Global Arena*, Charlotte, NC: Information Age Publishers, pp. 169–201.

Ansell, C. and J. Trondal (2017), 'Governing turbulence: An organizational-institutional agenda', *Perspectives on Public Management and Governance*, **1** (1), 43–57.

Ansell, C., A. Boin and A. Keller (2010), 'Managing transboundary crises: Identifying the building blocks of an effective response system', *Journal of Contingencies and Crisis Management*, **18** (4), 195–207.

Argyris, C. and D.A. Schön (1996), *Organizational Learning II: Theory, Method and Practice*, Reading, MA: Addison-Wesley.

Atkin, A. (2013), 'Peirce's theory of signs', in E.N. Zalta (ed.), *The Stanford Encyclopedia of Philosophy* (Summer Edition). http://plato.stanford.edu/archives/sum2013/entries/peirce-semiotics/ (accessed June 20, 2019).

Aven, T. (2013), 'On the meaning of a black swan in a risk context', *Safety Science*, **57**, 44–51.

Axilrod, S.H. (2009), *Inside the Fed: Monetary Policy and Its Management, Martin through Greenspan to Bernanke*, Cambridge, MA: MIT Press.

Bacon, M. (2010), 'The politics of truth: A critique of Peircean deliberative democracy', *Philosophy & Social Criticism*, **36** (9), 1075–91.

Bacon, M. (2012), *Pragmatism: An Introduction*, Cambridge, UK: Polity.

Bailey, H. (2009), 'Joe Biden, White House truth teller', *Newsweek*. http://www.newsweek.com/joe-biden-white-house-truth-teller-81181 (accessed September 22, 2014).

Bair, S. (2012), *Bull by the Horns: Fighting to Save Main Street from Wall Street and Wall Street from Itself*, New York: Free Press.

Bajaj, V. (2008), 'Wall St. goliath teeters amid fear of wider crisis', *New York Times*. http://www.nytimes.com/2008/09/14/business/14spiral.html (accessed March 30, 2016).

Baker, P. (2013), *Days of Fire: Bush and Cheney in the White House*, New York: Knopf Doubleday Publishing Group.

Bakker, J.H. (2011), 'The "semiotic self": From Peirce and Mead to Wiley and Singer', *The American Sociologist*, **42** (2–3), 187–206.

Baldwin, J.D. (1988), 'Habit, emotion, and self-conscious action', *Sociological Perspectives*, **31** (1), 35–57.

Ball, L. (2016), 'The Fed and Lehman Brothers', Paper prepared for a meeting of the NBER Monetary Economics Program, July 14. https://voxeu.org/article/fed-and-lehman-brothers (accessed June 20, 2019).

Banerjee, A.V. and E. Duflo (2009), 'The experimental approach to development economics', *Annual Review of Economics*, **1**, 151–78.

Bar-Joseph, U. and Z. Sheaffer (1998), 'Surprise and its causes in business administration and strategic studies', *International Journal of Intelligence and Counter Intelligence*, **11** (3), 331–49.

Baran, B.E. and C.W. Scott (2010), 'Organizing ambiguity: A grounded theory of leadership and sensemaking within dangerous contexts', *Military Psychology*, **22** (suppl. 1), S42–S69.

Barbalet, J. (2004), 'William James: Pragmatism, social psychology and emotions', *European Journal of Social Theory*, **7** (3), 337–53.

Barbalet, J. (2008), 'Pragmatism and economics: William James' contribution', *Cambridge Journal of Economics*, **32** (5), 797–810.

Bartenberger, M. and D. Sześciło (2016), 'The benefits and risks of experimental co-production: The case of urban redesign in Vienna', *Public Administration*, **94** (2), 509–25.

Beck, U. (1992), *Risk Society. Towards a New Modernity*, London; Newbury Park, CA: Sage Publications.

Beck, U. (2006), 'Living in the world risk society', *Economy and Society*, **35** (3), 329–45.

Beck, U. (2013), *German Europe*, Cambridge, UK; Malden, MA: Polity.

Becker, J., S.G. Stolberg and S. Labaton (2008), 'White House philosophy stoked mortgage bonfire', *New York Times*. http://www.nytimes.com/2008/ 12/21/ business/21admin.html (accessed May 9, 2014).

Beckert, J. (2003), 'Economic sociology and embeddedness: How shall we conceptualize economic action?', *Journal of Economic Issues*, **37** (3), 769–87.

Bendixen, P. (2010), 'The rationale of crisis management—on the handling of coincidence in economic situation', *Journal of Social Science Education*, **1**, 39–48.

Bendor, J. and T.H. Hammond (1992), 'Rethinking Allison's models', *American Political Science Review*, **86** (2), 301–22.

Benjamin, M. (2008), 'Senator Bunning says Paulson acts like socialist, should resign—Bloomberg', *Bloomberg*. http://web.archive.org/web/ 20150923133344/http://www.bloomberg.com/apps/news?pid=newsarchive &sid=alpUsTv3.upI&refer=home (accessed March 31, 2016).

Benjamin, W. (2003), 'On the concept of history', in H. Eiland and M.W. Jennings (eds), *Selected Writings. Volume 4, 1938–1940*, Cambridge, MA: Belknap Press of Harvard University Press, pp. 389–400.

Benjamin, W. (2007), *Reflections: Essays, Aphorisms, Autobiographical Writings*, New York: Schocken Books.

Benoit, W.L. and J.R. Henson (2009), 'President Bush's image repair discourse on Hurricane Katrina', *Public Relations Review*, **35** (1), 40–6.

Berenson, A. (2008), 'Wall St.'s turmoil sends stocks reeling', *New York Times*. http://www.nytimes.com/2008/09/16/business/worldbusiness/16mar kets.html (accessed April 1, 2016).

Bergman, M. (2009), 'Experience, purpose, and the value of vagueness: On CS Peirce's contribution to the philosophy of communication', *Communication Theory*, **19** (3), 248–77.

Berk, G. and D. Galvan (2009), 'How people experience and change institutions: A field guide to creative syncretism', *Theory and Society*, **38** (6), 543–80.

Berkes, F. (2007), 'Understanding uncertainty and reducing vulnerability: Lessons from resilience thinking', *Natural Hazards*, **41** (2), 283–95.

Bernanke, B. (2013), *The Federal Reserve and the Financial Crisis*, Princeton, NJ: Princeton University Press.

Bernanke, B. (2015), *The Courage to Act: A Memoir of a Crisis and Its Aftermath*, New York: W.W. Norton.

Bernstein, R.J. (1971), *Praxis and Action: Contemporary Philosophies of Human Activity*, Philadelphia, PA: University of Pennsylvania Press.

Bernstein, R.J. (2005), *The Abuse of Evil: The Corruption of Politics and Religion since 9/11*, Cambridge, UK: Polity.

Bernstein, R.J. (2006), 'The Pragmatic century', in S.G. Davaney and W.G. Frisina (eds), *The Pragmatic Century: Conversations with Richard J. Bernstein*, Albany, NY: State University of New York Press, pp. 1–14.

Bernstein, R.J. (2010), *The Pragmatic Turn*, Cambridge, UK: Polity.

Blackburn, S. (2005a), 'Dogma', *The Oxford Dictionary of Philosophy*, Oxford: Oxford University Press, p. 109.

Blackburn, S. (2005b), 'Pragmatism', *The Oxford Dictionary of Philosophy*, Oxford: Oxford University Press, p. 297.

Blackburn, S. (2005c), 'Rationalism', *The Oxford Dictionary of Philosophy*, Oxford: Oxford University Press, p. 318.

Blake, C.N. (2001), 'The Big Bang', *The American Scholar*, **70** (3), 148–51.

Bland, B. (2007), 'Bear Stearns hedge funds wiped out', *The Telegraph*. http://www.telegraph.co.uk/finance/markets/2812344/Bear-Stearns-hedge-funds-wiped-out.html (accessed February 23, 2016).

Blatter, J.K. (2008), 'Case study', in L.M. Given (ed.), *The SAGE Encyclopedia of Qualitative Research Methods*, Thousand Oaks, CA: Sage Publications. http://knowledge.sagepub.com/view/research/n39.xml (accessed March 11, 2015).

Blinder, A.S. (2013), *After the Music Stopped: The Financial Crisis, the Response, and the Work Ahead*, New York: Penguin.

Bohman, J. (2004), 'Realizing deliberative democracy as a mode of inquiry: Pragmatism, social facts, and normative theory', *The Journal of Speculative Philosophy*, **18** (1), 23–43.

Boin, A. (2008), 'Learning from crisis: NASA and the Challenger disaster', in A. Boin, A. McConnell and P. 't Hart (eds), *Governing After Crisis: The Politics of Investigation, Accountability and Learning*, Cambridge: Cambridge University Press, pp. 232–54.

Boin, A. and P. 't Hart (2003), 'Public leadership in times of crisis: Mission impossible?', *Public Administration Review*, **63** (5), 544–53.

Boin, A. and P. 't Hart (2007), 'The crisis approach', in H. Rodríguez, E.L. Quarantelli and R.R. Dynes (eds), *Handbook of Disaster Research*, New York: Springer, pp. 42–54.

Boin, A. and P. Nieuwenburg (2013), 'The moral costs of discretionary decision-making in crisis', *Public Integrity*, **15** (4), 367–84.

Boin, A. and C. Renaud (2013), 'Orchestrating joint sensemaking across government levels: Challenges and requirements for crisis leadership', *Journal of Leadership Studies*, **7** (3), 41–6.

Boin, A., C. Kofman-Bos and W. Overdijk (2004), 'Crisis simulations: Exploring tomorrow's vulnerabilities and threats', *Simulation & Gaming*, **35** (3), 378–93.

Boin, A., P. 't Hart, E. Stern and B. Sundelius (2005), *The Politics of Crisis Management: Public Leadership Under Pressure*, Cambridge: Cambridge University Press.

Boin, A., A. McConnell and P. 't Hart (2008), 'Governing after crisis', in A. Boin, A. McConnell and P. 't Hart (eds), *Governing After Crisis: The Politics of Investigation, Accountability and Learning*, Cambridge: Cambridge University Press, pp. 3–30.

Boin, A., P. 't Hart and A. McConnell (2009), 'Crisis exploitation: Political and policy impacts of framing contests', *Journal of European Public Policy*, **16** (1), 81–106.

Boin, A., P. 't Hart, A. McConnell and T. Preston (2010), 'Leadership style, crisis response and blame management: The case of Hurricane Katrina', *Public Administration*, **88** (3), 706–23.

Boin, A., M. Rhinard and M. Ekengren (2014), 'Managing transboundary crises: The emergence of European Union capacity', *Journal of Contingencies and Crisis Management*, **22** (3), 131–42.

Boisvert, R.D. (1999), 'The nemesis of necessity: Tragedy's challenge to Deweyan Pragmatism', in C. Haskins and D.I. Seiple (eds), *Dewey Reconfigured: Essays on Deweyan Pragmatism*, Albany, NY: State University of New York Press, pp. 151–68.

Bornstein, D. (2012), 'The dawn of the evidence-based budget', *New York Times*. http://opinionator.blogs.nytimes.com/2012/05/30/worthy-of-govern ment-funding-prove-it/ (accessed October 24, 2014).

Brändström, A., F. Bynander and P. 't Hart (2004), 'Governing by looking back: Historical analogies and crisis management', *Public Administration*, **82** (1), 191–210.

Bromley, D.W. (2008), 'Volitional pragmatism', *Ecological Economics*, **68** (1–2), 1–13.

Bromley, D.W. (2010), *Sufficient Reason: Volitional Pragmatism and the Meaning of Economic Institutions*, Princeton, NJ: Princeton University Press.

Burke, J.P. (2009), 'Organizational structure and presidential decision making', in G.C. Edwards and W.G. Howell (eds), *The Oxford Handbook of the American Presidency*, Oxford: Oxford University Press, pp. 501–27.

Burrough, B. (2008), 'Bringing down Bear Stearns', *Vanity Fair*. http://www .vanityfair.com/news/2008/08/bear_stearns200808-2 (accessed March 15, 2016).

Bush, G.W. (2008a), 'Address to the Economic Club of New York—March 14, 2008'. http://www.presidentialrhetoric.com/speeches/03.14.08.html (accessed January 21, 2016).

Bush, G.W. (2008b), 'Addressing the economy. Washington, DC, September 19, 2008'. http://www.presidentialrhetoric.com/speeches/09.19.08.html (accessed January 21, 2016).

Bush, G.W. (2008c), 'President Bush's Speech to the Nation on the Economic Crisis', *New York Times*. http://www.nytimes.com/2008/09/24/business/economy/24text-bush.html (accessed October 12, 2015).

Bush, G.W. (2008d), 'Remarks at the 2008 Conservative Political Action Conference—February 8, 2008'. http://www.presidentialrhetoric.com/speeches/02.08.08.html (accessed March 1, 2016).

Bush, G.W. (2010), *Decision Points*, New York: Crown Publishers.

Bytzek, E. (2008), 'Flood response and political survival: Gerhard Schröder and the 2002 Elbe flood in Germany', in A. Boin, A. McConnell and P. 't Hart (eds), *Governing After Crisis: The Politics of Investigation, Accountability and Learning*, Cambridge: Cambridge University Press, pp. 85–113.

Cambridge Dictionary (n.d.), https://dictionary.cambridge.org/us/ (accessed 2016).

Cameron, K.S., M.U. Kim and U.D.A. Whetten (1987), 'Organizational effects of decline and turbulence', *Administrative Science Quarterly*, **32** (2), 222–40.

Campbell, D.T. (1969), 'Reforms as experiments', *American Psychologist*, **24** (4), 409–29.

Campbell, J. (1995), *Understanding John Dewey: Nature and Cooperative Intelligence*, Chicago, IL: Open Court.

Campbell, J. (2008), 'The political philosophy of Pragmatism', in J.W. Garrison (ed.), *Reconstructing Democracy, Recontextualizing Dewey. Pragmatism and Interactive Constructivism in the Twenty-First Century*, Albany, NY: State University of New York Press, pp. 19–30.

Cartwright, N. (2010), 'What are randomised controlled trials good for?', *Philosophical Studies: An International Journal for Philosophy in the Analytic Tradition*, **147** (1), 59–70.

Cartwright, N. (2013), 'Evidence based policy', in B. Kaldis (ed.), *Encyclopedia of Philosophy and the Social Sciences*, Thousand Oaks, CA: Sage Publications, pp. 296–8.

Cartwright, N. and J. Hardie (2012), *Evidence-Based Policy: A Practical Guide to Doing It Better*, Oxford: Oxford University Press.

Cassidy, J. (2012), 'An inconvenient truth: It was George W. Bush who bailed out the automakers', *The New Yorker*. http://www.newyorker.com/news/john-cassidy/an-inconvenient-truth-it-was-george-w-bush-who-bailed-out-the-automakers (accessed April 26, 2016).

Chanley, V.A. (2002), 'Trust in government in the aftermath of 9/11: Determinants and consequences', *Political Psychology*, **23** (3), 469–83.

Cheney, R.B. (2011), *In My Time: A Personal and Political Memoir*, New York: Threshold Editions.

Cho, D. and N. Irwin (2008), 'In crucible of crisis, Paulson, Bernanke, Geithner forge a committee of three', *Washington Post*. http://www.washingtonpost.com/wp-dyn/content/article/2008/09/18/AR2008091804211.html (accessed April 12, 2016).

Christianson, M.K., M.T. Farkas, K.M. Sutcliffe and K.E. Weick (2009), 'Learning through rare events: Significant interruptions at the Baltimore & Ohio Railroad Museum', *Organization Science*, **20** (5), 846–60.

Clam, J. (2011), 'What is a crisis?', in P.F. Kjaer, G. Teubner and A. Febbrajo (eds), *The Financial Crisis in Constitutional Perspective: The Dark Side of Functional Differentiation*, Portland, OR: Hart Publishing, pp. 189–217.

Cleveland, K. (2014), 'Mobilizing nuclear bias: The Fukushima nuclear crisis and the politics of uncertainty', *The Asia-Pacific Journal*, **12** (20), 1–43.

CNN (2008), 'Transcripts of CNN Late Edition with Wolf Blitzer, 16 March 2008'. http://edition.cnn.com/TRANSCRIPTS/0803/16/le.01.html (accessed March 2, 2016).

Cohan, William D (2008), 'The weekend that changed Wall Street forever—Dec. 15, 2008', *Fortune*. http://archive.fortune.com/2008/12/12/magazines/fortune/3days_full.fortune/index.htm (accessed April 1, 2016).

Cohen, A. (2013), 'The most powerful dissent in American history', *The Atlantic*, August. http://www.theatlantic.com/national/archive/2013/08/the-most-powerful-dissent-in-american-history/278503/ (accessed June 17, 2014).

Cohen, M.D. (2007), 'Reading Dewey: Reflections on the study of routine', *Organization Studies*, **28** (5), 773–86.

Colapietro, V. (2006). 'Practice, agency, and sociality: An orthogonal reading of classical pragmatism', *International Journal for Dialogical Science*, **1** (1), 23–31.

Colapietro, V. (2011), 'Situation, meaning, and improvisation: An aesthetics of existence in Dewey and Foucault', *Foucault Studies*, **11**, 20–40.

Collier, D. (2011), 'Understanding process tracing', *PS: Political Science & Politics*, **44** (4), 823–30.

Colville, I., A. Pye and M. Carter (2013), 'Organizing to counter terrorism: Sensemaking amidst dynamic complexity', *Human Relations*, **66** (9), 1201–23.

Colvin, R. (2009). 'On Afghanistan, Joe Biden plays devil's advocate', *Reuters*. http://www.reuters.com/article/2009/10/22/us-afghanistan-biden-analysis-idUSTRE59L5A020091022 (accessed September 22, 2014).

Combe, I.A. and D.J. Carrington (2015), 'Leaders' sensemaking under crises: Emerging cognitive consensus over time within management teams', *The Leadership Quarterly*, **26** (3), 307–22.

Comfort, L.K., Y. Sungu, D. Johnson and M. Dunn (2001), 'Complex systems in crisis: Anticipation and resilience in dynamic environments', *Journal of Contingencies and Crisis Management*, **9** (3), 144–58.

Congressional Oversight Panel (2010). *Oversight Report. The AIG Rescue, Its Impact on Markets, and the Government's Exit Strategy*, Washington, DC. https://www.gpo.gov/fdsys/pkg/CPRT-111JPRT56698/pdf/CPRT -111JPRT56698.pdf (accessed June 20, 2019).

Conti-Brown, P. (2015a), 'Introducing guest blogger Philip Wallach, author of new book on law and the financial crisis', *Yale Journal on Regulation Blog*. http://www.yalejreg.com/blog/introducing-guest-blogger-philip-wallach -author-of-new-book-on-law-and-the-financial-crisis-by-peter (accessed April 8, 2016).

Conti-Brown, P. (2015b), 'Why the Fed's assertion that a Lehman bailout would have been illegal is wrong', *Yale Journal on Regulation Blog*. http:// www.yalejreg.com/blog/why-the-fed-s-assertion-that-a-lehman-bailout -would-have-been-illegal-is-wrong-by-peter-conti-brown (accessed April 8, 2016).

Cooke, E.F. (2011), 'Phenomenology of error and surprise: Peirce, Davidson, and McDowell', *Transactions of the Charles S. Peirce Society: A Quarterly Journal in American Philosophy*, **47** (1), 62–86.

Coombs, W.T. (2007), 'Protecting organization reputations during a crisis: The development and application of situational crisis communication theory', *Corporate Reputation Review*, **10** (3), 163–76.

Cornelissen, J.P., S. Mantere and E. Vaara (2014), 'The contraction of meaning: The combined effect of communication, emotions, and materiality on sensemaking in the Stockwell shooting', *Journal of Management Studies*, **51** (5), 699–736.

Corwin, E.S. (1917), 'War, the Constitution moulder', *The New Republic*, 153–5.

Corwin, E.S. (1947), *Total War and the Constitution*, New York: A.A. Knopf.

Creswell, J. and V. Bajaj (2007), '$3.2 billion move by Bear Stearns to rescue fund', *New York Times*. http://www.nytimes.com/2007/06/23/business/ 23bond.html (accessed February 23, 2016).

Cunliffe, A. and C. Coupland (2012), 'From hero to villain to hero: Making experience sensible through embodied narrative sensemaking', *Human Relations*, **65** (1), 63–88.

Czada, R.M. (1991), 'Muddling through a nuclear-political emergency: Multilevel crisis management in West Germany after radioactive fallout from Chernobyl', *Organization & Environment*, **5** (4), 293–322.

Dahl, R.A. and C.E. Lindblom (1992), *Politics, Economics, and Welfare*, New Brunswick, NJ: Transaction Publishers.

Daley, P. and D. O'Neill (1991), '"Sad is too mild a word": Press coverage of the Exxon Valdez oil spill', *Journal of Communication*, **41** (4), 42–57.

Dalton, B. (2004), 'Creativity, habit, and the social products of creative action: Revising Joas, incorporating Bourdieu', *Sociological Theory*, **22** (4), 603–22.

Damasio, A.R. 1994. *Descartes' Error: Emotion, Reason, and the Human Brain*, New York: Grosset/Putnam.

Danermark, B., M. Ekström, L. Jakobsen and J.K. Karlsson (2002), *Explaining Society: Critical Realism in the Social Sciences*, London; New York: Routledge.

Deaton, A. (2010). 'Instruments, randomization, and learning about development', *Journal of Economic Literature*, **48**, 424–55.

DeLeon, L. (2005), 'Public management, democracy, and politics', in E. Ferlie, L.E. Lynn and C. Pollitt (eds), *The Oxford Handbook of Public Management*, Oxford: Oxford University Press, pp. 103–30.

Denzin, N.K. (1985), 'Emotion as lived experience', *Symbolic Interaction*, **8** (2), 223–40.

Dequech, D. (2000), 'Fundamental uncertainty and ambiguity', *Eastern Economic Journal*, **26** (1), 41–60.

Dequech, D. (2003), 'Uncertainty and economic sociology: A preliminary discussion', *American Journal of Economics and Sociology*, **62** (3), 509–32.

Dequech, D. (2006), 'The new institutional economics and the theory of behaviour under uncertainty', *Journal of Economic Behavior & Organization*, **59** (1), 109–31.

Dewey, J. (1896), 'The reflex arc concept in psychology', *Psychological Review*, **3** (4), 357–70.

Dewey, J. (1902), 'The evolutionary method as applied to morality', *The Philosophical Review*, **11** (2), 107–24.

Dewey, J. (1909), *Studies in Logical Theory*, Chicago, IL: University of Chicago Press.

Dewey, J. (1910), *How We Think*, Boston: D.C. Heath & Co.

Dewey, J. (1911a), 'Adaption', in P. Monroe (ed.), *A Cyclopedia of Education, Volume One*, Detroit: Gale Research Co, p. 35.

Dewey, J. (1911b), 'Logic of experimentation', in P. Monroe (ed.), *A Cyclopedia of Education, Volume Two*, Detroit: Gale Research Co, p. 554.

Dewey, J. (1917), 'The need for a recovery of philosophy', in J. Dewey et al. (eds), *Creative Intelligence: Essays in the Pragmatic Attitude*, New York: H. Holt and Company, pp. 3–69.

Dewey, J. (1922), *Human Nature and Conduct: An Introduction to Social Psychology*, New York: Carlton House.

Dewey, J. (1933), *How We Think: A Restatement of the Relation of Reflective Thinking to the Educational Process*, Lexington, MA: Heath.

Dewey, J. (1938), *Experience & Education*, New York: Touchstone.

Dewey, J. (1979), 'Means and ends', in *Their Morals and Ours: Marxist Versus Liberal Views On Morality*, New York: Pathfinder Press, pp. 67–73.

Dewey, J. (1980), *The Middle Works, 1899–1924. Volume 16: 1916. Democracy and Education*, ed. J.A. Boydston, Carbondale, IL: Southern Illinois University Press.

Dewey, J. (1987), 'Democracy is radical', in J.A. Boydston (ed.), *The Later Works, 1925–1953. Volume 11: 1935–1937, Essays, Liberalism and Social Action*, Carbondale, IL: Southern Illinois University Press, pp. 296–300.

Dewey, J. (1990), *The Later Works, 1925–1953. Volume 4: 1929. The Quest for Certainty*, ed. J.A. Boydston, Carbondale, IL: Southern Illinois University Press.

Dewey, J. (1998a), 'Creative democracy—the task before us', in L.A. Hickman and T.M. Alexander (eds), *The Essential Dewey*, Bloomington, IN: Indiana University Press, pp. 340–3.

Dewey, J. (1998b), 'Pragmatic America', in LA. Hickman and T. M. Alexander (eds), *The Essential Dewey*, Bloomington, IN: Indiana University Press, pp. 29–32.

Dewey, J. (1998c), *The Essential Dewey Volume 1: Pragmatism, Education, Democracy*, Bloomington, IN: Indiana University Press.

Dewey, J. (2011), 'The influence of Darwinism on philosophy', in R.B. Talisse and S.F. Aikin (eds), *The Pragmatism Reader*, Princeton, NJ: Princeton University Press, pp. 141–9.

Dieleman, S. (2017), 'Pragmatist tools for public administration', *Administration & Society*, **49** (2), 275–95.

Donato, I.I. (2009), 'The United States: Crisis leadership in times of transition', in P. 't Hart and K. Tindall (eds), *Framing the Global Economic Downturn: Crisis Rhetoric and the Politics of Recessions*, Acton, ACT: ANU E Press, pp. 43–68.

Dorf, M.C. (2012), 'Could the occupy movement become the realization of democratic experimentalism's aspiration for pragmatic politics?', *Contemporary Pragmatism*, **9** (2), 263–71.

Dorf, M.C. and C.F. Sabel (1998), 'A constitution of democratic experimentalism', *Columbia Law Review*, **98** (2), 267–473.

Dowd, K. (2009), 'Moral hazard and the financial crisis', *Cato Journal*, **29** (1), 141–66.

Doyle, E.E., J. McClure, D. Paton and D.M. Johnston (2014), 'Uncertainty and decision making: Volcanic crisis scenarios', *International Journal of Disaster Risk Reduction*, **10**, 75–101.

Drnevich, P., R. Ramanujam, S. Mehta and A. Chaturvedi (2009), 'Affiliation or situation: What drives strategic decisionmaking in crisis response?', *Journal of Managerial Issues*, **21** (2), 216–31.

Duit, A. (2016), 'Resilience thinking: Lessons for public administration', *Public Administration*, **94** (2), 364–80.

Dunbar, R.L. and R. Garud (2009), 'Distributed knowledge and indeterminate meaning: The case of the Columbia shuttle flight', *Organization Studies*, **30** (4), 397–421.

Dunwoody, S. and R.J. Griffin (2015), 'Risk information seeking and processing model', in H. Cho, T. Reimer and K.A. McComas (eds), *SAGE Handbook of Risk Communication*, Thousand Oaks, CA: Sage Publications, pp. 102–16.

Dutton, J.E. (1986), 'The processing of crisis and non-crisis strategic issues', *Journal of Management Studies*, **23** (5), 501–17.

Dyson, S.B. and P. 't Hart (2013), 'Crisis management', in L. Huddy, D.O. Sears and J.S. Levy (eds), *The Oxford Handbook of Political Psychology*, Oxford: Oxford University Press, pp. 395–422.

Ebel, R.E. (1994), *Chernobyl and Its Aftermath: A Chronology of Events*, Washington, DC: CSIS.

Eckstein, H. (1992), *Regarding Politics: Essays on Political Theory, Stability, and Change*, Berkeley, CA: University of California Press.

Edelman, M. (1985), *The Symbolic Uses of Politics*, Chicago, IL: University of Illinois Press.

Edmondson, A.C., M.A. Roberto, R.M. Bohmer, E.M. Ferlins and L.R. Feldman (2005), 'The recovery window: Organizational learning following ambiguous threats', in W. Starbuck and M. Farjoun (eds), *Organization at the Limit: Lessons from the Columbia Disaster*, Malden, MA: Blackwell, pp. 220–45.

Efron, A. (2011), 'Reclaiming the Pragmatist legacy: Evolution and its discontents', in J.R. Shook and P. Kurtz (eds), *Dewey's Enduring Impact: Essays on America's Philosopher*, Amherst, NY: Prometheus Books, pp. 105–23.

Elkjaer, B. (2009), 'Pragmatism: A learning theory for the future', in K. Illeris (ed.), *Contemporary Theories of Learning*, Abington: Routledge, pp. 82–97.

Emery, F.E. and E.L. Trist (1965), 'The causal texture of organizational environments', *Human Relations*, **18**, 21–32.

Emirbayer, M. and A. Mische (1998), 'What is agency?', *American Journal of Sociology*, **103** (4), 962–1023.

Engdahl, E. and R. Lidskog (2014), 'Risk, communication and trust: Towards an emotional understanding of trust', *Public Understanding of Science*, **23** (6), 703–17.

Engel, A.K., A. Maye, M. Kurthen and P. König (2013), 'Where's the action? The pragmatic turn in cognitive science', *Trends in Cognitive Sciences*, **17** (5), 202–9.

Eriksson, K. and A. McConnell (2011), 'Contingency planning for crisis management: Recipe for success or political fantasy?', *Policy and Society*, **30** (2), 89–99.

Evening Standard (2010), 'Darling vetoed Lehman Bros takeover', *Evening Standard*. http://www.standard.co.uk/newsheadlines/darling-vetoed-lehma n-bros-takeover-6522847.html (accessed March 21, 2016).

Ezzy, D. (1998), 'Theorizing narrative identity: Symbolic interactionism and hermeneutics', *Sociological Quarterly*, **39** (2), 239–52.

Faraj, S. and Y. Xiao (2006), 'Coordination in fast-response organizations', *Management Science*, **52** (8), 1155–69.

Farjoun, M. (2010), 'Beyond dualism: Stability and change as a duality', *Academy of Management Review*, **35** (2), 202–25.

Farjoun, M. (2016), 'Contradictions, dialectics and paradoxes', in A. Langley and H. Tsoukas (eds), *The Sage Handbook of Process Organization Studies*, Thousand Oaks, CA: Sage Publications, pp. 87–109.

Faucheux, S. and G. Froger (1995), 'Decision-making under environmental uncertainty', *Ecological Economics*, **15** (1), 29–42.

Federal Reserve Bank (2008a), 'FRB: Press release—March 14, 2008'. http://www.federalreserve.gov/newsevents/press/monetary/20080314a.htm (accessed February 23, 2016).

Federal Reserve Bank (2008b), 'FRB: Press release—September 14, 2008'. http://www.federalreserve.gov/newsevents/press/monetary/20080914a.htm (accessed February 23, 2016).

Federal Reserve Bank (2008c), 'FRB: Press release, March 16, 2008'. http://www.federalreserve.gov/newsevents/press/monetary/20080316a.htm (accessed March 4, 2016).

Federal Reserve Bank (2008d), *Meeting of the Federal Open Market Committee on September 16, 2008*. http://www.federalreserve.gov/monetarypolicy/ files/FOMC20080916meeting.pdf (accessed June 16, 2016).

Federal Reserve Bank (2008e), *Minutes of the Board of Governors of the Federal Reserve System, March 16, 2008*. http://www.federalreserve.gov/ newsevents/press/other/other20080627a2.pdf (accessed June 16, 2016).

Federal Reserve Bank (2008f), 'Press release—Federal Reserve and other central banks announce specific measures designed to address liquidity pressures in funding markets, March 11, 2008'. http://www.federalreserve .gov/newsevents/press/monetary/20080311a.htm (accessed February 26, 2016).

Federal Reserve Bank (2008g), 'Report pursuant to Section 129 of the Emergency Economic Stabilization Act of 2008: Loan to facilitate the acquisition of the Bear Stearns Companies, Inc. by JPMorgan Chase & Co.' http://www .federalreserve.gov/monetarypolicy/files/129bearstearnsacquisitionloan.pdf (accessed February 24, 2016).

Federal Reserve Bank (2013), 'Federal Reserve Act—Section 13'. http://www.federalreserve.gov/aboutthefed/section13.htm (accessed February 23, 2016).

Federal Reserve Bank (2016a), 'FRB: Lending to depository institutions—credit and liquidity programs and the balance sheet'. http://www.federalreserve.gov/monetarypolicy/bst_lendingdepository.htm (accessed March 15, 2016).

Federal Reserve Bank (2016b), 'FRB: Primary Dealer Credit Facility (PDCF)'. http://www.federalreserve.gov/newsevents/reform_pdcf.htm (accessed February 26, 2016).

Federal Reserve Bank of New York (2008), 'Understanding the recent changes to Federal Reserve liquidity provision'. https://www.newyorkfed.org/markets/Understanding_Fed_Lending.html (accessed February 26, 2016).

Federal Reserve Bank of New York (2012), 'Actions related to AIG'. https://www.newyorkfed.org/aboutthefed/aig (accessed March 21, 2016).

Feduzi, A. and J. Runde (2014), 'Uncovering unknown unknowns: Towards a Baconian approach to management decision-making', *Organizational Behavior and Human Decision Processes*, **124** (2), 268–83.

Festenstein, M. (2001), 'Inquiry as critique: On the legacy of Deweyan pragmatism for political theory', *Political Studies*, **49** (4), 730–48.

Financial Crisis Inquiry Commission (2008a), *AIG Meeting Notes. FCIC-AIG0021217.* http://fcic-static.law.stanford.edu/cdn_media/fcic-docs/2008-09-12_Federal_Reserve_Bank_AIG_Meeting_Notes.pdf (accessed June 20, 2019).

Financial Crisis Inquiry Commission (2008b), *E-Mail from Ben Bernanke to Kevin Warsh, September 14, 2008. FCIC-155000.* http://fcic.law.stanford.edu/documents/view/470 (accessed June 16, 2016).

Financial Crisis Inquiry Commission (2008c), *FRBNY Internal Memo about AIG. FCIC-AIG0021567.* http://fcic-static.law.stanford.edu/cdn_media/fcic-docs/2008-09-14%20FRBNY%20Email%20re%20AIG%20and%20the%20Discount%20Window.pdf (accessed June 16, 2016).

Financial Crisis Inquiry Commission (2008d), *Liquidation Consortium Gameplan and Questions. FCIC-154768.* http://fcic-static.law.stanford.edu/cdn_media/fcic-docs/2008-09-11_Federal_Reserve_Bank_Email_from_Patrick_M_Parkinson_to_Don_Kohn_Scott_Alvarez_and_Brian_Madigan_Re_revised_Liquidation_Consortium_gameplan_questioins.pdf (accessed June 16, 2016).

Financial Crisis Inquiry Commission (2008e), *Mails 'Our Options in the Event of a Run on LB'. FCIC-154542.* http://fcic.law.stanford.edu/documents/view/433 (accessed June 16, 2016).

Financial Crisis Inquiry Commission (2008f), *Pros and Cons of Lending to AIG. FCIC-SSI0007443.* http://fcic-static.law.stanford.edu/cdn_media/fcic

-docs/2008-09-16%20Systemic%20Impact%20of%20AIG%20Bankruptcy %20attachment%20to%20FRBNY%20internal%20email%20from %20Alejandro%20LaTorre%20to%20Geithner.pdf (accessed June 16, 2016).

Financial Crisis Inquiry Commission (2008g), *Systemic Impact of AIG Bankruptcy. FCIC-SSI0007443.* http://fcic-static.law.stanford.edu/cdn _media/fcic-docs/2008-09-16%20Systemic%20Impact%20of%20AIG %20Bankruptcy%20attachment%20to%20FRBNY%20internal%20email %20from%20Alejandro%20LaTorre%20to%20Geithner.pdf (accessed June 16, 2016).

Financial Crisis Inquiry Commission (2010), *Chronology of Selected Events Related to Lehman Brothers and the Possibility of Government Assistance.* http://fcic-static.law.stanford.edu/cdn_media/fcic-testimony/2010-0901 -Lehman-Brothers-Chronology.pdf (accessed June 16, 2016).

Financial Crisis Inquiry Commission (2011), *The Financial Crisis Inquiry Report. Final Report of the National Commission on the Causes of the Financial and Economic Crisis in the United States, Authorized Edition*, New York: PublicAffairs.

Fiske, S.T. (1993), 'Social cognition and social perception', *Annual Review of Psychology*, **44** (1), 155–94.

Flach, J.M., M.A. Feufel, P.L. Reynolds, S.H. Parker and K.M. Kellogg (2017), 'Decisionmaking in practice: The dynamics of muddling through', *Applied Ergonomics*, **63**, 133–41.

Flaherty, M.G. and G.A. Fine (2001), 'Present, past, and future', *Time & Society*, **10** (2–3), 147–61.

Fletcher, M.A. and R. Morin (2005), 'Bush's approval rating drops to new low in wake of storm', *Washington Post*. http://www.washingtonpost.com/ wp-dyn/content/article/2005/09/12/AR2005091200668.html (accessed January 2, 2017).

Fligstein, N., J.S. Brundage and M. Schultz (2014), 'Why the Federal Reserve failed to see the financial crisis of 2008: The role of "macroeconomics" as a sense making and cultural frame', IRLE Working Paper 111-14, September.

Flin, R.H. (1996), *Sitting in the Hot Seat: Leaders and Teams for Critical Incident Management*, New York: John Wiley & Sons.

Forbes, I. (2004), 'Making a crisis out of a drama: The political analysis of BSE policy-making in the UK', *Political Studies*, **52** (2), 342–57.

Fox, J. (2008), 'Why the government wouldn't let AIG fail', *Time*. http:// content.time.com/time/business/article/0,8599,1841699,00.html (accessed April 25, 2016).

Frankel, A. (2015), 'The lawyer who talked too much—and lost the Fed privilege in AIG bailout suit', *Reuters Blogs*. http://blogs.reuters.com/

alison-frankel/2015/02/23/the-lawyer-who-talked-too-much-and-lost-the
-fed-privilege-in-aig-bailout-suit/ (accessed April 6, 2016).

Franklin, D.P. (2014), *Pitiful Giants: Presidents in Their Final Terms*, New York: Palgrave Macmillan.

Franks, D.D. (2010), *Neurosociology: The Nexus Between Neuroscience and Social Psychology*, New York: Springer.

Fredrickson, G.M. (2003), 'Review of the Metaphysical Club by Louis Menand', *The Journal of Southern History*, **69** (1), 205–6.

Frega, R. (2010), 'From judgment to rationality: Dewey's epistemology of practice', *Transactions of the Charles S. Peirce Society: A Quarterly Journal in American Philosophy*, **46** (4), 591–610.

Frega, R. (2012), *Practice, Judgment, and the Challenge of Moral and Political Disagreement: A Pragmatist Account*, Plymouth, UK: Lexington Books.

Frewer, L. (2004), 'The public and effective risk communication', *Toxicology Letters*, **149** (1–3), 391–7.

Frewer, L.J., S. Miles, M. Brennan, S. Kuznesof, M. Ness and C. Ritson (2002), 'Public preferences for informed choice under conditions of risk uncertainty', *Public Understanding of Science*, **11** (4), 363–72.

Frewer, L., S. Hunt, M. Brennan, S. Kuznesof, M. Ness and C. Ritson (2003), 'The views of scientific experts on how the public conceptualize uncertainty', *Journal of Risk Research*, **6** (1), 75–85.

Fung, A. (2006), 'Varieties of participation in complex governance', *Public Administration Review*, **66**, 66–75.

Funtowicz, S.O. and J.R. Ravetz (1994), 'Uncertainty, complexity and post-normal science', *Environmental Toxicology and Chemistry: An International Journal*, **13** (12), 1881–5.

Gallagher, S. (2014), 'Pragmatic interventions into enactive and extended conceptions of cognition', *Philosophical Issues*, **24** (1), 110–26.

Gallup (2008), 'Six in 10 oppose Wall Street bailouts'. http://www.gallup .com/poll/106114/six-oppose-wall-street-bailouts.aspx (accessed June 20, 2019).

Garber, D. (1999), 'Rationalism', in R. Audi (ed.), *The Cambridge Dictionary of Philosophy*, Cambridge: Cambridge University Press, pp. 771–2.

Garrison, J. (1996), 'Dewey, qualitative thought, and context', *International Journal of Qualitative Studies in Education*, **9** (4), 391–410.

Garrison, J. (1999), 'John Dewey's theory of practical reasoning', *Educational Philosophy and Theory*, **31** (3), 291–312.

Garrison, J. (2000), 'Pragmatism and public administration', *Administration & Society*, **32** (4), 458–77.

Gatens-Robinson, E. (1999), 'The private and its problem: A Pragmatic view of reproductive choice', in C. Haskins and D.I. Seiple (eds), *Dewey*

Reconfigured: Essays on Deweyan Pragmatism, Albany, NY: State University of New York Press, pp. 169–91.

Geithner, T.F. (2008), 'Reducing systemic risk in a dynamic financial system. Remarks at The Economic Club of New York, New York City'. https://www.newyorkfed.org/newsevents/speeches/2008/tfg080609 (accessed March 4, 2016).

Geithner, T.F. (2014), *Stress Test: Reflections on Financial Crises*, New York: Broadway Books.

Genovese, M.A. (1994), 'Crisis management', in L. Fisher and L.W. Levy (eds), *Encyclopedia of the American Presidency Vol. 1*, New York: Simon & Schuster, pp. 330–2.

George, A.L. (1979), 'Case studies and theory development: The method of structured, focused comparison', in P.G. Lauren (ed.), *Diplomacy: New Approaches in Theory, History, and Policy*, New York: Free Press, pp. 43–68.

George, A.L and A. Bennett (2005), *Case Studies and Theory Development in the Social Sciences*, Cambridge, MA: MIT Press.

George, A.L. and E.K. Stern (2002), 'Harnessing conflict in foreign policy making: From devil's to multiple advocacy', *Presidential Studies Quarterly*, **32** (3), 484–505.

Gerring, J. (2004), 'What is a case study and what is it good for?', *American Political Science Review*, **98** (2), 341–54.

Gerring, J. (2007), 'Is there a (viable) crucial-case method?', *Comparative Political Studies*, **40** (3), 231–53.

Gibson, D.R. (2011), 'Speaking of the future: Contentious narration during the Cuban missile crisis', *Qualitative Sociology*, **34** (4), 503–22.

Gilpin, D.R. and P.J. Murphy (2008), *Crisis Management in a Complex World*, New York: Oxford University Press.

Gioia, D.A. and K. Chittipeddi (1991), 'Sensemaking and sensegiving in strategic change initiation', *Strategic Management Journal*, **12** (6), 433–48.

Glaude, E.S. (2004), 'Tragedy and moral experience: John Dewey and Toni Morrison's Beloved', in B.E. Lawson and D.F. Koch (eds), *Pragmatism and the Problem of Race*, Bloomington, IN: Indiana University Press, pp. 89–121.

Glăveanu, V.P. (2012), 'Habitual creativity: Revising habit, reconceptualizing creativity', *Review of General Psychology*, **16** (1), 78–92.

Goertz, G. (2006), *Social Science Concepts: A User's Guide*, Princeton, NJ: Princeton University Press.

Gonzalez, M.E.Q. (2005), 'Creativity: Surprise and abductive reasoning', *Semiotica*, **153** (1), 325–42.

Goodman, R. (2013), 'William James', in E.N. Zalta (ed.), *The Stanford Encyclopedia of Philosophy*. http://plato.stanford.edu/archives/win2013/entries/james/ (accessed October 30, 2013).

Green, D.P. and I. Shapiro (1994), *Pathologies of Rational Choice Theory: A Critique of Applications in Political Science*, New Haven, CT: Yale University Press.

Greenspan, A. (2013), *The Map and the Territory: Risk, Human Nature, and the Future of Forecasting*, New York: Penguin.

Gross, N. (2009), 'A pragmatist theory of social mechanisms', *American Sociological Review*, **74** (3), 358–79.

Gross, M. (2010), *Ignorance and Surprise: Science, Society, and Ecological Design*, Cambridge, MA: MIT Press.

Greenstein, F.I. (2011), 'Barack Obama: The man and his presidency at the midterm', *PS: Political Science & Politics*, **44** (1), 7–11.

Grönvall, J. (2001), 'The mad cow crisis, the role of experts and European crisis management', in U. Rosenthal, A.R. Boin and L.K. Comfort (eds), *Managing Crises: Threats, Dilemmas, Opportunities*, Springfield, IL: Charles C. Thomas, pp. 155–74.

Habermas, J. (2010), 'Germany and the euro-crisis', *The Nation*. http://www.thenation.com/article/germany-and-euro-crisis/ (accessed December 10, 2015).

Hacker, J.S. (2002), *The Divided Welfare State. The Battle Over Public and Private Social Benefits in the United States*, Cambridge: Cambridge University Press.

Halper, S.A. and J. Clarke (2004), *America Alone: The Neo-Conservatives and the Global Order*, Cambridge; New York: Cambridge University Press.

Hands, D.W. (2006), 'Frank Knight and Pragmatism', *The European Journal of the History of Economic Thought*, **13** (4), 571–605.

Harknett, R.J. and J.A. Stever (2011), 'The new policy world of cybersecurity', *Public Administration Review*, **71** (3), 455–60.

't Hart, P. (2008), 'Symbols, rituals and power: The *lost* dimensions of crisis management', in A. Boin (ed.), *Crisis Management. Volume III*, London: Sage Publications, pp. 84–104.

't Hart (2010), 'Political psychology', in D. Marsh and G. Stoker (eds), *Theory and Methods in Political Science*, Houndmills, Basingstoke: Palgrave Macmillan, pp. 99–113.

't Hart (2011), 'Groupthink', in K. Dowding (ed.), *Encyclopedia of Power*, Thousand Oaks, CA: Sage Publications, pp. 297–8.

't Hart (2012), 'It depends: Examining the nexus between leaders and contexts', Paper for the Political Studies Association, Belfast, April. http://www.psa.ac.uk/journals/pdf/5/2012/846_171.pdf.

t'Hart, P.T. and K. Tindall (2009), 'Understanding crisis exploitation: Leadership, rhetoric and framing contests in response to the economic melt-down', in P.T. t'Hart and K. Tindall (eds), *Framing the Global Economic Downturn: Crisis Rhetoric and the Politics of Recessions*, Acton, ACT: ANU Press, pp. 21–42.

't Hart, P. and J. Uhr (2008), *Public Leadership Perspectives and Practices*, Acton, ACT: ANU Press.

't Hart, P., U. Rosenthal and A. Kouzmin (2008), 'Crisis decision making: The centralization thesis revisited', in A. Boin (ed.), *Crisis Management. Volume II*, London: Sage Publications, pp. 225–49.

Harvard Business School (2004), *Crisis Management: Master the Skills to Prevent Disasters*, Boston, MA: Harvard Business School Press.

Hauge, A.M. (2017), 'Organizing valuations: A Pragmatic inquiry', PhD dissertation, Copenhagen Business School.

Hay, C. (2002), *Political Analysis*. Houndmills, Basingstoke; New York: Palgrave Macmillan.

Head, B. (2010), 'Evidence-based policy: Principles and requirements', in *Strengthening Evidence-Based Policy in the Australian Federation, Roundtable Proceedings*, Canberra, pp. 13–26.

Hedtke, J.R. (2002), *Lame Duck Presidents—Myth or Reality*, Lewiston, NY: E. Mellen Press.

Helsloot, I., A. Boin, B. Jacobs and L.K. Comfort (eds) (2012), *Mega-Crises: Understanding the Prospects, Nature, Characteristics and Effects of Cataclysmic Events*, Springfield, IL: Charles C. Thomas.

Hermann, C.F. (1963), 'Some consequences of crisis which limit the viability of organizations', *Administrative Science Quarterly*, **8** (1), 61–82.

Hermann, M.G. (1979), 'Indicators of stress in policymakers during foreign policy crises', *Political Psychology*, **1** (1), 27–46.

Hermann, M.G. and B.W. Dayton (2009), 'Transboundary crises through the eyes of policymakers: Sense making and crisis management', *Journal of Contingencies and Crisis Management*, **17** (4), 233–41.

Hernes, T., B. Simpson and J. Soderlund (2013), 'Managing and temporality', *Scandinavian Journal of Management*, **29** (1), 1–6.

Hertwig, R. (2015), 'Decisions from experience', in G. Keren and G. Wu (eds), *The Wiley Blackwell Handbook of Judgment and Decision Making*, Vol. 2, Malden, MA: John Wiley & Sons, pp. 239–67.

Hickman, L.A. (1990), *John Dewey's Pragmatic Technology*, Bloomington, IN: Indiana University Press.

Hildebrand, D.L. (2003), *Beyond Realism and Antirealism: John Dewey and the Neopragmatists*, Nashville, TN: Vanderbilt University Press.

Hillyard, M.J. (2000), *Public Crisis Management: How and Why Organizations Work Together to Solve Society's Most Threatening Problems*, San Jose, CA: Writers Club Press.

Hilsenrath, J., J. Perry and S. Reddy (2008), 'Central bankers debate where to draw the line', *The Wall Street Journal Europe*. http://global.factiva.com/redir/default.aspx?P=sa&an=WSJE000020080915e49e00003&cat=a&ep=ASE (accessed March 31, 2016).

Hitlin, S. and G.H. Elder Jr (2007), 'Time, self, and the curiously abstract concept of agency', *Sociological Theory*, **25** (2), 170–91.

Hodgson, G.M. (2004), 'Reclaiming habit for institutional economics', *Journal of Economic Psychology*, **25** (5), 651–60.

Hodgson, G.M. (2009), 'The nature and replication of routines', in M. Becker and N. Lazaric (eds), *Organizational Routines: Advancing Empirical Research*, Cheltenham, UK and Northampton, MA, USA: Edward Elgar Publishing, pp. 26–46.

Holcomb, J. (2013), 'How the Lehman Bros. crisis impacted the 2008 presidential race', *Pew Research Center*. http://www.pewresearch.org/fact-tank/2013/09/19/how-the-lehman-bros-crisis-impacted-the-2008-presidential-race/ (accessed April 26, 2016).

Holmes, O.W. (1946), *Touched with Fire: Civil War Letters and Diary of Oliver Wendell Holmes Jr.*, ed. M. De Wolfe Howe, Cambridge, MA: Harvard University Press.

Holmwood, J. (2011), 'Pragmatism and the prospects of sociological theory', *Journal of Classical Sociology*, **11** (1), 15–30.

Holmwood, J. (2014), 'Reflexivity as situated problem-solving: A Pragmatist alternative to general theory', *Sociologica*, **8** (1), 1–25.

Holopainen, M. and M. Toivonen (2012), 'Weak signals: Ansoff today', *Futures*, **44** (3), 198–205.

Hood, C. (2011), *The Blame Game: Spin, Bureaucracy, and Self-Preservation in Government*, Princeton, NJ: Princeton University Press.

Hook, S. (2002), 'Pragmatism and the tragic sense of life', in R.B. Talisse and R. Tempio (eds), *Sidney Hook on Pragmatism, Democracy, and Freedom: The Essential Essays*, Amherst, NY: Prometheus Books, pp. 68–90.

Hookway, C. (2013), 'Pragmatism', in E.N. Zalta (ed.), *The Stanford Encyclopedia of Philosophy* (Winter Edition). http://plato.stanford.edu/archives/win2013/entries/pragmatism/ (accessed June 20, 2019).

Horkheimer, M. and T.W Adorno (1969), *Dialektik der Aufklärung. Philosophische Fragmente*, Frankfurt am Main: S. Fischer.

Houghton, D.P. (1996), 'The role of analogical reasoning in novel foreign-policy situations', *British Journal of Political Science*, **26** (4), 523–52.

Houghton, D.P. (2001), *US Foreign Policy and the Iran Hostage Crisis*, Cambridge: Cambridge University Press.

Howell, W.G. and T. Johnson (2009), 'War's contribution to presidential power', in G.C. Edwards and W.G. Howell (eds), *The Oxford Handbook of the American Presidency*, Oxford: Oxford University Press, pp. 724–46.

Howell, W.G., S.P. Jackman and J.C. Rogowski (2013), *The Wartime President: Executive Influence and the Nationalizing Politics of Threat*, Chicago, IL: University of Chicago Press.

Howitt, A.M. and H.B. Leonard (2009), *Managing Crises: Responses to Large-Scale Emergencies*, Washington, DC: CQ Press.

Huber, G.P. and K. Lewis (2010), 'Cross-understanding: Implications for group cognition and performance', *Academy of Management Review*, **35** (1), 6–26.

Huff, A.S. (1978), 'Consensual uncertainty', *Academy of Management Review*, **3** (3), 651–5.

Huff, A.S., F.J. Milliken, G P. Hodgkinson, R.J. Galavan and K.J. Sund (2016), 'A conversation on uncertainty in managerial and organizational cognition', in K.J. Sund, R.J. Galavan and A.S. Huff (eds), *Uncertainty and Strategic Decision Making*, Bingley, UK: Emerald Group Publishing Limited, pp. 1–31.

Hülsmann, J.G. (2008), 'Beware the moral hazard trivializers', *Mises Institute*. https://mises.org/library/beware-moral-hazard-trivializers (accessed October 12, 2015).

Hunter, S.T., K.E. Bedell-Avers, C.M. Hunsicker, M.D. Mumford and G.S. Ligon (2008), 'Applying multiple knowledge structures in creative thought: Effects on idea generation and problem-solving', *Creativity Research Journal*, **20** (2), 137–54.

Hutter, M. and D. Stark (2015), 'Pragmatist perspectives on valuation: An introduction', in A.B. Antal, M. Hutter and D. Stark (eds), *Moments of Valuation: Exploring Sites of Dissonance*, New York: Oxford University Press, pp. 1–14.

Ip, G. (2008), 'Fed's fireman on Wall Street feels some heat', *Wall Street Journal*. http://www.wsj.com/articles/SB121210816211631323 (accessed February 2, 2016).

Istook, E. (2008), 'Can American socialism ever be reversed?', *The Heritage Foundation. Commentary*. https://www.heritage.org/civil-society/commentary/can-american-socialism-ever-be-reversed (accessed June 20, 2019).

James, W. (1896), *The Sentiment of Rationality*, New York: Longmans, Green and Company.

James, W. (1900), *Talks to Teachers and Students*, New York: Henry Holt and Co.

James, W. (1910), 'The moral equivalent of war', *McClure's Magazine*, August, 463–8.

James, W. (1911), *Memories and Studies*, New York: Longmans, Green and Company.

James, W. (1997), 'The will to believe', in L. Menand (ed.), *Pragmatism: A Reader*, New York: Vintage Books, pp. 69–92.

James, W. (2000), *Pragmatism and Other Writings*, ed. G. Gunn, New York: Penguin.

James, W. (2005), 'Philosophical conceptions and practical results', in R.B. Goodman (ed.), *Pragmatism: Critical Concepts in Philosophy, Volume 1*, London; New York: Routledge, pp. 59–74.

James, W. (2010), *The Heart of William James*, ed. R. Richardson, Cambridge, MA: Harvard University Press.

Janis, I.L. (1982), *Groupthink*, Boston, MA: Houghton Mifflin.

Janis, I.L. (1989), *Crucial Decisions: Leadership in Policymaking and Crisis Management*, New York: Free Press.

Jervis, R. (2017), *Perception and Misperception in International Politics*, New Edition, Princeton, NJ: Princeton University Press.

Joas, H. (1990), 'The creativity of action and the intersubjectivity of reason: Mead's pragmatism and social theory', *Transactions of the Charles S. Peirce Society*, **26** (2), 165–94.

Joas, H. (1993), *Pragmatism and Social Theory*, Chicago, IL: University of Chicago Press.

Joas, H. (1997), *The Creativity of Action*, Chicago, IL: University of Chicago Press.

Joas, H. (2000), *The Genesis of Values*, Chicago, IL: University of Chicago Press.

Joas, H. and E. Kilpinen (2009), 'Creativity and society', in J.R. Shook and J. Margolis (eds), *A Companion to Pragmatism*, Malden, MA; Oxford: Wiley-Blackwell, pp. 323–35.

Johnson, B.B. and P. Slovic (1998), 'Lay views on uncertainty in environmental health risk assessment', *Journal of Risk Research*, **1** (4), 261–79.

Johnson, M. and T. Rohrer (2007), 'We are live creatures: American Pragmatism and the cognitive organism', in J. Zlatev, T. Ziemke, R. Frank and R. Dirven (eds), *Body, Language, and Mind*, Vol. 1, Berlin: Mouton de Gruyter, pp. 17–54.

Jones, J.M. (2008), 'Bush's approval rating drops to new low of 27%', *Gallup. com*. http://www.gallup.com/poll/110806/Bushs-Approval-Rating-Drops-New-Low-27.aspx (accessed April 27, 2016).

Jong, W., M.L. Dückers and P.G. van der Velden (2016), 'Leadership of mayors and governors during crises: A systematic review on tasks and effectiveness', *Journal of Contingencies and Crisis Management*, **24** (1), 46–58.

Jurkowitz, M. (2008), 'The latest campaign narrative—"It's The Economy, Stupid"', *Pew Research Center's Journalism Project*. http://www

.journalism.org/2008/09/22/pej-campaign-coverage-index-september-15
-21-2008/ (accessed April 26, 2016).

Kahneman, D. (2003), 'Maps of bounded rationality: Psychology for behavioral economics', *American Economic Review*, **93** (5), 1449–75.

Kahneman, D. (2012), *Thinking, Fast and Slow*, London: Penguin.

Kahneman, D. and G. Klein (2009), 'Conditions for intuitive expertise: A failure to disagree', *American Psychologist*, **64** (6), 515–26.

Kahneman, D. and A. Tversky (1982), 'Variants of uncertainty', *Cognition*, **11** (2), 143–57.

Kane, J. and H. Patapan (2009), 'The democratic legitimacy of bureaucratic leadership', in J. Kane, H. Patapan and P. 't Hart (eds), *Dispersed Democratic Leadership: Origins, Dynamics, and Implications*, Oxford; New York: Oxford University Press, pp. 119–39.

Kasperson, R.E., O. Renn, P. Slovic, H.S. Brown, J. Emel, R. Goble and S. Ratick (1988), 'The social amplification of risk: A conceptual framework', *Risk Analysis*, **8** (2), 177–87.

Kauffman, J. (2001), 'A successful failure: NASA's crisis communications regarding Apollo 13', *Public Relations Review*, **27** (4), 437–48.

Kelly, K. (2009), *Street Fighters: The Last 72 Hours of Bear Stearns, the Toughest Firm on Wall Street*, New York: Portfolio.

Kennedy, E. (1988), 'Introduction: Carl Schmitt's Parlamentarismus in its historical context', in *The Crisis of Parliamentary Democracy*, Cambridge, MA: MIT Press, pp. xiii–xlix.

Kennedy, J.F. (1964), *Public Papers of the Presidents of the United States: John F. Kennedy, 1963*, Washington, DC: US Government Printing Office.

Kenworthy, L. and L.A. Owens (2011), 'The surprisingly weak effect of recessions on public opinion', in D.B. Grusky, B. Western and C. Wimer (eds), *The Great Recession*, New York: Russell Sage Foundation, pp. 196–219.

Kilpinen, E. (2009), 'The habitual conception of action and social theory', *Semiotica*, **173**, 99–128.

Kilpinen, E. (2013), 'Pragmatic theory of action', *The International Encyclopedia of Ethics*, Hoboken, NJ: Blackwell, pp. 4020–6.

Kim, H.J. and G.T. Cameron (2011), 'Emotions matter in crisis: The role of anger and sadness in the publics' response to crisis news framing and corporate crisis response', *Communication Research*, **38** (6), 826–55.

King, G., R.O. Keohane and S. Verba (1994), *Designing Social Inquiry: Scientific Inference in Qualitative Research*, Princeton, NJ: Princeton University Press.

Klamer, A. (2003), 'A pragmatic view on values in economics', *Journal of Economic Methodology*, **10** (2), 191–212.

Klein, G.A. (1998). *Sources of Power: How People Make Decisions*, Cambridge, MA: MIT Press.

Klein, G.A. (2009), *Streetlights and Shadows: Searching for the Keys to Adaptive Decision Making*, Cambridge, MA: MIT Press.

Klein, G. and E. Eckhaus (2017), 'Sensemaking and sensegiving as predicting organizational crisis', *Risk Management*, **19** (3), 225–44.

Klinenberg, E. (2015), *Heat Wave: A Social Autopsy of Disaster in Chicago*, Chicago, IL: University of Chicago Press.

Kloppenberg, J.T. (1988), *Uncertain Victory: Social Democracy and Progressivism in European and American Thought, 1870–1920*, Oxford University Press on Demand.

Kloppenberg, J.T. (1996), 'Pragmatism: An old name for some new ways of thinking?', *The Journal of American History*, **83** (1), 100–38.

Knight, F.H. (1921), *Risk, Uncertainty and Profit*, Boston, MA: Houghton Mifflin.

Knight, J. and J. Johnson (1996), 'Political consequences of Pragmatism', *Political Theory*, **24** (1), 68–96.

Knight, J. and J. Johnson (1999), 'Inquiry into democracy: What might a pragmatist make of rational choice theories?', *American Journal of Political Science*, **43** (2), 566–89.

Kolb, R.W. (2011), *The Financial Crisis of Our Time*, Oxford: Oxford University Press. http://site.ebrary.com/id/10437691 (accessed October 16, 2015).

Kollewe, J. (2012), 'Angela Merkel's austerity postergirl, the thrifty swabian housewife', *Guardian*. http://www.theguardian.com/world/2012/sep/17/angela-merkel-austerity-swabian-housewives (accessed November 26, 2015).

Koopman, C. (2009), *Pragmatism as Transition: Historicity and Hope in James, Dewey, and Rorty*, New York: Columbia University Press.

Koopman, C. (2010), 'Historicism in pragmatism: Lessons in historiography and philosophy', *Metaphilosophy*, **41** (5), 690–713.

Koppenjan, J. and E.H. Klijn (2004), *Managing Uncertainties in Networks: Public Private Controversies*, Abingdon, UK: Routledge.

Koselleck, R. (2006), 'Crisis', *Journal of the History of Ideas*, **67** (2), 357–400.

Krieger, K., R. Amlôt and M.B. Rogers (2014), 'Understanding public responses to chemical, biological, radiological and nuclear incidents—driving factors, emerging themes and research gaps', *Environment International*, **72**, 66–74.

Kriner, D.L. (2010), *After the Rubicon: Congress, Presidents, and the Politics of Waging War*, Chicago, IL: University of Chicago Press.

Krugman, P. (1999), *The Return of Depression Economics*, New York: W.W. Norton.

Krugman, P. (2008), 'Cash for trash', *New York Times*. http://www.nytimes.com/2008/09/22/opinion/22krugman.html (accessed June 10, 2015).

Kudlow, L. (2008), 'Interview with President Bush, March 14 2008'. http://kudlowsmoneypolitics.blogspot.de/2008/03/my-interview-with-president-bush_14.html (accessed March 2, 2016).

Kuklick, B. (2001), 'Review of The Metaphysical Club: A story of ideas in America by Louis Menand', *Transactions of the Charles S. Peirce Society*, **37** (4), 635–8.

Kupers, W.M. (2011), 'Embodied pheno-pragma-practice-phenomenological and Pragmatic perspectives on creative "inter-practice" in organisations between habits and improvisation', *Phenomenology & Practice*, **5** (1), 100–39.

Kuruvilla, S. and P. Dorstewitz (2010), 'There is no "point" in decision-making: A model of transactive rationality for public policy and administration', *Policy Sciences*, **43** (3), 263–87.

La Porte, T.R. (1996), 'High reliability organizations: Unlikely, demanding and at risk', *Journal of Contingencies and Crisis Management*, **4** (2), 60–71.

La Porte, T.R. and P.M. Consolini (1991), 'Working in practice but not in theory: Theoretical challenges of "high-reliability organizations"', *Journal of Public Administration Research and Theory*, **1** (1), 19–48.

Labaton, S. (2008), 'Wall St. in worst loss since '01, despite reassurances from Washington', *New York Times*. http://www.nytimes.com/2008/09/16/business/16paulson.html (accessed March 30, 2016).

Labaton, S. and E.L. Andrews (2008), 'In rescue to stabilize lending, U.S. takes over mortgage finance titans', *New York Times*. http://www.nytimes.com/2008/09/08/business/08fannie.html (accessed April 20, 2016).

LaFollette, H. (2000), 'Pragmatic ethics', in H. LaFollette (ed.), *The Blackwell Guide to Ethical Theory*, Oxford: Blackwell, pp. 400–19.

Lagadec, P. (2004), 'Understanding the French 2003 heat wave experience: Beyond the heat, a multi-layered challenge', *Journal of Contingencies and Crisis Management*, **12** (4), 160–9.

Lalonde, C. (2004), 'In search of archetypes in crisis management', *Journal of Contingencies and Crisis Management*, **12** (2), 76–88.

Landler, M. and E. Dash (2008), 'Drama behind a $250 billion banking deal', *New York Times*. http://www.nytimes.com/2008/10/15/business/economy/15bailout.html (accessed October 7, 2015).

Landon, T. (2008a), 'Fears that Bear Stearns's downfall may spread', *New York Times*. http://www.nytimes.com/2008/03/17/business/17econ.html (accessed January 27, 2016).

Landon, T. (2008b), 'Run on big Wall St. bank spurs rescue backed by U.S', *New York Times*. http://www.nytimes.com/2008/03/15/business/15bear.html (accessed January 27, 2016).

Lauren, P.G. (1979), 'Crisis management: History and theory in international conflict', *The International History Review*, **1** (4), 542–56.

Lawder, D. (2008), 'Paulson adamant no goverment funds for Lehman: Source', *Reuters*. http://www.reuters.com/article/us-lehman-treasury -idUSWAT01003520080912 (accessed April 8, 2016).

Lawlor, M.S. (2006), 'William James's psychological Pragmatism: Habit, belief and purposive human behaviour', *Cambridge Journal of Economics*, **30** (3), 321–45.

Lehman Brothers (2008a), 'Lehman Brothers Holdings Inc. announces it intends to file Chapter 11 bankruptcy petition'. http://www.lehman.com/ press/pdf_2008/091508_lbhi_chapter11_announce.pdf (accessed June 20, 2019).

Lehman Brothers (2008b), 'Quarterly earnings—second quarter 2008'. http:// www.lehman.com/press/qe/past/2_08qe.htm (accessed March 21, 2016).

Lewitt, M. (2008), 'Why the Fed can't let A.I.G. go under', *New York Times*. http://www.nytimes.com/2008/09/16/opinion/16lewitt.html (accessed April 25, 2016).

Lewis, M. (2011). *The Big Short: Inside the Doomsday Machine*, London: Penguin UK.

Li, Y., N.M. Ashkanasy and D. Ahlstrom (2014), 'The rationality of emotions: A hybrid process model of decision-making under uncertainty', *Asia Pacific Journal of Management*, **31** (1), 293–308.

Lincoln, A. (1953), 'To Albert G. Hodges', in R.P. Basler (ed.), *Collected Works of Abraham Lincoln. Volume 7*, New Brunswick, NJ: Rutgers University Press, pp. 281–3.

Lincoln, A. (1992), 'Second Inaugural Address', in *Selected Speeches and Writings*, New York: Vintage Books, pp. 449–50.

Lindblom, C.E. (1959), 'The science of "muddling through"', *Public Administration Review*, **19** (2), 79–88.

Lindblom, C.E. (1977), *Politics and Markets: The World's Political Economic Systems*, New York: Basic Books.

Lindblom, C.E. (1979), 'Still muddling, not yet through', *Public Administration Review*, **39** (6), 517–26.

Lindblom, C.E. (1988), *Democracy and Market System*, Oslo: Norwegian University Press.

Lindblom, C.E. and E.J. Woodhouse (1993), *The Policy-Making Process*, Englewood Cliffs, NJ: Prentice Hall.

Lipshitz, R. and O. Strauss (1997), 'Coping with uncertainty: A naturalistic decision-making analysis', *Organizational Behavior and Human Decision Processes*, **69** (2), 149–63.

Lipshitz, R., G. Klein, J. Orasanu and E. Salas (2001), 'Taking stock of naturalistic decision making', *Journal of Behavioral Decision Making*, **14** (5), 331–52.

Liu, B.F., L. Bartz and N. Duke (2016), 'Communicating crisis uncertainty: A review of the knowledge gaps', *Public Relations Review*, **42** (3), 479–87.

Lodge, M. (2013), 'Crisis, resources and the State: Executive politics in the age of the depleted State', *Political Studies Review*, **11** (3), 378–90.

Lodge, M. and K. Wegrich (2012), *Executive Politics in Times of Crisis*, Houndmills, Basingstoke: Palgrave Macmillan.

Lovejoy, A.O. (1908), 'The thirteen Pragmatisms', *The Journal of Philosophy, Psychology and Scientific Methods*, **5** (1), 5–12.

Lovell, J. and J. Kluger (2006), *Apollo 13*, Boston, MA: Houghton Mifflin Harcourt.

Lynn, G.S., J.G. Morone and A.S. Paulson (1996), 'Marketing and discontinuous innovation: The probe and learn process', *California Management Review*, **38** (3), 8–37.

Mahoney, J. and G. Goertz (2006), 'A tale of two cultures: Contrasting quantitative and qualitative research', *Political Analysis*, **14** (3), 227–49.

Maines, D.R., N.M. Sugrue and M.A. Katovich (1983), 'The sociological import of GH Mead's theory of the past', *American Sociological Review*, **48** (2), 161–73.

Maitlis, S. and M. Christianson (2014), 'Sensemaking in organizations: Taking stock and moving forward', *The Academy of Management Annals*, **8** (1), 57–125.

Maitlis, S. and S. Sonenshein (2010), 'Sensemaking in crisis and change: Inspiration and insights from Weick (1988)', *Journal of Management Studies*, **47** (3), 551–80.

Mann, J. (2015), *George W. Bush: The American Presidents Series: The 43rd President, 2001–2009*, New York: Times Books.

March, J.G. (1978), 'Bounded rationality, ambiguity, and the engineering of choice', *The Bell Journal of Economics*, **9** (2), 587–608.

Markie, P. (2013), 'Rationalism vs. empiricism, in E.N. Zalta (ed.), *The Stanford Encyclopedia of Philosophy*. http://plato.stanford.edu/archives/sum2013/entries/rationalism-empiricism/ (accessed January 2, 2015).

Markon, M.P.L. and L. Lemyre (2013), 'Public reactions to risk messages communicating different sources of uncertainty: An experimental test', *Human and Ecological Risk Assessment: An International Journal*, **19** (4), 1102–26.

Marsh, D. and P. Furlong (2010), 'A skin not a sweater: Ontology and epistemology in political science', in D. Marsh and G. Stoker (eds), *Theory and Methods in Political Science*, Houndmills, Basingstoke: Palgrave Macmillan, pp. 184–211.

Massecar, A. (2011), 'An ethics of intelligently informed habits: How theory informs practice in Charles S. Peirce's writings', PhD dissertation, University of Guelph.

Massecar, A. (2012), 'Peirce's interesting associations', *Transactions of the Charles S. Peirce Society: A Quarterly Journal in American Philosophy*, **48** (2), 191–208.

Masters, A. and P. 't Hart (2012), 'Prime ministerial rhetoric and recession politics: Meaning making in economic crisis management', *Public Administration*, **90** (3), 759–80.

Masur, G. (1968), 'Crisis in history', in P.P. Wiener (ed.), *Dictionary of the History of Ideas, Volume I*, New York: Macmillan, pp. 589–96.

McCain, J. and S. Palin (2008), 'We'll protect taxpayers from more bailouts', *Wall Street Journal*. http://www.wsj.com/articles/SB122091995349512749 (accessed January 16, 2016).

McCall, G.J. (2013), 'Interactionist perspectives in social psychology', in J. DeLamater and A. Ward (eds), *Handbook of Social Psychology*, Dordrecht: Springer Netherlands, pp. 3–29.

McComas, K.A. (2006), 'Defining moments in risk communication research: 1996–2005', *Journal of Health Communication*, **11** (1), 75–91.

McConnell, A. (2003), 'Overview: Crisis management, influences, responses and evaluation', *Parliamentary Affairs*, **56** (3), 363–409.

McConnell, A. (2008), 'Overview: Crisis management, influences, responses and evaluation', in A. Boin (ed.), *Crisis Management. Volume III*, London: Sage Publications, pp. 187–201.

McConnell, A. (2011), 'Success? Failure? Something in-between? A framework for evaluating crisis management', *Policy and Society*, **30** (2), 63–76.

McConnell, A. and A. Stark (2002), 'Foot-and-Mouth 2001: The politics of crisis management', *Parliamentary Affairs*, **55** (4), 664–81.

McDermid, D. (2006), *The Varieties of Pragmatism: Truth, Realism, and Knowledge from James to Rorty*, London; New York: Continuum.

McDermott, R., J. Cowden and C. Koopman (2002), 'Framing, uncertainty, and hostile communications in a crisis experiment', *Political Psychology*, **23** (1), 133–49.

McGowan, J. (1998), 'Toward a Pragmatist theory of action', *Sociological Theory*, **16** (3), 292–7.

Mead, G.H. (1925), 'The genesis of the self and social control', *The International Journal of Ethics*, **35** (3), 251–77.

Mead, G.H. (1929), 'The nature of the past', in J. Coss (ed.), *Essays in Honor of John Dewey*, New York: Henry Holt & Co., pp. 235–42.

Mead, G.H. (1932), *The Philosophy of the Present*, Chicago, IL: University of Chicago Press.

Menand, L. (1997), 'An introduction to Pragmatism', in L. Menand (ed.), *Pragmatism: A Reader*, New York: Vintage Books, pp. xi–xxxiv.

Menand, L. (2001), *The Metaphysical Club*, New York: Farrar, Straus, and Giroux.

Menary, R. (2016), 'Pragmatism and the pragmatic turn in cognitive science', in K. Friston, A. Andreas and D. Kragic (eds), *Pragmatism and the Pragmatic Turn in Cognitive Science*, Cambridge, MA: MIT Press, pp. 219–36.

Mendonça, S., M.P. Cunha, J. Kaivo-Oja and F. Ruff (2004), 'Wild cards, weak signals and organisational improvisation', *Futures*, **36** (2), 201–18.

Merriam Webster (n.d.), 'Definition of Pragmatism', *Merriam Webster Dictionary*. http://www.merriam-webster.com/dictionary/pragmatism (accessed April 27, 2016).

Meyer, R. and H. Kunreuther (2017), *The Ostrich Paradox: Why We Underprepare for Disasters*, Philadelphia, PA: Wharton Digital Press.

Miettinen, R. (2006), 'Epistemology of transformative material activity: John Dewey's Pragmatism and cultural-historical activity theory', *Journal for the Theory of Social Behaviour*, **36** (4), 389–408.

Miettinen, R. (2000), 'The concept of experiential learning and John Dewey's theory of reflective thought and action', *International Journal of Lifelong Education*, **19** (1), 54–72.

Miettinen, R., S. Paavola and P. Pohjola (2012), 'From habituality to change: Contribution of Activity Theory and Pragmatism to practice theories', *Journal for the Theory of Social Behaviour*, **42** (3), 345–60.

Mill, J.S. (1989), 'On Liberty', in S. Collini (ed.), *J. S. Mill: 'On Liberty' and Other Writings*, Cambridge: Cambridge University Press, pp. 1–116.

Milliken, F.J. (1987). 'Three types of perceived uncertainty about the environment: State, effect, and response uncertainty', *Academy of Management Review*, **12** (1), 133–43.

Mirbabaie, M. and S. Youn (2018), 'Exploring sense-making activities in crisis situations', in *Proceedings of the 10th Multikonferenz Wirtschaftsinformatik* (MKWI), Lüneburg, Germany, pp. 1656–67.

Misak, C. (2004), 'Making disagreement matter: Pragmatism and deliberative democracy', *The Journal of Speculative Philosophy*, **18** (1), 9–22.

Misak, C. (2014), 'Review of pragmatism and inquiry: Selected essays, by Isaac Levi', *European Journal of Philosophy*, **22** (S1), e11–e14.

Mitchell, D. (2005), *Making Foreign Policy: Presidential Management of the Decision-Making Process*, Burlington, VT: Ashgate Publishing.

Mollenkamp, C. (2008), 'Lehman deal could come soon as high-level talks continue', *Wall Street Journal*. http://www.wsj.com/articles/SB122132019771832253 (accessed March 30, 2016).

Montibeller, G. and D. Von Winterfeldt (2015), 'Cognitive and motivational biases in decision and risk analysis', *Risk Analysis*, **35** (7), 1230–51.

Mooney, M. (2008), 'Bush "battered down" in economic crisis', *ABC News*. http://abcnews.go.com/Politics/Vote2008/story?id=5977264&page=1 (accessed April 26, 2016).

Morgan, I. (2010), 'Bush's political economy: Deficits, debt, and depression', in I. Morgan and P. Davies (eds), *Assessing George W. Bush's Legacy: The Right Man?* New York: Palgrave Macmillan, pp. 185–206.

Morgenson, G. and D. Van Natta (2009), 'During crisis, Paulson's calls to Goldman posed ethics test', *New York Times*. http://www.nytimes.com/2009/08/09/business/09paulson.html (accessed February 26, 2016).

Morse, D. (2010), 'Dewey on the emotions', *Human Affairs*, **20** (3), 224–31.

Morton, R.B. (2009), 'Formal modeling and empirical analysis in political science', in S. Pickel, G. Pickel, H-J. Lauth and D. Jahn (eds), *Methoden Der Vergleichenden Politik- Und Sozialwissenschaft*, Wiesbaden: VS Verlag für Sozialwissenschaften, pp. 27–35.

Mousavi, S. and J. Garrison (2003), 'Toward a transactional theory of decision making: Creative rationality as functional coordination in context', *Journal of Economic Methodology*, **10** (2), 131–56.

Mousavi, S. and G. Gigerenzer (2014), 'Risk, uncertainty, and heuristics', *Journal of Business Research*, **67** (8), 1671–8.

Moynihan, D.P. (2008), 'Learning under uncertainty: Networks in crisis management', *Public Administration Review*, **68** (2), 350–65.

Moynihan, D.P. (2009), 'The network governance of crisis response: Case studies of incident command systems', *Journal of Public Administration Research and Theory*, **19** (4), 895–915.

Mullins, P. (2002), 'Peirce's abduction and Polanyi's tacit knowing', *The Journal of Speculative Philosophy*, **16** (3), 198–224.

Mumford, M.D., S. Connelly and B. Gaddis (2003), 'How creative leaders think: Experimental findings and cases', *The Leadership Quarterly*, **14** (4–5), 411–32.

Mumford, M.D., T.L. Friedrich, J.J. Caughron and C.L. Byrne (2007), 'Leader cognition in real-world settings: How do leaders think about crises?', *The Leadership Quarterly*, **18** (6), 515–43.

Muniesa, F. (2012), 'A flank movement in the understanding of valuation', *The Sociological Review*, **59** (s2), 24–38.

Myers, S.L. (2008), 'Bush, praising Fed's move, faces criticism', *New York Times*. http://www.nytimes.com/2008/03/17/business/17cnd-bush.html (accessed March 3, 2016).

Nash, J.S. (2003), 'On Pragmatic philosophy and Knightian uncertainty', *Review of Social Economy*, **61** (2), 251–72.

Nelson, S.C. and P.J. Katzenstein (2014), 'Uncertainty, risk, and the financial crisis of 2008', *International Organization*, **68** (2), 361–92.

Nocera, J. (2011), 'Sheila Bair's exit interview', *New York Times*. http://www.nytimes.com/2011/07/10/magazine/sheila-bairs-exit-interview.html (accessed April 20, 2016).

Nolan, L. (2011), 'Descartes' ontological argument', in E.N. Zalta (ed.), *The Stanford Encyclopedia of Philosophy*. http://plato.stanford.edu/archives/sum2011/entries/descartes-ontological/ (accessed October 29, 2013).

Nöth, W. (2010), 'The criterion of habit in Peirce's definitions of the symbol', *Transactions of the Charles S. Peirce Society: A Quarterly Journal in American Philosophy*, **46** (1), 82–93.

NPR (2009), 'Interview with Alan Greenberg'. http://www.pbs.org/wgbh/pages/frontline/ meltdown/interviews/greenberg.html (accessed March 1, 2016).

Nubiola, J. (2005), 'Abduction or the Logic of surprise', *Semiotica*, **153** (1), 117–30.

OECD (2015), *The Changing Face of Strategic Crisis Management*. Paris: Organisation for Economic Co-operation and Development.

Olmeda, J.A. (2008), 'A reversal of fortune: blame games and framing contests after the 3/11 terrorist attacks in Madrid', in A. Boin, A. McConnell and P. 't Hart (eds), *Governing After Crisis: The Politics of Investigation, Accountability and Learning*, Cambridge: Cambridge University Press, pp. 62–84.

Oppenheimer, J.A. (2010), 'Rational choice theory', in M. Bevir (ed.), *Encyclopedia of Political Theory*, Thousand Oaks, CA: Sage Publications.

Ornstein, N.J. (2009), 'George W. Bush's gentlemanly goodbye', *New York Times*. http://www.nytimes.com/2009/01/20/opinion/20iht-edornstein.1.19525297.html (accessed April 26, 2016).

Orszag, P. (2009), 'Building rigorous evidence to drive policy', *The White House*. http://www.whitehouse.gov/omb/blog/09/06/08/buildingrigorousevidencetodrivepolicy (accessed October 24, 2014).

Paavola, S. (2005), 'Peircean abduction: Instinct or inference?', *Semiotica*, **153** (4), 131–54.

Page, S.E. (2008), 'Uncertainty, difficulty, and complexity', *Journal of Theoretical Politics*, **20** (2), 115–49.

Parker, C.F. and E.K. Stern (2002), 'Blindsided? September 11 and the origins of strategic surprise', *Political Psychology*, **23** (3), 601–30.

Parkhurst, J.O. and S. Abeysinghe (2014), 'What constitutes 'good' evidence for public health and social policy making? From hierarchies to appropriateness', *Social Epistemology Review and Reply Collective*, **3** (10), 40–52.

Parsons, S.D. (2005), *Rational Choice and Politics: A Critical Introduction*, London; New York: Continuum.

Patterson, J.T. (2010), 'Transformative economic policies. Tax cutting, stimuli, and bailouts', in J.E. Zelizer (ed.), *The Presidency of George W. Bush: A First Historical Assessment*, Princeton, NJ: Princeton University Press, pp. 115–38.

Paulson, H.M. (2010), *On the Brink: Inside the Race to Stop the Collapse of the Global Financial System*, New York: Business Plus.

PBS (2009), 'Inside the meltdown. Interview with Barney Frank'. http://www .pbs.org/wgbh/pages/frontline/meltdown/interviews/frank.html (accessed April 6, 2016).

Peirce, C.S. (1868), 'Some consequences of four incapacities', *The Journal of Speculative Philosophy*, **2** (3), 140–57.

Peirce, C.S. (1932), *Collected Papers of Charles Sanders Peirce. Volume II: Elements of Logic*. C. Hartshorne and P. Weiss (eds), Cambridge, MA: Harvard University Press.

Peirce, C.S. (1934), *Collected Papers of Charles Sanders Peirce. Volume V: Pragmatism and Pragmaticism*, ed. C. Hartshorne and P. Weiss, Cambridge, MA: Harvard University Press.

Peirce, C.S. (1992), *The Essential Peirce: Selected Philosophical Writings, Vol. 1 (1867–1893)*, ed. N. Houser and C. Kloesel, Bloomington, IN: Indiana University Press.

Peirce, C.S. (1997a), 'A definition of Pragmatism', in L. Menand (ed.), *Pragmatism: A Reader*, New York: Vintage Books, pp. 56–8.

Peirce, C.S. (1997b), 'The fixation of belief', in L. Menand (ed.), *Pragmatism: A Reader*, New York: Vintage Books, pp. 7–25.

Peirce, C.S. (1998), *The Essential Peirce: Selected Philosophical Writings, Vol. 2 (1893–1913)*, ed. Peirce Edition Project, Bloomington, IN: Indiana University Press.

Peltola, T. and I. Arpin (2017), 'How we come to value nature? A Pragmatist perspective', *Ecological Economics*, **142**, 12–20.

Perrow, C. (1984), *Normal Accidents: Living with High-Risk Technolgies*, New York: Basic Books.

Perrow, C. (2001), 'Accidents, normal', in N.J. Smelser and P.B. Baltes (eds), *International Encyclopedia of the Social & Behavioral Sciences*, Oxford: Pergamon, pp. 33–8.

Perrow, C. (2008), 'Disasters evermore? Reducing our vulnerabilities to natural, industrial, and terrorist disasters', *Social Research*, **75** (3), 733–52.

Perrow, C. and M.F. Guillen (1990), *The AIDS Disaster: The Failure of Organizations in New York and the Nation*, New Haven, CT: Yale University Press.

Pew Research Center (2008), '57% of public favors Wall Street bailout', *Pew Research Center for the People and the Press*. http://www.people-press .org/2008/09/23/57-of-public-favors-wall-street-bailout/ (accessed April 27, 2016).

Pfiffner, J.P. (2009), 'The contemporary presidency: Decision making in the Bush White House', *Presidential Studies Quarterly*, **39** (2), 363–84.

Pfiffner, J.P. (2011), 'Decision making in the Obama White House', *Presidential Studies Quarterly*, **41** (2), 244–62.

Pious, R.M. (2008), *Why Presidents Fail: White House Decision Making from Eisenhower to Bush II*, Lanham, MD: Rowman & Littlefield.

Polasky, S., S.R. Carpenter, C. Folke and B. Keeler (2011), 'Decision-making under great uncertainty: Environmental management in an era of global change', *Trends in Ecology & Evolution*, **26** (8), 398–404.

Polkinghorne, D.E. (2000). 'Psychological inquiry and the pragmatic and hermeneutic traditions', *Theory & Psychology*, **10** (4), 453–79.

Polsky, A.J. (2012), *Elusive Victories: The American Presidency at War*, Oxford; New York: Oxford University Press.

Poortinga, W. and N.F. Pidgeon (2003), 'Exploring the dimensionality of trust in risk regulation', *Risk Analysis: An International Journal*, **23** (5), 961–72.

Popper, K. (2002), *The Logic of Scientific Discovery*, London: Routledge.

Posner, R.A. (2003), *Law, Pragmatism, and Democracy*, Cambridge, MA: Harvard University Press.

Powell, M., S. Dunwoody, R. Griffin and K. Neuwirth (2007), 'Exploring lay uncertainty about an environmental health risk', *Public Understanding of Science*, **16** (3), 323–43.

Power, N. and L. Alison (2017). 'Redundant deliberation about negative consequences: Decision inertia in emergency responders', *Psychology, Public Policy, and Law*, **23** (2), 243–58.

Prawat, R. (2000), 'The two faces of Deweyan Pragmatism: Inductionism versus social constructivism', *The Teachers College Record*, **102** (4), 805–40.

Preston, T. (2001), *The President and His Inner Circle: Leadership Style and the Advisory Process in Foreign Policy Making*, New York: Columbia University Press.

Proulx, P.L.D. (2016), 'Early forms of metaethical constructivism in John Dewey's Pragmatism', *Journal for the History of Analytical Philosophy*, **4** (9), 1–13.

Putnam, H. (1995), *Word and Life*, ed. J. Conant, Cambridge, MA: Harvard University Press.

Quarantelli, E.L. (1998), *What Is a Disaster? Perspectives on the Question*, London; New York: Routledge.

Quarantelli, E.L. (2000), 'Emergencies, disasters and catastrophes are different phenomenon', *DRC Preliminary Papers*. http://udspace.udel.edu/handle/19716/674 (accessed December 6, 2013).

Rasmussen Reports (2008a), '78% say other investment firms likely to suffer Bear Stearns fate'. http://www.rasmussenreports.com/content/pdf/9735 (accessed June 16, 2016).

Rasmussen Reports (2008b), 'Lehman Brothers—September 15–16, 2008'. http://www.rasmussenreports.com/public_content/business/econ_survey _questions/september_2008/toplines_lehman_brothers_september_15_16 _2008 (accessed April 22, 2016).

Raum T. (2008), 'Analysis: Bush's lame-duck status limits clout', *USA Today*. http://usatoday30.usatoday.com/news/washington/2008-10-01 -1462473548_x.htm (accessed April 26, 2016).

Ravallion, M. (2009), 'Should the randomistas rule?', *The Economists' Voice*, **6** (2), 1–5.

Reinhart, V. (2008), 'Secretary Paulson makes the right call', *Wall Street Journal*, September 16. https://www.wsj.com/articles/SB122152364444339757 (accessed June 20, 2019).

Rerup, C. (2009), 'Attentional triangulation: Learning from unexpected rare crises', *Organization Science*, **20** (5), 876–93.

Rescher, N. (2000), *Realistic Pragmatism: An Introduction to Pragmatic Philosophy*, Albany, NY: State University of New York Press.

Rescher, N. (2004), 'Pragmatism and practical rationality', *Contemporary Pragmatism*, **1** (1), 43–60.

Rescher, N. (2005), 'Pragmatism', in T. Honderich (ed.), *The Oxford Companion to Philosophy*, Oxford: Oxford University Press, pp. 747–51.

Resodihardjo, S.L., B.J. Carroll, C.J. Van Eijk and S. Maris (2016), 'Why traditional responses to blame games fail: The importance of context, rituals, and sub-blame games in the face of raves gone wrong', *Public Administration*, **94** (2), 350–63.

Reuters (2008), 'Paulson defends U.S. rescue of Bear Stearns', *Reuters*. http://www.reuters.com/article/businesspro-usa-economy-paulson-dc -idUSN1761686520080317 (accessed March 2, 2016).

Reuters (2010), 'Full text of President Obama's BP Oil Spill Speech', *Reuters*. http://www.reuters.com/article/2010/06/16/us-oil-spill-obama-text -idUSTRE65F02C20100616 (accessed December 1, 2015).

Richardson, G., A. Komaj and M. Gou (2013), 'Gold Reserve Act of 1934—a detailed essay on an important event in the history of the Federal Reserve', *Federal Reserve History*. http://www.federalreservehistory.org/ Events/DetailView/13 (accessed April 5, 2016).

Riegler, T. (2011), *Im Fadenkreuz: Österreich und der Nahostterrorismus 1973 bis 1985*, Göttingen: Vienna University Press.

Roberts, K.H. (1990), 'Some characteristics of one type of high reliability organization', *Organization Science*, **1** (2), 160–76.

Robinson, J.A. (1968), 'Crisis', in D.L. Sills (ed.), *International Encyclopedia of the Social Sciences*, Vol. 3, New York: Macmillan, pp. 510–14.

Robinson, M., K. Jones and H. Janicke (2015) 'Cyber warfare: Issues and challenges', *Computers & Security*, **49**, 70–94.

Rochlin, G.I., T.R. La Porte and K.H. Roberts (1987), 'The self-designing high-reliability organization: Aircraft carrier flight operations at sea', *Naval War College Review*, **40** (4), 76–90.

Rodríguez, H., J. Trainor and E.L. Quarantelli (2006), 'Rising to the challenges of a catastrophe: The emergent and prosocial behavior following Hurricane Katrina', *Annals of the American Academy of Political and Social Science*, **604**, 82–101.

Rodrik, D. (2010), 'The new development economics: We shall experiment, but how shall we learn?', in J. Cohen and W. Easterly (eds), *What Works in Development? Thinking Big and Thinking Small*, Washington, DC: Brookings Institution Press, pp. 24–47.

Roe, E. and P.R. Schulman (2008), *High Reliability Management: Operating on the Edge*, Palo Alto, CA: Stanford University Press.

Roe, E. and P.R. Schulman (2016). *Reliability and Risk: The Challenge of Managing Interconnected Infrastructures*, Stanford, CA: Stanford University Press.

Rogers, M.B., R. Amlôt, G.J. Rubin, S. Wessely and K. Krieger (2007), 'Mediating the social and psychological impacts of terrorist attacks: The role of risk perception and risk communication', *International Review of Psychiatry*, **19** (3), 279–88.

Rogers, M.L. (2007), 'Action and inquiry in Dewey's philosophy', *Transactions of the Charles S. Peirce Society: A Quarterly Journal in American Philosophy*, **43** (1), 90–115.

Rolfe, G. (2014), 'Rethinking reflective education: What would Dewey have done?', *Nurse Education Today*, **34** (8), 1179–83.

Rorty, R. (1979), *Philosophy and the Mirror of Nature*, Princeton, NJ: Princeton University Press.

Rosenhek, Z. (2013), 'Diagnosing and explaining the global financial crisis: Central banks, epistemic authority, and sense making', *International Journal of Politics, Culture, and Society*, **26** (3), 255–72.

Rosenthal, S.B. (1996), 'Continuity, contingency, and time: The divergent intuitions of Whitehead and Pragmatism', *Transactions of the Charles S. Peirce Society*, **32** (4), 542–67.

Rosenthal, U. and P. 't Hart (1991), 'Experts and decision makers in crisis situations', *Knowledge*, **12** (4), 350–72.

Rosenthal, U. and P. 't Hart (2008), 'Experts and decision makers in crisis situations', in A. Boin (ed.), *Crisis Management. Volume II*, London: Sage Publications, pp. 250–66.

Rosenthal, U. and A. Kouzmin (1997), 'Crises and crisis management: Toward comprehensive government decision making', *Journal of Public Administration Research and Theory*, **7** (2), 277–304.

Rosenthal, U., M.T. Charles and P. 't Hart (1989), *Coping with Crises: The Management of Disasters, Riots, and Terrorism*, Springfield, IL: Charles C. Thomas.

Rosenthal, U., A. Boin and L.K. Comfort (2001), 'The changing world of crises and crisis management', in U. Rosenthal, A. Boin and L.K. Comfort (eds), *Managing Crises: Threats, Dilemmas, Opportunities*, Springfield, IL: Charles C. Thomas, pp. 5–27.

Rosenthal, U., P. 't Hart and A. Kouzmin (2008), 'The bureau-politics of crisis management', in A. Boin (ed.), *Crisis Management. Volume II*, London: Sage Publications, pp. 326–47.

Rossiter, C. (1948), *Constitutional Dictatorship: Crisis Government in the Modern Democracies*, Princeton, NJ: Princeton University Press.

Rossiter, C. (1956), *The American Presidency*, New York: Harcourt, Brace.

Rumsfeld, D. (2002), 'Transcript of DoD news briefing—Secretary Rumsfeld and Gen. Myers'. http://www.defense.gov/transcripts/transcript.aspx ?transcriptid=2636 (accessed July 10, 2014).

Russill, C. (2005), 'The road not taken: William James's radical empiricism and communication theory', *The Communication Review*, **8** (3), 277–305.

Russill, C. (2008), 'Through a public darkly: Reconstructing Pragmatist perspectives in communication theory', *Communication Theory*, **18** (4), 478–504.

Ryan, F.X. (2003), 'Values as consequences of transaction: Commentary on "Reconciling homo economicus and John Dewey's ethics"', *Journal of Economic Methodology*, **10** (2), 245–57.

Sabel, C.F. and J. Zeitlin (2010), *Experimentalist Governance in the European Union: Towards a New Architecture*, Oxford: Oxford University Press.

Sabel, C.F. and J. Zeitlin (2012), 'Experimentalist governance', in D. Levi-Faur (ed.), *Oxford Handbook of Governance*, Oxford: Oxford University Press, pp. 169–83.

Sagan, S.D. (1994), 'Toward a political theory of organizational reliability', *Journal of Contingencies and Crisis Management*, **2** (4), 228–40.

Sandberg, J. and H. Tsoukas (2015), 'Making sense of the sensemaking perspective: Its constituents, limitations, and opportunities for further development', *Journal of Organizational Behavior*, **36** (S1), S6–S32.

Sarasvathy, S.D. (2001), 'Causation and effectuation: Toward a theoretical shift from economic inevitability to entrepreneurial contingency', *Academy of Management Review*, **26** (2), 243–63.

Sawyer, R.K. (2000), 'Improvisation and the creative process: Dewey, Collingwood, and the aesthetics of spontaneity', *The Journal of Aesthetics and Art Criticism*, **58** (2), 149–61.

Sayegh, L., W.P. Anthony and P.L. Perrewé (2004), 'Managerial decision-making under crisis: The role of emotion in an intuitive decision process', *Human Resource Management Review*, **14** (2), 179–99.

Sayer, A. (2010), *Method in Social Science. A Realist Approach*, London; New York: Routledge.

Scarry, E. (2011), *Thinking in an Emergency*, New York: W.W. Norton & Co.

Schaefer, S. (2013), 'A look back at Bear Stearns, five years after its shotgun marriage to JPMorgan', *Forbes*. http://www.forbes.com/sites/steveschaefer/2013/03/14/a-look-back-at-bear-stearns-five-years-after-its-shotgun-marriage-to-jpmorgan/ (accessed December 9, 2015).

Scheuerman, B. (1995), 'Is Parliamentarism in crisis? A response to Carl Schmitt', *Theory and Society*, **24** (1), 135–58.

Scheuerman, W.E. (1999), 'Free market anti-formalism: The case of Richard Posner', *Ratio Juris* **12** (1), 80–95.

Schlesinger, A.M. (1973), *The Imperial Presidency*, Boston, MA: Houghton Mifflin.

Schlesinger, A.M. (2004), *War and the American Presidency*, New York: W.W. Norton.

Schmidt-Thomé, P. (2013), 'Uncertainty', in P.T. Bobrowsky (ed.), *Encyclopedia of Natural Hazards*, Dordrecht: Springer Science + Business Media, pp. 1055–6.

Schmitt, C. (1964), *Die Diktatur, von den Anfängen des modernen Souveränitätsgedanken bis zum proletarischen Klassenkampf*, Berlin: Duncker & Humblot.

Schmitt, C. (1985), *Political Theology: Four Chapters on the Concept of Sovereignty*, Cambridge, MA: MIT Press.

Schmitt, C. (1988), *The Crisis of Parliamentary Democracy*, Cambridge, MA: MIT Press.

Schmitt, C. (1996), *Politische Theologie*, Berlin: Duncker & Humblot.

Schneider, S.H., B.L. Turner and H.M. Garriga (1998), 'Imaginable surprise in global change science', *Journal of Risk Research*, **1** (2), 165–85.

Schön, D.A. (1983), *The Reflective Practitioner: How Professionals Think in Action*, New York: Basic Books.

Schön, D.A. (1992), 'The theory of inquiry: Dewey's legacy to education', *Curriculum Inquiry*, **22** (2), 119–39.

Schulkin, J. (2011), 'Dewey and Darwin on evolution and natural kinds: A Pragmatist perspective', in J.R. Shook and P. Kurtz (eds), *Dewey's Enduring Impact: Essays on America's Philosopher*, Amherst, NY: Prometheus Books, pp. 87–103.

Schulman, P.R. and E. Roe. (2007), 'Designing infrastructures: Dilemmas of design and the reliability of critical infrastructures', *Journal of Contingencies and Crisis Management*, **15** (1), 42–9.

Schultz, F. and J. Raupp (2010). 'The social construction of crises in governmental and corporate communications: An inter-organizational and inter-systemic analysis', *Public Relations Review*, **36** (2), 112–19.

Schultz, F., J. Kleinnijenhuis, D. Oegema, S. Utz and W. Van Atteveldt (2012), 'Strategic framing in the BP crisis: A semantic network analysis of associative frames', *Public Relations Review*, **38** (1), 97–107.

Schwab, G. (1985), 'Introduction', in C. Schmitt (ed.), *Political Theology: Four Chapters on the Concept of Sovereignty*, Cambridge, MA: MIT Press, pp. xi–xxvi.

Schwarz, A. (2012), 'How publics use social media to respond to blame games in crisis communication: The Love Parade tragedy in Duisburg 2010', *Public Relations Review*, **38** (3), 430–7.

Schwartz, A.J. (1996), 'From obscurity to notoriety: A biography of the Exchange Stabilization Fund', National Bureau of Economic Research Working Paper. http://www.nber.org/papers/w5699 (accessed April 5, 2016).

Schwarz, B. (2013), 'The real Cuban missile crisis', *The Atlantic*. http://www .theatlantic.com/magazine/archive/2013/01/the-real-cuban-missile-crisis/ 309190/ (accessed January 2, 2017).

Seawright, J. and J. Gerring (2008), 'Case selection techniques in case study research: A menu of qualitative and quantitative options', *Political Research Quarterly*, **61** (2), 294–308.

Seeger, M.W. (2006), 'Best practices in crisis communication: An expert panel process', *Journal of Applied Communication Research*, **34** (3), 232–44.

Seidl, R. (2014), 'The shape of ecosystem management to come: Anticipating risks and fostering resilience', *BioScience*, **64** (12), 1159–69.

Selznick, P. (1996), 'Institutionalism "old" and "new"', *Administrative Science Quarterly*, **41** (2), 270–7.

Sen, F. and W.G. Egelhoff (1991), 'Six years and counting: Learning from crisis management at Bhopal', *Public Relations Review*, **17** (1), 69–83.

Shafie, D.M. (2013), *Eleventh Hour: The Politics of Policy Initiatives in Presidential Transitions*, College Station, TX: Texas A & M University Press.

Shalin, D.N. (2007), 'Signing in the flesh: Notes on Pragmatist hermeneutics', *Sociological Theory*, **25** (3), 193–224.

Shapiro, K. (2008), *Carl Schmitt and the Intensification of Politics*, Lanham, MD: Rowman & Littlefield.

Sharma, S. (2015), '"It Is Horror": French President Hollande's remarks after Paris attacks', *Washington Post*. https://www.washingtonpost.com/ news/worldviews/wp/2015/11/13/it-is-horror-french-president-hollandes -remarks-after-paris-attacks/ (accessed November 30, 2015).

Sherwin-White, A.N. and A.W. Lintott (2014), 'Dictator', in S. Hornblower and A. Spawforth (eds), *The Oxford Companion to Classical Civilization*, Oxford: Oxford University Press, p. 236.

Shiller, R.J. (2008), *The Subprime Solution: How Today's Global Financial Crisis Happened and What to Do About It*, Princeton, NJ: Princeton University Press.

Shrivastava, P. (1987), *Bhopal: Anatomy of Crisis*, Cambridge, MA: Ballinger Publishing Co.

Shusterman, R. (2012), 'Thought in the strenuous mood: Pragmatism as a philosophy of feeling', *New Literary History*, **43** (3), 433–54.

Sidel, R., G. Ip, M.M. Philipp and K. Kelly (2008), 'The week that shook Wall Street: Inside the demise of Bear Stearns—as trouble deepened, a herculean effort to limit its spread', *Wall Street Journal*. https://global .factiva.com/redir/default.aspx?P=sa&NS=16&AID=9LEI000700&an= WSJE000020080319e43j00002&cat=a&ep=ASI (accessed January 28, 2016).

Siegel, J. (2008), 'The resilience of American finance', *Wall Street Journal*, September 16. https://www.wsj.com/articles/SB122152085270539225 (accessed June 20, 2019).

Siemers, D.J. (2004), 'Principled Pragmatism: Abraham Lincoln's method of political analysis', *Presidential Studies Quarterly*, **34** (4), 804–27.

Sigel, K., B. Klauer and C. Pahl-Wostl (2010), 'Conceptualising uncertainty in environmental decision-making: The example of the EU water framework directive', *Ecological Economics*, **69** (3), 502–10.

Sigelman, L. and P. Johnston Conover (1981), 'The dynamics of presidential support during international conflict situations: The Iranian hostage crisis', *Political Behavior*, **3** (4), 303–18.

Simon, H.A. (1957), *Models of Man: Social and Rational. Mathematical Essays on Rational Human Behavior in a Social Setting*, New York: Wiley.

Simpson, B. (2009), 'Pragmatism, Mead and the practice turn', *Organization Studies*, **30** (12), 1329–47.

Simpson, B. (2011), 'Rational choice theories', in G. Ritzer and J.M. Ryan (eds), *The Concise Encyclopedia of Sociology*, Malden, MA: John Wiley & Sons, pp. 494–5.

Slovic, P. (1993), 'Perceived risk, trust, and democracy', *Risk Analysis*, **13** (6), 675–82.

Slovic, P. (1999), 'Trust, emotion, sex, politics, and science: Surveying the risk-assessment battlefield', *Risk Analysis*, **19** (4), 689–-701.

Slovic, P., M.L. Finucane, E. Peters and D.G. MacGregor (2004), 'Risk as analysis and risk as feelings: Some thoughts about affect, reason, risk, and rationality', *Risk Analysis*, **24** (2), 311–22.

Small, W.J. (1991), 'Exxon Valdez: How to spend billions and still get a black eye', *Public Relations Review*, **17** (1), 9–25.

Smart, C. and I. Vertinsky (1977), 'Designs for crisis decision units', *Administrative Science Quarterly*, **22** (4), 640–57.

Smith, A. and F. Graetz (2006), 'Organizing dualities and strategizing for change', *Strategic Change*, **15** (5), 231–9.

Smithson, M. and Y. Ben-Haim (2015), 'Reasoned decision making without math? Adaptability and robustness in response to surprise', *Risk Analysis*, **35** (10), 1911–18.

Snook, S.A. and J.C. Connor (2009), 'The price of progress: Structurally induced inaction', in W. Starbuck and M. Farjoun (eds), *Organization at the Limit: Lessons from the Columbia Disaster*, Malden, MA: John Wiley & Sons, pp. 178–201.

Solnit, R. (2009), *A Paradise Built in Hell: The Extraordinary Communities that Arise in Disasters*, New York: Penguin.

Solomon, D., D.K. Berman, S. Craig and C. Mollenkamp (2008), 'Ultimatum by Paulson sparked frantic end', *Wall Street Journal*, September 15. https://www.wsj.com/articles/SB122143670579134187 (accessed June 20, 2019).

Sommer, S.C. and C.H. Loch (2004), 'Selectionism and learning in projects with complexity and unforeseeable uncertainty', *Management Science*, **50** (10), 1334–47.

Sommer, S.C., C.H. Loch and J. Dong (2009), 'Managing complexity and unforeseeable uncertainty in startup companies: An empirical study', *Organization Science*, **20** (1), 118–33.

Sonenshein, S. (2016), 'Routines and creativity: From dualism to duality', *Organization Science*, **27** (3), 739–58.

Sorkin, A.R. (2008), 'Lehman files for bankruptcy; Merrill is sold', *New York Times*. http://www.nytimes.com/2008/09/15/business/15lehman.html (accessed March 30, 2016).

Sorkin, A.R. (2009), *Too Big to Fail: The Inside Story of How Wall Street and Washington Fought to Save the Financial System from Crisis—and Themselves*, New York: Viking.

Spence, P.R., K.A. Lachlan and J. Burke (2008), 'Crisis preparation, media use, and information seeking: Patterns across Katrina evacuees and lessons learned for crisis communication', *Journal of Emergency Management*, **6** (2), 11–23.

Starbuck, W.H. (2009), 'Perspective—cognitive reactions to rare events: Perceptions, uncertainty, and learning', *Organization Science*, **20** (5), 925–37.

Stark, D. 2011. *The Sense of Dissonance: Accounts of Worth in Economic Life*, Princeton, NJ: Princeton University Press.

Starn, R. (2005), 'Crisis', in M.C. Horowitz (ed.), *New Dictionary of the History of Ideas*, Vol. 2, New York: Charles Scribner's Sons, pp. 500–1.

Stern, E. (1997), 'Crisis and learning: A conceptual balance sheet', *Journal of Contingencies and Crisis Management*, **5** (2), 69–86.

Stern, E. (1999), 'Crisis decisionmaking: A cognitive institutional approach', Doctoral dissertation, University of Stockholm, Department of Political Science.

Stern, E. and B. Sundelius (1997), 'Sweden's twin monetary crises of 1992: Rigidity and learning in crisis decision making', *Journal of Contingencies and Crisis Management*, **5** (1), 32–48.

Stewart, J.B. 2009. 'Eight days', *The New Yorker*. http://www.newyorker.com/magazine/2009/09/21/eight-days (accessed March 21, 2016).

Stewart, J.B. and P. Eavis (2014), 'Revisiting the Lehman Brothers bailout that never was', *New York Times*. http://www.nytimes.com/2014/09/30/business/revisiting-the-lehman-brothers-bailout-that-never-was.html (accessed April 22, 2016).

Stieglitz, S., M. Mirbabaie and M. Milde (2018), 'Social positions and collective sense-making in crisis communication', *International Journal of Human–Computer Interaction*, **34** (4), 328–55.

Stiglitz, J.E. (2010), *Freefall: America, Free Markets, and the Sinking of the World Economy*, New York: W.W. Norton & Co.

Stiglitz, J.E. (2012), *The Price of Inequality: How Today's Divided Society Endangers Our Future*, New York: W.W. Norton & Co.

Stock, J.H. and M.W. Watson (2012), 'Disentangling the channels of the 2007–2009 recession', National Bureau of Economic Research Working Paper 18094.

Stoker, G. and P. John (2009), 'Design experiments: Engaging policy makers in the search for evidence about what works', *Political Studies*, **57** (2), 356–73.

Stolberg, S.G. (2008), 'Bush emerges after days of financial crisis', *New York Times*. http://www.nytimes.com/2008/09/19/business/19bush.html (accessed March 30, 2016).

Strauss, A.L. (1993), *Continual Permutations of Action*, New York: Aldine de Gruyter.

Strauss, D.A. (2007), 'The anti-formalist', *Chicago Law Review*, **74**, 1885–94.

Strömbäck, J. and L.W. Nord (2006), 'Mismanagement, mistrust and missed opportunities: A study of the 2004 Tsunami and Swedish political communication', *Media, Culture & Society*, **28** (5), 789–800.

Stuhr, J.J. (2003), 'Pragmatism about values and the valuable: Commentary on "A pragmatic view on values in economics"', *Journal of Economic Methodology*, **10** (2), 213–21.

Summers, L. (2007), 'Beware moral hazard fundamentalists', *Financial Times*. http://www.ft.com/cms/s/0/5ffd2606-69e8-11dc-a571-0000779fd2ac.html (accessed December 8, 2015).

Sund, K.J., R.J. Galavan and A.S. Huff (eds), *Uncertainty and Strategic Decision Making*, Bingley, UK: Emerald Group Publishing.

Swagel, P. (2009), 'The financial crisis: An inside view', *Brookings Papers on Economic Activity*, Spring, 1–78.

Sylves, R.T. (2006), 'President Bush and Hurricane Katrina: A presidential leadership study', *Annals of the American Academy of Political and Social Science*, **604**, 26–56.

Taleb, N.N. (2007), *The Black Swan: The Impact of the Highly Improbable*, New York: Random House.

Talisse, R.B. (2007), *A Pragmatist Philosophy of Democracy*, New York: Routledge.

Teo, W.L., M. Lee and W.S. Lim (2017), 'The relational activation of resilience model: How leadership activates resilience in an organizational crisis', *Journal of Contingencies and Crisis Management*, **25** (3), 136–47.

Thayer, H.S. (1968), *Meaning and Action: A Critical History of Pragmatism*, Indianapolis: Bobbs-Merrill.

The Economist (2009), 'Did we need to bail out AIG?', *The Economist*. http://www.economist.com/blogs/freeexchange/2009/04/did_we_need_to_bail_out_aig (accessed April 25, 2016).

Timiraos, N. and E. Holmes (2008), 'McCain, Obama confront the market', *Wall Street Journal*, September 16. https://www.wsj.com/articles/SB122151017079138227 (accessed June 20, 2019).

Torres, C. (2008), 'Fed "rogue operation" spurs further bailout calls'. http://www.bloomberg.com/apps/news?pid=email_en&sid=axSyA04372Fw (accessed October 12, 2015).

Turner, B. (1978), *Man-Made Disasters*, London: Wykeham Publications.

Tversky, A. and D. Kahneman (1974), 'Judgment under uncertainty: Heuristics and biases', *Science*, **185** (4157), 1124–31.

Twomey, P. (1998), 'Reviving Veblenian economic psychology', *Cambridge Journal of Economics*, **22** (4), 433–48.

Tyson, C.J. (2006), 'Satisficing behavior', in M. Bevir (ed.), *Encyclopedia of Governance*, Thousand Oaks, CA: Sage Publications, pp. 851–2.

Underhill, J.B. (2008). 'Review of The Politics of Crisis Management: Public leadership under pressure', *Political Psychology*, **29** (1), 139–43.

United States Senate (2014), *Senate Manual Containing the Standing Rules, Orders, Laws, and Resolutions Affecting the Business of the United States Senate*. https://www.gpo.gov/fdsys/pkg/SMAN-113/pdf/SMAN-113.pdf (accessed June 16, 2016).

United States v Marshall (1990), https://h2o.law.harvard.edu/cases/4699 (accessed June 20, 2019).

US Congress (1934), *Gold Reserve Act of 1934. Public Law 73-87, 73d Congress, H.R. 6976*. https://fraser.stlouisfed.org/scribd/?title_id=1085& filepath=/docs/historical/congressional/goldreserveact1934.pdf (accessed April 5, 2016).

US Congress (2008a), *The Future of Financial Services: Exploring Solutions for the Market Crisis, Hearing Before the Committee on Financial Services, U.S. House of Representatives, September 24, 2008*, Washington, DC. https://www.gpo.gov/fdsys/pkg/CHRG-110hhrg45625/pdf/CHRG-110hhrg45625 .pdf (accessed June 16, 2016).

US Congress (2008b), *The Recent Actions Taken by the Federal Regulatory Agencies to Contain the Financial Crisis, the Current State of the Financial Markets, and Proposals to Address the Crisis. Hearing Before the Committee on Banking, Housing, and Urban Affairs, United States Senate, September 23, 2008*, Washington, DC. https://www.gpo.gov/fdsys/pkg/ CHRG-110shrg50414/pdf/CHRG-110shrg50414.pdf (accessed June 16, 2016).

US Congress (2008c), *Turmoil in U.S. Credit Markets: Examining the Recent Actions of Federal Finance Regulators. Hearing Before the Committee on Banking, Housing, and Urban Affairs, United States Senate, April 3, 2008*, Washington, DC. https://www.gpo.gov/fdsys/pkg/CHRG-110shrg50394/ pdf/CHRG-110shrg50394.pdf (accessed June 16, 2016).

US Department of Treasury (2008a), 'Paulson statement on SEC and Federal Reserve actions surrounding Lehman Brothers'. https://www.treasury.gov/ press-center/press-releases/Pages/hp1134.aspx (accessed March 21, 2016).

US Department of Treasury (2008b), 'Statement by Secretary Henry M. Paulson, Jr. on Treasury and Federal Housing Finance Agency action to protect financial markets and taxpayers'. https://www.treasury.gov/press -center/press-releases/Pages/hp1129.aspx (accessed March 21, 2016).

US Department of Treasury (2008c), 'Treasury announces guaranty program for money market funds'. https://www.treasury.gov/press-center/press -releases/Pages/hp1147.aspx (accessed March 22, 2016).

Valukas, A.R. (2010), *Report of Anton R. Valukas. In Re Lehman Brothers Holdings Inc., et al. Volume 2 of 9*, Chicago: United States Bankruptcy Court Southern District of New York.

Van Buuren, A., M. Vink and J. Warner (2016), 'Constructing authoritative answers to a latent crisis? Strategies of puzzling, powering and framing in Dutch climate adaptation practices compared', *Journal of Comparative Policy Analysis: Research and Practice*, **18** (1), 70–87.

van den Heuvel, C., L. Alison and N. Power (2014). 'Coping with uncertainty: Police strategies for resilient decision-making and action implementation', *Cognition, Technology & Work*, **16** (1), 25–45.

Van Eeten, M. and J.M. Bauer (2009), 'Emerging threats to internet security: Incentives, externalities and policy implications', *Journal of Contingencies and Crisis Management*, **17** (4), 221–32.

Van Esch, F. (2014), 'Exploring the Keynesian–ordoliberal divide: Flexibility and convergence in French and German Leaders' economic ideas during the euro-crisis', *Journal of Contemporary European Studies*, **22** (3), 288–302.

Van Esch, F. and M. Swinkels (2015), 'How Europe's political leaders made sense of the euro crisis: The influence of pressure and personality', *West European Politics*, **38** (6), 1203–25.

Vaughan, D. (1997), *The Challenger Launch Decision: Risky Technology, Culture, and Deviance at NASA*, Chicago, IL: University of Chicago Press.

Vaughn, J.S. and J.D. Villalobos (2011), 'White House staff', in L.C. Han (ed.), *New Directions in the American Presidency*, London: Routledge, pp. 120–35.

Vecchiato, R. (2012), 'Environmental uncertainty, foresight and strategic decision making: An integrated study', *Technological Forecasting and Social Change*, **79** (3), 436–47.

Vendelo, M.T. and C. Rerup (2009), 'Weak cues and attentional triangulation: The Pearl Jam concert accident at Roskilde Festival', Paper presented at the Academy of Management Annual Meeting, Chicago, IL.

Walker, S.G. (2009), 'The psychology of presidential decision making', in G.C. Edwards and W.G. Howell (eds), *The Oxford Handbook of the American Presidency*, Oxford: Oxford University Press, pp. 550–74.

Walker, W.E., P. Harremoës, J. Rotmans, J.P. van der Sluijs, M.B. van Asselt, P. Janssen and M.P. Krayer von Krauss (2003), 'Defining uncertainty: A conceptual basis for uncertainty management in model-based decision support', *Integrated Assessment*, **4** (1), 5–17.

Walker, W.E., V.A. Marchau and J.H. Kwakkel (2013), 'Uncertainty in the framework of policy analysis', in *Public Policy Analysis*, Boston, MA: Springer, pp. 215–61.

Wallach, P.A. (2015a), 'Lehman the lemon, or Lehman the forsaken?', *Yale Journal on Regulation Blog*. http://www.yalejreg.com/blog/lehman-the -lemon-or-lehman-the-forsaken-by-philip-wallach (accessed April 8, 2016).

Wallach, P.A. (2015b), *To the Edge: Legality, Legitimacy, and the Responses to the 2008 Financial Crisis*, Washington, DC: Brookings Institution Press.

Walsh, K.T. (2008), 'In this economic crisis, President Bush finds himself short of political capital', *US News & World Report*. http://www.usnews .com/news/articles/2008/10/06/in-this-economic-crisis-president-bush -finds-himself-short-of-political-capital (accessed April 26, 2016).

Walsh, M.W. and M.J. De La Merced (2008), 'Wall St.'s turmoil sends stocks reeling', *New York Times*. http://www.nytimes.com/2008/09/16/business/16aig.html (accessed April 1, 2016).

Washington Post (2006), 'Timeline of events from September 11, 2001', *Washington Post*. http://www.washingtonpost.com/wp-dyn/content/article/2006/09/11/AR2006091100450.html (accessed July 26, 2016).

Washington Post (2008), 'The Lehman lesson', September 16. http://www.washingtonpost.com/wp-dyn/content/article/2008/09/15/AR2008091502703.html (accessed June 20, 2019).

Watkins, M.D. and M.H. Bazerman (2003), 'Predictable surprises: The disasters you should have seen coming', *Harvard Business Review*, **81** (3), 72–85.

Webb, J.L. (2007), 'Pragmatisms (plural) part 1: Classical pragmatism and some implications for empirical inquiry', *Journal of Economic Issues*, **41** (4), 1063–86.

Weber, M. (1949), *The Methodology of the Social Sciences*, ed. E.A. Shils and H.A. Finch, Glencoe, IL: Free Press.

Weick, K.E. (1988), 'Enacted sensemaking in crisis situations', *Journal of Management Studies*, **25** (4), 305–17.

Weick, K.E. (1993), 'The collapse of sensemaking in organizations: The Mann Gulch disaster', *Administrative Science Quarterly*, **38** (4), 628–52.

Weick, K.E. (1995), *Sensemaking in Organizations*, Thousand Oaks, CA: Sage Publications.

Weick, K.E. (2006), 'Faith, evidence, and action: Better guesses in an unknowable world', *Organization Studies*, **27** (11), 1723–36.

Weick, K.E. (2007), 'The generative properties of richness', *Academy of Management Journal*, **50** (1), 14–19.

Weick, K.E. (2015), 'Ambiguity as grasp: The reworking of sense', *Journal of Contingencies and Crisis Management*, **23** (2), 117–23.

Weick, K.E. and K.H. Roberts (1993), 'Collective mind in organizations: Heedful interrelating on flight decks', *Administrative Science Quarterly*, **38** (3), 357–81.

Weick, K.E. and K.M. Sutcliffe (2011), *Managing the Unexpected: Resilient Performance in an Age of Uncertainty*, San Francisco, CA: John Wiley & Sons.

Weick, K.E., K.M. Sutcliffe and D. Obstfeld (2005), 'Organizing and the process of sensemaking', *Organization Science*, **16** (4), 409–21.

Weick, K.E., K.E. Sutcliffe and D. Obstfeld (2008), 'Organizing for high reliability: Processes of collective mindfulness', in A. Boin (ed.), *Crisis Management. Volume III*, London: Sage Publications, pp. 31–66.

Weisæth, L., Ø. Knudsen Jr and A. Tønnessen (2002), 'Technological disasters, crisis management and leadership stress', *Journal of Hazardous Materials*, **93** (1), 33–45.

Wells, P. (2007), 'New Labour and evidence based policy making: 1997–2007', *People, Place and Policy*, **1** (1), 22–9.

Wessel, D. (2009), *In Fed We Trust: Ben Bernanke's War on the Great Panic*, New York: Crown Business.

West, C. (1982), 'Book review: Philosophy and the Mirror of Nature', *Union Seminary Quarterly Review*, **37** (1&2), 179–85.

West, C. (1989), *The American Evasion of Philosophy: A Genealogy of Pragmatism*, New York: Springer.

West, C. (2000), 'Pragmatism and the sense of the tragic', in *The Cornel West Reader*, New York: Basic Civitas Books, pp. 174–82.

Wheaton, S. (2010), 'Oil spill remedies: Trial and error in Deep Water', *New York Times*. http://www.nytimes.com/interactive/2010/05/28/us/20100528 _GULF_TIMELINE.html?_r=0 (accessed December 1, 2015).

White House (2008a), 'Press briefing by Dana Perino, 17 March 2008'. http:// georgewbush-whitehouse.archives.gov/news/releases/2008/03/20080317-5 .html (accessed January 27, 2016).

White House (2008b), 'Press briefing by Dana Perino and Secretary of the Treasury Henry Paulson'. http://georgewbush-whitehouse.archives.gov/ news/releases/2008/09/20080915-8.html (accessed January 27, 2016).

Whitford, J. (2002), 'Pragmatism and the untenable dualism of means and ends: Why rational choice theory does not deserve paradigmatic privilege', *Theory and Society*, **31** (3), 325–63.

Wiggins, R.Z., T. Piontek and A. Metrick (2014), *The Lehman Brothers Bankruptcy A: Overview*, Rochester, NY: Social Science Research Network. SSRN Scholarly Paper. http://papers.ssrn.com/abstract=2588531 (accessed March 21, 2016).

Wildavsky, A. (1988), *Searching for Safety*, New Brunswick, NJ: Transaction Books.

Wiley, N. (1994), *The Semiotic Self*, Chicago, IL: University of Chicago Press.

Wiley, N. (2003), 'The self as self-fulfilling prophecy', *Symbolic Interaction*, **26** (4), 501–13.

Williams, D.E. and G. Treadaway (1992), 'Exxon and the Valdez accident: A failure in crisis communication', *Communication Studies*, **43** (1), 56–64.

Williams, J.J. (2001), 'New York intellectual: An interview with Louis Menand', *Minnesota Review*, **52** (1), 141–57.

Willihngaz, S., J.L. Hart and G.B. Leichty (2004), 'Telling the story of organizational change', in D.P. Millar and R.L. Heath (eds), *Responding to Crises: A Rhetorical Approach to Crisis Communication*, Mahwah, NJ: Lawrence Erlbaum Associates, pp. 213–31.

Wills, G. (1999), 'Lincoln's Greatest Speech', *The Atlantic*, September. http://www.theatlantic.com/past/issues/99sep/9909lincoln.htm.

Wilson, W. (1887), 'The study of administration', *Political Science Quarterly*, **2** (2), 197–222.

Winther, R.G. (2014), 'James and Dewey on abstraction', *The Pluralist*, **9** (2), 1–28.

Wirth, A.G. (1966), 'The psychological theory for experimentation in education at John Dewey's Laboratory School, the University of Chicago, 1896–1904', *Educational Theory*, **16** (3), 271–80.

Wittneben, B.F. (2012), 'The impact of the Fukushima nuclear accident on European energy policy', *Environmental Science & Policy*, **15** (1), 1–3.

Wohlstetter, R. (1962), *Pearl Harbor: Warning and Decision*, Palo Alto, CA: Stanford University Press.

Woodward, B. (2010), *Obama's Wars*, New York: Simon & Schuster.

Wynne, B. (1989), 'Sheepfarming after Chernobyl: A case study in communicating scientific information', *Environment: Science and Policy for Sustainable Development*, **31** (2), 10–39.

Wynne, B. (1992), 'Misunderstood misunderstanding: Social identities and public uptake of science', *Public Understanding of Science*, **1** (3), 281–304.

Zegart, A.B. (2009), *Spying Blind: The CIA, the FBI, and the Origins of 9/11*, Princeton, NJ: Princeton University Press.

Zeldin, X. (1991), 'John Dewey's role on the 1937 Trotsky Commission', *Public Affairs Quarterly*, **5** (4), 387–94.

Zeelenberg, M. and R. Pieters (2006), 'Feeling is for doing: A Pragmatist approach to the study of emotions in economic behavior', in D. De Cremer, M. Zeelenberg and J.K. Murnighan (eds), *Social Psychology and Economics*, New York: Psychology Press, pp. 117–37.

Žižek, S. (2004), 'What Rumsfeld doesn't know that he knows about Abu Ghraib', *In These Times*. http://inthesetimes.com/article/747 (accessed June 13, 2014).

Zumbrun, J. (2008), 'Paulson's line in the sand', *Forbes*. http://www.forbes.com/2008/09/15/lehman-bernanke-paulson-biz-beltway-cx_jz_0915paulson.html (accessed March 30, 2016).

Zwanenberg, P. van and E. Millstone (2005), *BSE: Risk, Science, and Governance*, Oxford: Oxford University Press.

Index

Printed and bound by CPI Group (UK) Ltd, Croydon, CR0 4YY

23/04/2025

14660963-0005